The Many Costs
of Racism

The Many Costs of Racism

Joe R. Feagin and Karyn D. McKinney

ROWMAN & LITTLEFIELD PUBLISHERS, INC.
Lanham • Boulder • New York • Oxford

ROWMAN & LITTLEFIELD PUBLISHERS, INC.

Published in the United States of America
by Rowman & Littlefield Publishers, Inc.
A Member of the Rowman & Littlefield Publishing Group
4720 Boston Way, Lanham, Maryland 20706
www.rowmanlittlefield.com

PO Box 317, Oxford, OX2 9RU, United Kingdom

Distributed by NATIONAL BOOK NETWORK

British Library Cataloguing in Publication Information Available

Library of Congress Cataloging-in-Publication Data

Feagin, Joe R.
  The many costs of racism / Joe R. Feagin and Karyn D. McKinney.
    p. cm.
  Includes bibliographical references (p.   ) and index.
  ISBN 0-7425-1117-0 (cloth)
    1. African Americans—Social conditions. 2. African Americans
  —Psychology. 3. African Americans—Health and hygiene.
    4. United States—Race relations. 5. United States—Race relations
  —Psychological aspects. 6. Racism—United States.
    7. Racism—United States—Psychological aspects. 8. Racism
  —Health aspects—United States. I. McKinney, Karyn D., 1969– . II. Title.
  E185.86.F434 2003
  305.896'073'0019—dc21   2002009703

Printed in the United States of America

♾™ The paper used in this publication meets the minimum requirements of American National Standard for Information Sciences—Permanence of Paper for Printed Library Materials, ANSI/NISO Z39.48-1992.

Contents

Acknowledgments   **vi**

Introduction   **1**

1 The Many Costs of White Racism   **6**

2 The Psychological and Energy Costs of   **39**
Contemporary Racism

3 The Physical Health Consequences of Racism   **65**

4 The Family and Community Costs of Racism   **94**

5 Fighting and Managing Everyday Racism: **119**
An Array of Strategies

6 Combating Racism: Active Behavioral Strategies   **147**

7 Racism and the U.S. Health Care System   **180**

Notes   **211**

Index   **243**

About the Authors   **250**

Acknowledgments

WE HAVE BEEN FORTUNATE to know a number of fine scholars willing to give us their sage advice or read significant portions of earlier versions of this book. We are particularly indebted to Linda Clayton, W. Michael Byrd, Roy Brooks, Leslie Houts, Sheila Jeffers, Katisha Greer, Bette Woody, Kristi Lowery, Yvonne Combs, Melvin Sikes, Sharon Rush, Diane Brown, and Amir Marvasti. We would particularly like to thank John McKnight and Kevin Early for doing excellent work in moderating our focus groups and Dean Birkenkamp, our editor, for his strong support throughout this project. Earlier versions of some arguments and data in chapters 1 through 4 and chapter 7 appeared in our article, "The Many Costs of Discrimination: The Case of Middle Class African Americans," *Indiana Law Review* 34 (2001): 1313–1360 (with Kevin Early). The material is used here by permission.

We owe much gratitude to the many African American women and men who have explained patiently in interviews and focus groups the painful and continuing reality and impact of racial discrimination in their lives. We would like to dedicate this book to them, as they are some of society's finest, and unsung, heroes.

We would also like to thank our families for their loving support and patience throughout this long project.

Introduction

OVER THE LAST DECADE, the federal government's Equal Employment Opportunity Commission (EEOC) has received tens of thousands of complaints of racial harassment in U.S. workplaces. These accounts represent only a small portion of a bigger problem, for many more accounts of racial harassment and other forms of racial discrimination are reported daily in the mass media across the United States.

Here are a few recent illustrations from our files. A food company in Texas settled a lawsuit in which African American employees reported a racially hostile work climate where, to take one example, a white supervisor told a black employee that "all black people are crack heads" and that they should "go back to Africa."[1] A federal judge in Pennsylvania recently allowed an African American police sergeant to pursue his case against local white officials for allowing a racially hostile work environment in which his complaints of racist actions resulted in retaliation against him.[2] At a major power company worksite, numerous hangman's nooses were put out with the apparent goal of threatening the black employees. In another workplace in the Midwest, two white workers, including a supervisor, dressed up and paraded around in Ku Klux Klan costumes.[3] Several African American workers at a major aerospace company filed a discrimination lawsuit charging the company with allowing whites to put nooses in their lockers, write racist graffiti, and use racist epithets. According to the lawsuit, managers ignored the situation, fabricated statements about the black workers, or assigned them to menial tasks.[4] At a West Coast dairy, six African American employees recently reported unequal pay along racial lines and racial threats, including Ku Klux Klan and Nazi symbols and racist pictures and epithets.[5] In many other U.S. workplaces, African American employees have reported problems with hangman's nooses, racist graffiti on walls, racist cartoons, racist jokes, booklets making fun of African Americans, and white employees in KKK hoods or sheets. White workers have displayed effigies (such as coconuts made up in "blackface") of black workers and their families, with racist epithets written on the effigies.

To make these actions even more painful for their targets, whites who engage in this hostile harassment—and sometimes white bystanders—often make light of it. In addition, numerous white employers have allowed racial harassment to continue in worksites even after black employees have called it to their attention. These blatant actions are the type of discrimination that many whites assert has all but disappeared in the United States. Such assertions, if sincere, border on foolishness. Even a cursory search of a newspaper database yields numerous examples of discrimination against African Americans in worksites across the country.

One would think that whites, for fear of punishment, would be careful not to indulge in such blatantly racist actions because such commonplace racial harassment is a violation of U.S. civil rights laws. Indeed, many white Americans would likely recognize this as discrimination and believe that such racial discrimination is improper. However, what most whites do *not* usually see is the array of stress-related psychological, physical, and family costs that are imposed on the targets of racial discrimination. Certainly, much of this damage is intended by the white perpetrators, often in an attempt to drive African Americans out of workplaces or neighborhoods—and such racist actions do in fact result in much harm.

Why are these common, racist actions by white Americans so harmful? The reason should be obvious to those familiar with this country's long racist history. To most African Americans, hangman's nooses, other KKK symbols, and racist epithets suggest the brutal violence that they and their ancestors have endured at the hands of white supremacists for several centuries. In a later chapter, we recount the reaction of an African American psychologist, now in his eighties. He explained that when he hears hostile, antiblack epithets, he often sees, in the back of his mind, a black man hanging from a tree. He grew up when lynchings of black men were much more common than they are today, and racist acts carried out by whites in the present recall his past experience with this bloody form of racism.

Most African Americans know that white supremacist groups, such as the Ku Klux Klan, have long participated in violence against African Americans—now for more than a century and continuing to the present day. They also know that favored white supremacist icons, such as hangman's nooses and burning crosses, still intend intimidation and signal threats of violence and death to African Americans. Yet the white supremacist groups that have historically perpetrated so much violence against African Americans are still legal in every state in the United States, and their threatening actions generally get little attention from local and federal police agencies.

It is not just active members of white supremacist groups who engage in this behavior. Many other whites feel that they, too, can engage in openly racist behavior. Indeed, outrageous acts of discrimination often generate copycat actions by other white Americans. Commonplace acts of overt racial discrimination signal to all Americans that whites usually can still get away with such actions, and with only sporadic police or other government response. This country, in general, only weakly enforces its civil rights laws.

Moreover, it is not only these blatant acts of discrimination that African Americans must endure. As we demonstrate in this book, the racial discrimination that causes psychological and physical harm for African Americans includes a range of covert and subtle acts of discrimination, as well. The evidence we assess indicates that in recent years many white Americans at all class levels have come to feel that they can discriminate against African Americans and other Americans of color with little or no fear of punishment.

Powerful whites are often part of the problem. Consider how seldom the mass media actually deal with the backstage actions of powerful whites. Recall, for example, the "Texaco tape" case in which several Texaco executives were recorded commenting negatively about their African American employees.[6] This case is a rare instance of covert discrimination that became overt only because the discussion of the discriminatory action was secretly tape-recorded, and subsequently made public. In this discussion, major executives were heard discussing black employees, metaphorically referring to them as "black jellybeans" that remain stuck to the "bottom of the bag." The taped conversation made public what usually remains behind closed doors in major companies: African American and other employees of color face discrimination, including a "glass ceiling," in major U.S. corporations. Often, African Americans are allowed to reach certain levels of employment and then are not allowed to rise further. Whites in U.S. workplaces perpetrate covert and subtle discrimination every day, and it greatly increases the work-related stress faced by African Americans. Because some of these discriminatory practices are covert, it is difficult to provide the hard evidence that they have occurred, as many of our respondents indicate in the chapters that follow. In the workplace, African American employees often must spend a lot of time and energy documenting their own work as well as the actions taken by others.

Another source of hidden discrimination for many African Americans is the one-way assimilation characteristic of most employment settings. Most historically white workplaces, including corporations, are still predominantly white with modest numbers of African Americans and other employees of color. People of color who work in such environments are often forced to assimilate to white norms and styles. Generally, they are not allowed to change the work environment, in a two-way assimilation process, to accept their own values as well as the predominant values. For example, a female African American executive might need to forgo her dreadlocks or braids (hairstyles that originated as strong African American cultural expressions) to work comfortably in a predominantly white, corporate workplace. Additionally, simply being the only person of color, or one of only a few people of color, in a predominantly white workplace can mean added stress. In such situations, employees of color usually feel that they must take on the sometimes uncomfortable cloak of white workplace norms and that they cannot really be themselves until they get home. Moreover, they may be the targets of assumptions that they are just "token" hires or undeserving beneficiaries of affirmative action policies. Constantly working with others who doubt one's qualifications involves a type of subtle discrimination that greatly increases stress over a period of time.

Although many sensitive whites recognize the more blatant forms of discrimination as wrong and unjust, many do not see the hidden, recurring "woodwork" discrimination that African American workers endure in most white-dominated workplaces every day. Nor do most whites see the broad range of personal, family, and community costs that stem from this racial discrimination. In the chapters that follow, respondents vividly describe what it is like to deal with workplace discrimination of all kinds—blatant, covert, and subtle. It is the central purpose of this book to delineate the extensive range of harm inflicted by discriminatory actions that occur routinely in many U.S. workplaces.

1

The Many Costs
of White Racism

BEING BLACK IN AMERICA comes with many costs. In a previous study, Joe Feagin and Melvin Sikes asked a successful entrepreneur, "What is it like to be a black person in white America today?" She replied sharply:

> One step from suicide! What I'm saying is—the psychological warfare games that we have to play everyday just to survive. We have to be one way in our communities, and one way in the workplace or in the business sector. We can never be ourselves all around. I think that may be a given for all people, but us particularly; it's really a mental health problem. It's a wonder we haven't all gone out and killed somebody or killed ourselves. . . . We learn the rules of the games, and by the time we have mastered them, to really try to get into the mainstream, and I mean economic mainstream . . . then they change the rules of the game. The game becomes something else, because now you have learned how to play it.[1]

This eloquent answer to a question about life in white America is full of insight, as well as anguish, frustration, and pain. This woman is a creative and successful businessperson, and she is not actually contemplating suicide. Yet she describes her life as a black person in the white business world as a game of psychological warfare that she needs to play just to survive. The racist "game" necessitates a constant struggle on the part of black Americans to survive and be successful in their individual lives and their families. Because of continuing racism, living black in America usually involves confronting a range of physical and mental health problems that are not of one's own making.

RACISM AND HUMAN HEALTH

No matter how hard African Americans work, no matter what their hard-earned achievements may be, they still face high levels of discrimination, and this discrimination usually leads to additional life stress, stress-related health problems, and the development of a necessary repertoire of counter-responses to deal with the problems of everyday racism. African Americans "are alternately baffled, frustrated, shocked, and outraged that the strong evidence of their hard work and personal achievements does not protect them from white discrimination. . . . Racial stereotyping, prejudice, and hostility still operate indiscriminately, despite the actual identities and achievements of the black individuals discriminated against."[2]

The World Health Organization defines "human health" as a state of complete physical, mental, and social well-being.[3] Thus, human health is much more than the absence of infirmity and disease; it involves positive well-being and the active possession of basic human rights, such as the right to be free of racial discrimination in employment, housing, and public accommodations, and the right to fairness and social justice in one's everyday life. Attaining this well-being is very difficult, however, because of the continuing reality of widespread discrimination. A recent report by the National Medical Association reviewed extensive data on the health conditions of African Americans in the past and in the present and came to this conclusion:

> According to the latest available data, African Americans are plagued with persistent race-based health disparities that . . . have existed for centuries. . . . The scientific literature is documenting increasing evidence that links compromised health status with biases based on

race, class, gender, ethnicity, and culture that ultimately translates
to discrimination in the health system. . . . As we enter the 21st century, institutional racism remains an insidious obstacle to improving and eliminating the disparate health status of African Americans
in America.[4]

Racial inequalities in health and health care have lasted for centuries
because of *systemic racism*—a concept central to our analysis of the costs
of contemporary racism. We show that contemporary racism—which
includes both racial antipathy and active discrimination—is systemic and
generates major barriers to the full health and well-being of African
Americans, as well as of other Americans of color. This systemic racism
has serious, negative consequences for the health of society as a whole.

Over the last decade, a growing number of research studies in the
social and health sciences have demonstrated some of the personal health
costs of systemic racism—of racial stereotyping, discrimination, and exclusion.[5] We cite these numerous studies in later chapters. However, as of
today, relatively little in-depth field research has examined the substantial
range of the costs of racial discrimination for African Americans, including
the personal, psychological, and physical costs, as well as the major family
and community costs. We focus on the everyday discrimination directed
by whites against African Americans, its consequences for those whom it
targets, and African Americans' resistance and counteractions toward this
recurring discrimination. While workplace discrimination is our primary
focus, racial discrimination outside the workplace is regularly an element
of our respondents' multifaceted accounts. It is this accumulation of discrimination inside and outside the workplace that, in the long run, likely
accounts for the most enduring and harmful effects on African Americans'
lives and health. Our goal here is to begin an in-depth examination of the
substantial range of costs that African Americans still pay for the contemporary racism that interferes with many aspects of their everyday lives.

The African American respondents we quote are almost entirely middle class. Economically successful African Americans are most often
viewed by white Americans as having achieved equality, success in their
workplace, full comfort and happiness, and the American dream to at least
the same degree as middle-class whites. However, as we demonstrate,

these views are generally well off the mark. For example, workplace "integration" for African Americans has, in most cases, been token or only one-way. Black white- and blue-collar employees are often made to adapt to white workplace norms while few of their distinctive and important cultural understandings, especially in regard to racial matters, are incorporated in these workplaces. "Integration" has often created stressful work situations for African American employees because of the many acts of blatant, covert, and subtle discrimination by whites that await them on the job.

In addition, for many poor and working-class African Americans, psychological and physical health problems often arise not only from the direct discrimination in workplaces but also from physically difficult jobs or the lack of access to decent-paying jobs and to adequate and safe housing and neighborhoods. Difficult economic and housing conditions usually are linked directly or indirectly to the fact that many generations of African Americans have had to face institutionalized racism, and these economic difficulties link directly to health problems. In a comprehensive analysis of the privileges of whiteness, George Lipsitz found that the hazards in the living environments of many African Americans put their health at risk on a continuing basis:

> Environmental racism makes the possessive investment in whiteness literally a matter of life and death; if African Americans had access to the nutrition, wealth, health care, and protection against environmental hazards offered routinely to whites, seventy-five thousand fewer of them would die each year.[6]

In his analysis, Lipsitz demonstrates how large-scale job discrimination in the distant or recent past can mean lower income for present and future generations of black families. In central cities, governmental urban redevelopment programs, racially discriminatory home loan programs, and environmental hazards like toxic-waste dumping still increase the health risks for working-class African Americans. Many white-controlled organizations and institutions are involved in these patterns of urban development, not just a few isolated bigots. This is what is meant by racism being institutionalized and systemic.

For the most part, our predominantly middle-class respondents do not face the direct health damage that comes from working in dangerous blue-collar jobs, or that stems from not having a decent family income and adequate housing. In this sense, middle-class African Americans represent a test case of whether living not-white in America is, directly and in itself, dangerous to one's health.

A STATE OF DENIAL

In spite of the painful reality of everyday racism—which time spent in candid discussions with even a few black acquaintances should make clear—most white Americans and many other nonblack Americans insist on denying the reality of antiblack attitudes and discriminatory practices in the contemporary United States. One reason for this is that most whites' lives are racially segregated, and thus they have few substantial or enduring (especially equal-status) contacts with black Americans. Many, if not most, whites never become close enough to their few black acquaintances to have candid and consequential discussions about the racism these acquaintances face. Whites may see, in their workplaces or in the media, some African Americans discussing personal experiences with racism. However, most whites seem to view such discussions as "black paranoia," "playing the race card," or "blacks always complaining." Most do not go beyond these usually wrongheaded images to try to understand the continuing realities of racial oppression. In addition, few white Americans seem aware of, or are willing to acknowledge, the scale of the negative consequences of ongoing racist attitudes, practices, and institutions.

White Views: Health and Economic Conditions

The evidence of white denial and ignorance of the reality of discrimination and its heavy costs is substantial. For example, a recent *Washington Post*/Kaiser/Harvard national survey of 779 whites found that the majority (61 percent) viewed the average black person as having health care access that is *equal to or better than* that of the average white person.[7] However, contrary to this white majority opinion, the data show that whites are far more likely to have good health insurance and adequate or better medical care than black Americans (see chapter 7). This ignorance is particularly serious in light of the many serious health problems faced by African Americans. In addition, about half the white respondents felt that blacks had a level of education similar to or better than that of whites. Yet, white adults are much more likely to be college graduates, and are a little more likely to be high school graduates, than black adults are. Half the white respondents also felt that, on the average, whites and blacks are about as well off in the jobs they hold. Once again, the data show that whites are much more likely than blacks to hold professional, managerial, or well paying blue-collar jobs. Moreover, some 42 percent of the whites in this survey thought that the average black worker earned at least as much as the average white worker, although there is in fact a *large* gap in actual earnings.[8] When the results of the four questions were combined, 70 percent of these white respondents were found to hold one or more erroneous beliefs about white/black differentials. Overall, most whites hold a fictional view of at least some aspects of the economic and health status of African Americans today.

On a general question in the same survey about opportunities in life, 71 percent of the white respondents thought that African Americans had opportunities that were equal to or better than those of whites. Moreover, only *one in five* among the white respondents evaluated the current societal situation accurately on a general question about how much discrimination African Americans faced—that is, they agreed that the situation today is one in which African Americans face "a lot of discrimination."[9] Yet, as we and other researchers have demonstrated in previous studies, and as we show throughout this book, African Americans still face much racial discrimination.[10]

Why Do Many Whites Deny the Reality of Everyday Racism?

Judging from this and other recent opinion surveys, a substantial majority of white Americans are *greatly* out of touch with social reality when it comes to estimations of the difficult health care and economic conditions faced by African Americans. These whites are either ignorant of these disparate and discriminatory conditions or are unwilling to fully acknowledge that they exist. Thus, it is not just African Americans who are paying a price for continuing racism in the United States. The majority of white Americans are confused or troubled in their thinking about racial matters because they deny easily ascertainable social realities—probably because they are generally conforming and lacking in introspection when it comes to many of their racial attitudes and views.[11] Also, for many of these whites, it would likely be too disruptive of their self-concepts to accept the fact that they live in a very unfair and non-meritocratic society. If these whites admitted that significant black *disadvantages* existed, then, conversely, they would have to acknowledge that significant white *privileges* also exist. Denial of the continuing reality of racial discrimination and its negative impact allows many whites to keep their own self-conceptions intact, as well as their belief that they live in a meritocratic society.

Another reason that whites downplay or deny the reality and costly impact of racism on African Americans is that they "blame the victims." Many whites hold stereotypes that, directly or indirectly, blame black Americans for their lack of achievement or their difficult socioeconomic situations. The common view is that black Americans bring whatever problems they still have on themselves. Indeed, most whites admit they still hold to negative images of African Americans. In one recent national survey of whites by Harvard researchers, 58 percent of the white respondents agreed with one or more of these listed traits as being applicable to African Americans: lazy, aggressive or violent, prefer to live on welfare, or complaining. Some 34 percent agreed with two or more of these negative traits.[12] Other surveys show a similar pattern of majority white acceptance of antiblack stereotypes and images.[13] Clear in these stereotypes is the idea that if African Americans would work harder and get rid of their "poor values," they would do much better in society.

Most whites also hold individualistic values that lend themselves to de-emphasizing the racist realities of the society. Thus, white Americans often emphasize "free will," the supposed ability of each individual to select freely from among the many choices permitted in society. Again, those whites who deny that there is significant antiblack racism in society likely believe themselves to have generally "made it" on their own—and believe that others are able to do the same. Whites may see a few successful middle-class or upper-income African Americans in the mass media and extend generalizations from these examples to African Americans as a group. However, the routine assertion of the view that there are fully equal opportunities in the United States communicates that many whites do not understand that African Americans and other Americans of color are seriously limited by the contours and barriers of systemic racism.[14] Such a view is also supportive of white views that there is no need for aggressive government programs to eradicate racial discrimination.

Denial of Racism in Health Care

A recent book titled *PC, M.D.* attempts to make the case that the "racial disparities in health are real, but data do not point convincingly to systemic racial bias as a determinant."[15] The author, Sally Satel, is a white psychiatrist and fellow at the conservative American Enterprise Institute. She reviews selected studies on racial differences in health care procedures and notes some flaws in a few studies. However, she downplays the findings that show clear racial differentials and, more importantly, she ignores many other studies that point to racial discrimination, both subtle and blatant, on the part of health care practitioners and institutions (see chapter 3). Like other conservative commentators, Satel also ignores the preponderance of data showing that a majority of white Americans, including many who are well-educated, harbor antiblack and other racial stereotypes, and that many whites still regularly discriminate against African Americans in such areas as housing and employment. Even without the studies showing discrimination in health care, one should strongly entertain the possibility that the pervasive discrimination against African Americans perpetrated by whites in numerous other institutional arenas might well spill over into health care institutions. At a number of points, Satel notes serious racial and economic differentials in health and health care, but does not see these issues as significantly linked to continuing racial or class bias in health care.[16]

At one point, Satel raises the question as to whether black respondents in one study "overreported episodes of discrimination."[17] This comment suggests the standard stereotype of African Americans as being "paranoid" about discrimination. Indeed, many whites reject or seriously play down black employees' reports of racial discrimination and its related stresses inside or outside their workplaces, even though white employees' reports of health-damaging stress in the workplace are more likely to be taken at face value. Research studies on workplace stress generally accept (the usually white) workers' reports of job strain, daily work problems, and troubling life events.[18] Researchers or commentators rarely question these latter reports as involving "over reporting" by the respondents or "only their perceptions."

Moreover, like many whites who attempt to explain the causes of continuing inequality, Satel reiterates the theme that this inequality problem is mainly the result of African Americans and other people of color not taking responsibility for their lives. It is easy for an affluent white person to lecture those who are oppressed along racial and class lines on the need to take "personal responsibility over their health."[19] However, since Americans of color have little control over the character and structure of the important institutions in U.S. society, there is only so much personal control that a person of color can exert over a range of important work, health, and healthcare matters. As groups and individuals, African Americans and most other Americans of color still have relatively little influence over corporate workplaces, real estate firms, or healthcare organizations. As we see in the data presented throughout this book, African Americans struggle daily with the barriers placed in their paths by white individuals and white-dominated institutions. Most do take responsibility for dealing with their own employment and health problems and, equally as important, for fighting the recurring white-generated racism they encounter. Given all that they face, and their remarkable perseverance in the face of major barriers, most African Americans do *not* need conservatives or others lecturing them about morality, especially from the discredited "blaming the victim" perspective.

At this point, we might add a more general note. Many well-educated conservatives deny the evidence of the many racial barriers that criss-cross U.S. society and seriously damage their targets. For example, the conservative Asian-Indian American journalist, Dinesh D'Souza, has written that, for groups like African Americans, "Irrational discrimination . . . is, as we have seen, a relatively infrequent occurrence." He also says that "it does exist, but we can live with it."[20] Critical to such an analysis is denial of the many reported experiences of African Americans who attest to the widespread character of the discrimination that they face. Conservative foundations and institutes fund much of this conservative analysis denying racial discrimination. Like D'Souza, Satel acknowledges financial and institutional assistance from a number of right-wing and conservative organizations—in her case, the American Enterprise Institute, the Earhart Foundation, the Ethics and Policy Center, and the Center for Equal Opportunity. Since the 1980s, these and similar white-funded conservative organizations have intentionally generated a large-scale effort to shape the way Americans think about many important public policy issues, including racial and gender discrimination, immigration, welfare reform, and health care institutions and programs.[21]

Denial of Racism and Its Costs: A Recent Court Case

Most white, American leaders seem to share, to some degree, denial of the seriousness of racism in U.S. society. Not surprisingly, in both the past and the present, the overwhelmingly white and male elites at the helm of powerful corporate, political, media, and academic organizations have played the key roles in generating many stereotyped views of African Americans, and in blocking or weakening government programs and decisions that might redress patterns of racial discrimination.

Take, for example, some white judges who, in recent cases, are back-pedaling on government remedies for racial discrimination targeting African Americans.[22] For example, in a 1998 case, *Etter v. Veriflo Corporation*, the California Court of Appeals decided that frequent racist epithets directed at a black male employee (Etter) were not "severe or pervasive" enough to warrant a legal remedy under either federal or California employment discrimination law.[23] Etter reported that a white supervisor directed racially derogatory terms—among them "Buckwheat," "Jemima," "boy"—at him and other black employees, and that she mocked blacks' pronunciation of certain words. However, the court asserted that Etter was referred to as "Buckwheat" by a supervising white employee "only" twice, and also noted that Etter could not remember the precise dates when he was called "boy." The court missed a major problem faced by many black employees: Racial insults are common and are often ignored or repressed in order for the person to continue daily functioning—and, thus, may be hard to recall later.[24] Because subtle and blatant insults are recurring, it may be particularly difficult to remember specific dates. Furthermore, the court opinion referred twice to the fact that Etter had himself laughed at racially insulting comments, thereby implying that the negative impact of the racist comments was not serious or was only "in the head" of the victim, and thus was beyond legal remedy. However, Etter may have laughed only in an attempt to get along with fellow white employees at the time, a common reaction of black employees who fear for their jobs.[25] Indeed, his laughter could also have been because of nervousness, shock, or disbelief.

The *Etter* court also questioned black reports of discrimination when they found it relevant, as in their noting that Etter had previously filed discrimination charges against another employee. The apparent reason for mentioning this fact is to suggest that Etter is overly sensitive. They also may be suggesting that he is using his racial classification—that is, "playing the race card"— for the financial gain that might be won through a successful discrimination lawsuit. In this case, it apparently did not occur to these prominent white judges that racial discrimination could be a common occurrence at a black man's workplace—or in his life generally.

The original *Etter* trial took place in Contra Costa County, California, and thus it is likely that the jury was predominantly white. The jury was specifically instructed by the lower court judge to consider whether "a reasonable person of the Plaintiff's race would have found the racial conduct complained of to be sufficiently severe or pervasive to alter the conditions of the person's employment and create a hostile or abusive working environment."[26] However, one might question whether many whites (and other nonblacks), as judges or a jury, are able to determine accurately what is "reasonable" for an African American. In this case, the three appellate court judges acted, in effect, as a higher-level jury, and all three were white men, as was the original district court judge.

Since they are overwhelmingly white in composition, the California and U.S. courts do not ordinarily embed in their general understandings of workplace life the perspectives of the African American targets of racial discrimination. Instead, the white-dominated courts often embed the white (here, the perpetrator's) perspective in their understandings. This is ironic since U.S. civil rights laws are supposed to take into full account *the perspectives of those who are the targets of everyday discrimination. Etter* suggests the reality of institutionalized racism in the U.S. justice system, what a leading constitutional scholar Roy Brooks calls "juridical subordination."[27] As a rule, a jury or group of judges with a significant representation of African Americans would be better able to reach a fair judgment about the character and impact of the workplace discrimination facing an African American.

The majority of whites do not have the knowledge or experience to make such judgments. It has been shown in surveys that a majority of whites do not have a significant understanding of the severity of the racism faced by black Americans.[28] The *Etter* court, in deciding that the plaintiff's experiences were merely "episodic," and not "pervasive," failed to understand the severity and impact of those experiences for black employees.

This court case stands as an important guide for judges in regard to the "reasonable person" standard under both federal and California employment discrimination law. Clearly, the white judges here, and others with this view, are out of touch with the relevant social reality. Many, if not most, historically white workplaces have a difficult or hostile racial climate largely because the majority of whites still harbor at least a few racist images and stereotypes, and because many harbor propensities to discriminate against African Americans.[29] Under the right circumstances, such stereotypes and prejudices play themselves out in subtly racist actions by these whites. In yet other cases, the stereotypical images and related notions erupt in more overt and direct racist practices.

Discrimination in the workplace at the hands of fellow employees is serious enough, but when it is colluded in or made light of by higher-level, more powerful authorities—including immediate supervisors, top corporate executives, political leaders, and judges—its impact can be even more lasting and painful. Discrimination that is supported or ignored by higher-level authorities can be very negative in its effects because the targets of the discrimination do not know where to turn for help or redress. In many settings, most whites orient their actions to signals from these higher-level authorities, and racist behavior that is winked at or rewarded tends to be repeated.[30] The lack of significant remedial action by higher authorities to end discrimination can contribute significantly to the damage it generates both immediately and in the long run.

THE THEORETICAL FRAMEWORK: RACISM AS INSTITUTIONALIZED AND SYSTEMIC

There is a tendency in much analysis of racial matters in the United States to limit the concept of *racism* to just racial prejudices and stereotypes. However, we use here the original meaning of the term, and thus accent the *structural* and *systemic* character of contemporary racism. When Magnus Hirschfeld first used the term "racism" (in German) to describe the anti-Semitism directed against Jews in the 1930s, he had in mind more than individual prejudices and stereotypes.[31] From the beginning, this term *racism* was intended to denote a *system* of racialized oppression. A systemic perspective on racism directs us to pay attention to the particular social settings surrounding and generating racial discrimination and other forms of racial oppression. We can speak meaningfully of systemic racism because there are literally hundreds of thousands of social settings in which discrimination or other racial oppression is imposed regularly on African Americans and other Americans of color. These social settings include a myriad of private and governmental workplaces, educational classrooms, voluntary organizations, public accommodations, and other institutional settings.

In the structural regime that is everyday racism, whites act overtly, subtly, or covertly in order to single out and harm African Americans or other Americans of color. *Discrimination* thus involves *actions*, as well as one or more *discriminators* and one or more *targets*. In this book, we focus mainly on antiblack discrimination and its many consequences. Broadly viewed, the system of antiblack discrimination includes (1) the motivations of the discriminator, such as stereotyping and prejudice, (2) the discriminatory actions, (3) the costs and benefits of discrimination, (4) the immediate social-institutional context, and (5) the surrounding community, societal, and global contexts.

In the late 1960s, Kwame Ture and Charles Hamilton made an important distinction between *individual racism,* such as the discriminatory actions of one bigoted white individual, and *institutional racism,* such as the institutional practices that result in large numbers of black children suffering from inadequate nutrition.[32] This distinction is at the core of a deeper understanding of contemporary racism. In most organizations and other societal settings, whites have the ability and opportunity to discriminate as individuals, yet much of their power to harm African Americans or other Americans of color comes from their membership in larger white-dominated social networks and organizations, what have been termed "enforcement coalitions."[33] As we see in later chapters, these white-dominated networks, coalitions, and other organizations typically undergird the discriminatory actions of individual whites. Additionally, even if a white person does not discriminate individually, he or she benefits from white privilege based on group membership.

Today, antiblack discrimination is commonplace, recurring, and institutionalized. In many U.S. workplaces, a racial hierarchy of dominant white workers supervising subordinate African Americans is part of the ongoing organizational structure. This often lends itself to workplace discrimination of a blatant, subtle, or covert type. In addition, institutionalized racism can be found in the local cultures of organizations—in the informal rules, the implicit protocols for workplace interaction, and the organizational memories. More generally, the racist culture of the larger society—seen in everything from the language of antiblack joking and epithets, to negative media images of black bodies, to distorted accounts of U.S. racial history—constantly interacts with, and reinforces, the social structures of racism.[34] Social psychologist James Jones suggests that cultural racism "comprises the cumulative effects of a racialized worldview, based on belief in essential racial differences that favor the dominant racial group over others."[35] This worldview penetrates most areas of U.S. society.

In recent decades, a number of scholars have shown how racial oppression intersects and interacts with other types of social oppression, such as class and gender discrimination and domination. For example, social psychologist Philomena Essed has used data from interviews with black women in the United States and the Netherlands to show that racism and sexism regularly interact in the lives of these women. As we see in some of the comments of our respondents, the oppression of black women sometimes takes the form of racism, sometimes of sexism, and sometimes of *gendered racism.*[36] Scholars like Essed, Patricia Hill Collins, and Yanick St. Jean and Joe Feagin have, in their research on the situations of black women and other women of color, emphasized the importance of liberating these women from racial, gender, *and* gendered-racist stereotypes and discrimination.[37] In addition, Denise Segura has suggested the concept of *triple oppression,* the mutually reinforcing and interactive set of racial, class, and gender forces, the cumulative effects of which "place women of color in a subordinate social and economic position relative to men of color and the white population."[38]

In the routines of everyday life, the racist and gendered-racist norms imposed by white (or white male) enforcement coalitions are usually linked to, and perpetuated by, the antiblack stereotypes held by the majority of white Americans. Many whites still *think* and *feel* in racialized terms when they choose neighborhoods, mates, employees, and workplace buddies. Prejudice is not simply antipathy possessed by individual whites but is "rooted in a sense of group position."[39] As we discussed earlier, opinion polls and social science research demonstrate that antiblack hostility persists among whites today, not because of a few isolated bigots, but because a majority of whites still cling to antiblack stereotypes or images. These images and stereotypes likely lie behind most of the discriminatory actions of whites—who are linked together in white networks and generally dominant in white-controlled workplaces and many other societal settings.

For nearly four centuries now, systemic racism has included a diverse assortment of exploitative, exclusionary, and other discriminatory practices targeting African Americans and other Americans of color. Some of this racialized mistreatment, as we see in the accounts in later chapters, takes a direct and overt form, while other mistreatment is subtle or covert. Much of the racism encountered by African Americans today takes the form of what might be termed "woodwork" racism—that is, the racist incidents are so commonplace and recurring that many African Americans take them as an everyday aspect of their lives. If asked in a survey whether they have faced discrimination recently, many African Americans may not mention the many little racist events that cross their paths daily, but rather accent only the larger-scale and more dramatic incidents. In a previous study, a retired schoolteacher in a Southwestern city recounted her experience with a racist epithet yelled by a clerk in a mall shop, then characterized the many recurring incidents of racism as the "little murders every day" that have made her long life so difficult.[40] It is clear in this statement that the everyday events, which might seem small and unimportant to outside white observers, in reality can cause *great* pain and stress. Racist practices are chronic stressors for most African Americans, stressors with often dangerous and deadly impacts. This system of everyday racism is buttressed by white-racist ideologies, hostile prejudices, and negative images and stereotypes, and is deeply imbedded in societal institutions that generate and preserve racial advantages for most white Americans.

UNJUST ENRICHMENT AND UNJUST IMPOVERISHMENT: A BRIEF LOOK AT A LONG HISTORY

Historically, European adventurers and entrepreneurs from countries such as Portugal, Spain, Holland, and England generated worldwide economic expansion involving colonial domination over many other peoples across the globe. This colonialism and imperialism involved seizing the land and labor of those who were soon seen as racialized "others." In the North American case, the European invaders subordinated or destroyed Native American societies, seized their lands, and then imported Africans as enslaved laborers used to help generate white wealth. They soon rationalized this theft of land and labor in extensive racist stereotypes and ideologies.

The Costs of Slavery

At the center of systemic racism are the many economic and political resources unjustly gained by whites over some fifteen generations since the seventeenth century. This unjust enrichment has included more or less exclusive white access to major social, economic, and political resources that were, until recently, denied to African Americans by slavery and segregation. Think for a moment about the length of time that African Americans have been in North America—largely as the result of involuntary immigration as enslaved workers, beginning in 1619. For *nearly two thirds* of their total time in North America, African Americans were enslaved as the *chattel property* of white Americans. From the end of slavery in 1865 until the end of legal segregation in 1968, there was roughly another century of overt and blatant segregation (often a system of near-slavery) for most African Americans. It was only about a third of a century ago that legalized racial oppression of an extreme type was abolished in the United States.[41]

Beginning in the early to mid-seventeenth century, African Americans were brutally and aggressively exploited in a growing, increasingly slavery-centered economic system that brought a range of benefits for white Americans. Over nearly two and a half centuries, millions of enslaved black Americans labored for white slaveholders, large and small. Yet slaveholders were not the only beneficiaries of the slavery system. Those whites who held plantation jobs, those trading in products bought from or sold to plantations, and those working in support sectors such as shipbuilding, banking, and insurance also benefited from the slavery-centered economic system of the long period up to 1865. In this slavery system, many white Americans gained significant income and wealth unjustly, and at a high cost for African Americans.

The costs of slavery were *far more* than just economic, as one of the greatest Americans, Frederick Douglass, often indicated in his writings

about his own enslavement. Writing in reference to a new white owner, he noted in an autobiography that:

> We were worked in all weathers. It was never too hot or too cold; it could never rain, blow, hail, or snow, too hard for us to work in the field. Work, work, work, was scarcely more the order of the day than of the night. The longest days were too short for him, and the short-est nights too long for him. I was somewhat unmanageable when I first went there, but a few months of this discipline tamed me. Mr. Covey succeeded in breaking me. I was broken in body, soul, and spirit. My natural elasticity was crushed, my intellect languished, the disposition to read departed, the cheerful spark that lingered about my eye died; the dark night of slavery closed in upon me. . . . At times I would rise up, a flash of energetic freedom would dart through my soul, accompanied with a faint beam of hope, that flickered for a moment, and then vanished. I sank down again, mourning over my wretched condition. I was sometimes prompted to take my life, and that of Covey, but was prevented by a combination of hope and fear.[42]

From the beginning, the system of enslavement had physical and psychological costs, as well as severe economic costs, for those enslaved. Moreover, under slavery, African American women not only suffered what Douglass described, but also faced the added oppression of sexual victimization and violence from white slaveholders and other white men. Angela Davis describes well the lives of millions of enslaved black women "who toiled under the lash for their masters, worked for and pro-tected their families, fought against slavery, and who were beaten and raped, but never subdued."[43]

We should also underscore the important point that many enslaved African Americans engaged in ongoing resistance to this racial oppres-sion. For example, one day Frederick Douglass had a two-hour fight with his white owner, Mr. Covey. After an intense struggle, Covey decided to abandon the fight, and because of the resistance did not try to whip Douglass thereafter:

> This battle with Mr. Covey was the turning-point in my career as a slave. It rekindled the few expiring embers of freedom, and revived

within me a sense of my own manhood. It recalled the departed self-confidence, and inspired me again with a determination to be free. . . . My long-crushed spirit rose, cowardice departed, bold defiance took its place; and I now resolved that, however long I might remain a slave in form, the day had passed forever when I could be a slave in fact. I did not hesitate to let it be known of me, that the white man who expected to succeed in whipping, must also succeed in killing me.[44]

The person subjected to racial oppression usually develops a range of resistance strategies. W. E. B. DuBois captured the reality of this resistance long ago when he underscored the point that it was not only white abolitionists and Abraham Lincoln, who "freed the slaves," but also enslaved African Americans who helped to free themselves "by armed rebellion, by sullen refusal to work, by poison and murder, by running away to the North and Canada, by giving point and powerful example to the agitation of the abolitionists and by furnishing 200,000 soldiers and many times as many civilian helpers in the Civil War."[45] From the beginning, and now for centuries, African Americans have played a central role in their own liberation, both as individuals and as a group. As we see in many of our respondents' accounts in later chapters, racial oppression operates in dialectical tension and interaction with acts of everyday resistance.

White Privileges and Black Oppression under Legal Segregation

After slavery, the white majority continued to benefit, directly and indirectly, economically and psychologically, from an extensive system of legal (in the South) and informal (in the North) segregation, a system that lasted in most areas until the 1960s. This white-maintained segregation had physical, psychological, and economic costs for African Americans. These costs involved continuing violence against black men and black women, including widespread police brutality and some six thousand lynchings of African Americans by white lynchers often operating in mobs. Many whites, both men and women and workers at various class levels, gained economically under legal and de facto (informal) segregation. We do not have the space here to demonstrate the substantial economic evidence of white benefits and black costs under legal segregation, so one dramatic illustration will suffice: Millions of white Americans are the contemporary beneficiaries of very large giveaways of federal lands to their farming ancestors. The Homestead Act, passed in the 1860s, eventually provided some 246 million acres at minimal cost for some 1.5 million homesteads. Research by Trina Williams suggests that the number of *current* beneficiaries is perhaps in the range of about 46 million, almost all of whom are white because of restrictions on African American access to such lands during the land-giveaway period that lasted up to about 1930.[46] Until the 1960s, many other federal giveaways of wealth-generating resources—airline routes, radio and television frequencies, mineral resources, and government contracts and licenses—more or less exclusively benefited whites.

Under legal segregation in the South, and similar de facto segregation in the North, whites also secured almost all of the jobs above the menial level, whether in the blue- or white-collar sectors, outside black communities. After World War II, whites enjoyed privileged or exclusive access to a range of major government programs, including guaranteed home loans favoring homebuyers in white suburban areas, and veteran's (GI) programs for higher education. Under legal and de facto segregation, few people but whites were able to attend most of the nation's historically white colleges and universities, at least until the 1950s and 1960s. This privileged educational access enabled many whites whose parents had modest means to secure the "cultural capital" that they then translated into good-paying jobs, decent houses, and many consumer goods. These educated whites, in turn, could translate their own prosperity into good educational and other major socioeconomic benefits for their children and grandchildren. Today, most whites continue to benefit not only from the unjust enrichment of their ancestors, but also from the large-scale discrimination that still targets African Americans in housing, workplaces, public accommodations, and educational and political institutions.[47] While working-class whites usually have not been as well off as middle- and upper-class whites, they too have had access to a range of benefits— such as white skin privilege and related benefits such as freedom from police brutality—that no African Americans have had.

Once the structure of racial oppression was firmly in place, white privileges and enrichment came to be seen as natural, as they are usually seen today by white Americans. The country's white leadership, strongly supported by most, but not all, ordinary whites, has long worked to maintain by discriminatory and exclusionary means this longstanding structure of unjust enrichment for white Americans. Individually and as a group, whites have helped to maintain the system of racism by subtle, blatant, and covert means.[48]

The other side of unjust enrichment for whites is unjust deprivation and impoverishment for African Americans. Over time, the wealth-generating system of white racism has cost African Americans enormous amounts of economic resources and other forms of wealth. One economic analyst estimates that the dollar value of the labor taken from enslaved African Americans for just the years 1790 through 1860 is in the $7 to 40 billion range, depending on certain historical assumptions.[49] One might use these amounts as rough estimates of the value of the wages lost to African American workers over this period. Moreover, we should add to the value of this stolen labor the income and wealth that would have been generated by these African American workers—and, subsequently, by generations of their descendants—if they had been able, like many whites during this period, to put some earned wages into income-generating investments such as land, farms, other business enterprises, and education. Viewed over many generations, the lost wealth and other economic losses for African Americans that are rooted in the slavery period are doubtless enormous. In addition, under the system of legal and intensive de facto segregation that was in effect from the late 1800s to the 1960s in the South and much of the North, even more income and wealth was lost because of high levels of discrimination perpetrated by whites in many areas, such as employment, education, and housing. Yet more income and wealth has been lost to most African Americans since the end of that legal segregation as a result of contemporary patterns of discrimination, especially in such areas as employment and housing. Systemic racism has meant not only much less income and wealth for some fifteen generations of African American families, but also fewer opportunities to overcome these huge losses because of *continuing* discrimination to the present day. Today, the economic debt alone owed to African Americans is probably in the trillions of dollars. And this substantial cost does not include the emotional costs of centuries of personal and familial pain and suffering, or the many shortened lives.

Discrimination Today: A Brief Overview

In previous books, we describe in detail the data that show conclusively the widespread character of the racial discrimination that still afflicts African Americans today.[50] Because this is not the main focus of this book, we only briefly note recent evidence of continuing racial discrimination. Discriminatory practices that create heavy costs for African Americans today remain commonplace and pandemic. They are found in all major employment sectors. For example, one study in Los Angeles found that about 60 percent of more than a thousand black respondents reported discriminatory barriers in workplaces in just the previous year.[51] Those with more education, like many of our respondents, were *more likely* than those with less income to report such discrimination at their workplaces. In addition, a recent national survey found that more than a third of black respondents reported discrimination in regard to jobs or promotions.[52] Another recent, large-scale survey of forty thousand military personnel by the Department of Defense found that nearly half, or more, of the black respondents had encountered racist jokes, offensive racial discussions, or racial condescension in the last year alone. Significant proportions also had experienced racist comments, racist publications, hostile racial stares, and racial barriers in regard to career-related decisions. Still, employment in the military is considered by many African Americans to mean *fewer* problems with racism than they encounter in the civilian sector.[53]

Reports of unfair racialized treatment by white police officers are commonplace. African American pedestrians and motorists are much more likely than whites to be stopped, questioned, or searched by the police. One urban survey found that black respondents were much more likely than whites to report being unfairly stopped and checked by the police.[54] In addition, one ACLU study of Interstate 95 in Maryland found that, while black drivers made up just 18 percent of those in violation of traffic laws, they were about three quarters of all those stopped and searched by police.[55]

One recent national survey found that more than 80 percent of the black respondents reported facing hostile racial acts in public spaces or public accommodations; these acts by whites included poor service, racial slurs, fearful or defensive behavior, and lack of respect.[56] Another recent survey of 131 black alumni of the University of Florida found that most had been victims of discrimination while traveling. They experienced discrimination while shopping, dining, or staying in a hotel. Nearly eight in ten had experienced discrimination at a restaurant, while about seven in ten reported discrimination in hotels and while shopping.[57] Other major research studies have found serious levels of discrimination for African Americans shopping for new cars, in bail-setting by judges, and in medical treatment by physicians.[58]

Several recent housing audit studies have found high rates of discrimination for black renters and homebuyers seeking decent housing for themselves and their families. In field research in several cities, when their experiences were compared with those of white test-renters, black test-renters were found to have faced discrimination some 61 to 80 percent of the time depending on the city. For example, a 2001 rental audit study in Houston, using forty paired white and black testers, found that racial discrimination occurred in 80 percent of the attempts to rent by the black testers. This racial mistreatment took the form of openly stated discriminatory policies, misinformation about the housing, and differential treatment in regard to appointments, applications, and terms of contracts. Audit studies have also found discrimination against homebuyers. A 2001 Boston audit study included apartment complexes and real estate agencies. In 60 percent of the thirty-five phone and in-person tests, black testers received discriminatory treatment compared to the paired white testers.[59] In addition, a recent national survey asked 1,663 whites about their likely home buying choices. Each white respondent was given a statement asking them to consider how they would react if they were looking for a new house, and found one in their price range that was much better than any other. The researchers then varied what they told the respondents about the racial composition of the hypothetical neighborhood, the quality of local schools, the stability of property values, and the local crime rate. Controlling for other factors, the researchers found that—while the percentage of the neighborhood that was Latino or Asian had no independent effect on white housing choices—the percentage of black people living in the neighborhood, controlling for other factors like crime and school quality, had a strong and independent effect on white housing choices. At low black percentages, the average white respondent would buy the house. However, "after about 15 percent black, net of the variables for which race serves as a proxy, the average white is unlikely to buy the house."[60]

A major reason for the extensive residential segregation along racial lines in U.S. towns and cities lies in the unwillingness of many whites—

including the owners of many apartment complexes and many owners or salespeople in real estate firms—to sell or rent to African Americans (especially in historically white residential areas), as well as the unwillingness of many white families to consider housing areas with more than a small percentage of African Americans living there. The consequent residential segregation is a key underlying factor that links to or generates other problems facing African Americans. Segregation of neighborhoods and communities often means, for African Americans, less access to schools with excellent resources, key job networks, quality public services such as hospital care, and quality housing. The latter factor, less access to quality housing, also limits the ability of African American families to build up substantial housing equity, a major source for the wealth passed along by white families now for several generations.

In addition to the most serious and dramatic incidents of racial discrimination, such as being victimized by police brutality, turned down for a job, or excluded from housing, there are the many everyday hassles— the aforementioned "woodwork" discrimination that creates much stress because it is so commonplace. For example, in a recent Detroit study of African American women, researchers found that most of their 331 respondents reported facing everyday types of discrimination—with 62 percent reporting moderate to high levels of this more mundane discrimination. This everyday mistreatment included verbal insults, various types of disrespect, and poor service from whites. Moreover, the consequences of this everyday discrimination were found to be serious; there was a significant relationship between the level of experience with this discrimination and psychological distress.[61]

Economic and Other Social Costs Today

An early 1990s United Nations report discussed the living conditions endured by African Americans compared to people in many other countries around the globe. This report used a Human Development Index (HDI) to measure the quality of life. This index included data on education, income, and life expectancy. Among all of the countries (and major subgroups within countries) examined in the report, U.S. whites, taken separately, ranked *first* in overall quality of life. However, taken separately, African Americans ranked *just thirty-first* in the long list of countries and country subgroups.[62]

Why is there such a huge disparity in quality of life between white and black Americans after three decades of attempts by the federal government to eliminate discrimination and its effects? In the U.S., the remedies for racial discrimination, segregation, and other racial oppression implemented since the 1960s civil rights movements have not brought the significant socioeconomic changes and redistribution that most African Americans and their white and other nonblack allies have long hoped for. Today, there are huge and continuing inequalities in wealth and income between white and black Americans.

We have previously demonstrated that these inequalities are in part, as the distinguished Supreme Court Justice William O. Douglas once noted in a 1968 court case, the continuing consequences of past racial oppression: "Some badges of slavery remain today. While the institution has been outlawed, it has remained in the minds and hearts of many white men. Cases which have come to this Court depict a *spectacle of slavery unwilling to die.*"[63] In addition, these racial inequalities are in part the legacy of the long era of legal segregation. Black Americans today pay a heavy economic price for centuries of racial oppression, a price perhaps most dear for those with low-wage jobs. Thus, over the last decade or two, black families have had a median family income only about 55 to 63 percent of that of white families. Today, African American families also continue to endure poverty conditions at a much greater rate than white families, and black workers face an unemployment rate that is typically twice that of whites. Black workers are often the first laid off during economic recessions and the last to be recalled. Perhaps more serious is the fact that today, the wealth (net worth) of the average black family is only *about 10 percent* or so of that of the average white family, a clear indication of the impact of unjust enrichment over many generations—unjust enrichment that has taken the form of privileged if not exclusive white access to critical material, educational, and cultural resources, often for many generations.[64]

More than Economic Losses: Physical, Psychological, Family, and Community Costs

Historically, and in the present, antiblack racism has had a great impact well beyond the economic. Many African Americans lived shortened lives under slavery and segregation from the poor economic and housing conditions and the violence, including lynchings, by individual and organized whites. Later, those who participated in the civil rights movements of the 1950s and 1960s were harassed or attacked, and sometimes injured or killed, just for seeking basic civil rights and an end to de jure and de facto segregation in education, housing, and other institutional arenas. Indeed, many brave black children were on the cutting edge of school desegregation in the North and the South, and they often paid a heavy price. In one interview study, a Chicago mother who does counseling discussed how she learned of her daughter's borderline epilepsy: "I moved out here in '69. We were one of the first black families. My daughter attended a predominantly white school that was becoming integrated. My neighbors were fighting it. I'd never seen a mob of whites until that time. Never in my whole life. . . . There were maybe four hundred, five hundred whites protesting the black children." Then she noted the impact on her daughter, who was only fourteen and in the first year of high school: "She began to get really nervous and didn't want to go to school. It got so bad that I thought maybe it was drugs. So I had taken her to a psychiatrist. We come to find out that it was just the fear of going to school there. I didn't know she was a borderline epileptic. The pressure brought it out."[65] The child and her family had to suffer through the extraordinarily intense pressures the daughter faced while simply trying to fulfill the traditional American dream of receiving a good education.

Today, antiblack discrimination and other aspects of racial oppression continue to have much more than just an economic impact on African American individuals, families, and communities. There are still physical, psychological, family, and community costs, as we document in later chapters. In his provocative and widely read book, African American journalist Ellis Cose began his analysis with this comment: "Despite its very evident prosperity, much of America's black middle class is in excruciating pain. And that distress—although most of the country does not see it—illuminates a serious American problem."[66]

The aforementioned United Nations HDI (Human Development Index) included life expectancy, a statistic that is sharply different for black and white Americans. On the average, white Americans live about 6 to 7 years longer than black Americans. That is perhaps one summary indicator of the long-term, present-day effects of slavery and segregation unwilling to die.

Since the mid-1990s, an increasing number of health and social science researchers have focused their work on the consequences of racial discrimination for the psychological and physical health of African Americans. For example, a recent metropolitan Detroit study looked in some detail at the situations of white and black women and found that black women had fewer economic resources, more experience with unfair and discriminatory treatment, and more serious life crises than did the white women. They also found that racial differentials in discriminatory treatment and life crises significantly, and independently of certain control variables, contributed to racial differences in health status.[67] In addition, one 1990s survey found that the level of discrimination reported over the lifetimes of black respondents was linked to psychological problems, overall well-being, and number of days sick in bed.[68] As we see in later chapters, the physical reactions to racial discrimination often take the form of all-day headaches, stomach problems, chest pains, stress diabetes, and hypertension. In addition, a study of 1980s longitudinal data from black respondents found that experience with racial discrimination at one point in time was associated with high levels of psychological stress at a later point in time.[69] And several recent studies of black respondents have analyzed detailed inventories of racial incidents and found that the more discrimination a person reported, the greater the level of psychological distress.[70] The psychological reactions to discrimination take many forms— ranging from anger and bitterness, to anxiety and frustration, to a sense of fear or hopelessness. And these often link to physical health problems as well.

Some Linkages: Discrimination Translates into Health Consequences

Exactly how does everyday discrimination translate into negative physical and psychological health consequences? One recent model suggested by Rodney Clark, Norman Anderson, Vanessa Clark, and David Williams, proposes that the environmental stressors of racial discrimination are translated through the mindsets of the people targeted, which in turn generate coping responses in those people and consequent negative health impacts from discrimination. In this proposed model, lying between the environmental stressors and the understandings and perceptions of individuals are an array of sociodemographic, psychological, and physical-constitution characteristics that can shape how the racism is received and understood by its targets—all of which factors, in turn, shape subsequent coping responses and personal health consequences.[71]

While a full understanding of how past and present discrimination is translated into negative health consequences is not yet possible, there is general agreement that one central way this happens is through the generation of *additional, often high, levels of stress beyond those faced by white people* in the same or similar social settings—added stress that, in its turn, creates or aggravates psychological and physical problems. Racial or ethnic discrimination in the workplace often generates additional stress on top of the ordinary stress that comes from the commonplace problems that all workers face.[72] In the case of this ordinary workplace stress, an employee frequently feels that the stress is caused by something that makes some sense in terms of their place or purpose in the workplace. Additionally, such a worker can often take some action to gain more control over her or his situation, and thus lower the stress level. In the case of stress in the workplace caused by racial discrimination, however, the source of the stress typically makes no sense in terms of the worker's purpose in the workplace. Even more importantly, despite many attempts, an African American worker may never find a way to gain some control over the source of racially generated stress in the workplace. Thus, stress caused by racial hostility or discrimination is typically different in kind or intensity from normal workplace stress.

While there are few medical studies dealing directly with the linkage running from discrimination to stress to physical effects, there is substantial research showing that serious stress of other kinds can have negative effects on a person's cardiovascular, immune, and neurological functioning. Research shows that stress can create problems with breast cancer survival, heart disease, pulmonary disease, and respiratory infections.[73] Numerous research studies show that major life crises (for example, divorce), recurring role strain (for example, in the workplace), and economic problems (for example, unemployment or underemployment) are stressors that can have serious effects on any person's psychological or physical health.[74] It seems very likely that the stress from racism's many incarnations—stress that is often great—has a similarly negative effect on psychological and physical health. We see much evidence on this point in later chapters.

The everyday stressors that target African Americans at work and in other social settings include specific overt, subtle, and covert acts of discrimination by white supervisors, peers, clients, and subordinates. In addition, experiencing white racism is not confined to a few isolated events over a black person's lifetime. It almost always entails a long string of discriminatory events with accumulating consequences. In *Living with Racism*, Joe Feagin and Melvin Sikes developed the idea "that experiences with serious discrimination not only are very painful and stressful in the immediate aftermath but also have a *cumulative* impact on particular individuals, their families, and their communities. A black person's life is regularly disrupted by mistreatment suffered personally or by family members."[75] When one faces a long series of discriminatory incidents over the course of a lifetime, totaling hundreds if not thousands of incidents, these crises disturb an individual's life trajectory and force adaptations and countering responses. This long series of discriminatory events typically has significant family and community consequences. A person who suffers a discriminatory attack often shares the burden of this event with family and friends, and this in turn can create "a domino effect of anguish and anger rippling across an extended group. An individual's discrimination becomes a family matter."[76] Particular instances of discrimination may seem minor to some outside (especially white) observers, particularly if they are considered in isolation. However, when blatant racist actions and overt mistreatment combine with discrimination in more subtle and covert forms, and when these discriminatory practices accumulate over weeks, months, and years, the effect on African Americans is more than what a simple summing of the impact of particular incidents might suggest. There is often a significant multiplier effect, from recurring racial hostility, on a black person's work, health, and social relationships.

In addition, related stress stems from the institutionalized racism deeply imbedded in the socioeconomic background that results in differential treatment for black and white Americans. Institutional racism includes the relative lack of economic and other social resources bequeathed to many black families as a result of the multigenerational legacy of slavery, legal segregation, and contemporary discrimination. Past and present discrimination can be translated into negative health consequences by means of a reduction in the socioeconomic resources available to many black families and individuals, resources that might be used to protect or buttress economic, psychological, and physical health. These resources include economic and educational capital. And they can also involve critical stores of personal, intellectual, and motivational energy. In *Living with Racism,* a retired black psychologist suggested that each human being gets one hundred ergs of energy to live out their lives. Then he added this sharp follow-up: "Now a black person also has one hundred ergs; he uses fifty percent the same way a white man does, dealing with what the white man has [to deal with], so he has fifty percent left. But he uses twenty-five percent fighting being black, [with] all the problems being black and what it means."[77] The negative consequences of racism include a sapping of critical human energy, which can affect one's level of success in a variety of endeavors.

A century ago, the pioneering social psychologist William James noted that human isolation and marginalization are "the greatest of evils" for human beings.[78] Among those who are marginalized in social interaction, "impotent despair" and other psychological problems may develop. Writing in the 1940s in his influential book *An American Dilemma,* social scientist Gunnar Myrdal underscored the link between widespread antiblack discrimination and social isolation and caste-like marginalization. In recent decades, social scientists have further documented the negative effects that marginalization and dehumanization can have on the physical and emotional health of human beings in a variety of settings.[79] The serious damage that racial discrimination inflicts on its African American targets includes such marginalization and dehumanization, which in turn can have serious physical and psychological consequences.

Fighting Back

White-generated discrimination and its costs do not occur without major countering and contenting responses from African Americans. As we see in chapters 5 and 6, African Americans have had to craft an extensive array of ways to fight everyday racism—from withdrawal to fight another day, to sharing strategies with family and friends, to humor and laughter, to open confrontation with white discriminators, to protesting through official channels and lawsuits. The majority of African Americans, and most middle-class African Americans, live their lives in two different communities. As Howard Ramseur has put it, "While most blacks live, have families, social friends and churches within the black community, they still must adapt to white-run schools, workplaces, military settings, and media, an adaptation that often requires them to juggle different values, behavioral styles and aspirations."[80] The social reality of racism is pervasive and destructive, and most African Americans must develop strong, and often successful, ways of coping and contending with that everyday discrimination. For centuries, African Americans have been faced, as individuals and families, with developing an extensive array of strategies for fighting back against continuing oppression.

OUR RESPONDENTS

To begin a serious sociological examination of the many costs of racial discrimination, we conducted exploratory focus groups in the mid-1990s with economically successful African Americans—two in the Midwest and three in the Southeast. We used informants in several communities as starting points to suggest economically successful African Americans who were likely to have significant experience in predominantly white workplaces. Our sample ranges from lower to upper middle class, and most respondents are over the age of thirty. We secured 37 participants, 16 in the Midwest and 21 in the Southeast. Of those reporting their age, the majority were between 31 and 40 years of age, with 5 between 21 and 30, and 12 between 41 and 60. Among those reporting their education, the majority had pursued graduate work beyond a four-year college degree, while thirteen others had completed some college work or earned a college degree. Only one reported not having gone to college at all. Among those who reported family income, the majority had an income that was $31,000 a year or more, with fourteen reporting it above $50,000. The respondents reported a variety of occupations, mostly professional, managerial, and other white-collar positions.[81] Twenty-seven were female, and ten were male. In the analysis, we quote from most of the focus group participants. A central feature of these focus groups was a set of questions probing how the respondents deal with racial discrimination in their everyday lives, and what the costs of that discrimination are in personal, family, and community terms. Over the course of these focus groups, it became clear that these African Americans had long thought about the causes and consequences of the discrimination they regularly face at the hands of whites. Most had well-developed and considered answers to our questions about the contemporary realities of racial discrimination. They are indeed sage theorists of their own experiences.

In addition, we have supplemented these focus group data with some individual interview data from another research study conducted by Feagin and Sikes. This study involved in-depth interviews with more than two hundred middle-class African Americans across the country. They were selected in a snowball design involving various starting points in numerous cities, with about two thirds in cities of the South and Southwest. This sample is roughly equal in men and women, and just over half are in the 36 to 50 age bracket—with another third younger, and a sixth older, than that. Most are employed in white-collar positions, head their own small businesses, or are college students. Nearly one third had household incomes of $35,000 or less; about a fifth in the $36,000 to 55,000 range; and about half in the over-$55,000 bracket. This group is well educated as well, with most having completed at least some college work.[82] The questions asked in this national interview study covered more topics than were brought up in the focus group study, and we use here only their commentaries on the costs of the discrimination and the strategies they use to contend with discrimination (chapters 5 and 6). In addition, we should note that in the following chapters, we have kept the respondents from both studies anonymous by deleting or disguising names and places.[83]

CONCLUSION

Recall that in several recent opinion surveys, a majority of whites still speak of African Americans as lazy, violent, or desirous of living on welfare. Among whites, in homes, bars, offices, and school corridors, the work efforts and other assumed characteristics of African Americans are often denigrated. Ironically, however, African Americans have always provided much of the hard labor that built the United States into a world economic and political power. Certainly, in the first two centuries, African Americans provided much of the labor that enabled the fledgling nation to become prosperous. Their labor under slavery, and later under legal segregation, enabled this country to continue to prosper over several centuries, and their labor still remains very important to the prosperity of the nation.

Many white Americans seem to believe that economically successful, middle-class African Americans such as our respondents are doing well in fully integrated workplaces and living the American dream. As we demonstrate, however, such views are wrongheaded. For most African

American employees, workplace integration has brought continuing and recurring discrimination and a sense of being constantly watched or controlled. Historically, workplace integration has generally required African Americans and other racially oppressed people to accept white norms without the power to significantly affect workplace cultures.[84] Some research has shown that this is certainly the case for middle-class African Americans like our respondents. Susan Toliver makes this pertinent observation: "There was a time in the very recent past when all or most of the social interactions experienced by black middle-class Americans were with other blacks, and included other blacks from all walks of life. . . . Blacks in the middle class who were doctors, lawyers, or ministers not only had a black constituency or clientele but tended to be autonomous in the context of work. For example, those who were middle class and employed in occupations such as those mentioned here were often their own bosses. Today, black middle-class managers do not have such autonomy on the job and work in companies that are white controlled."[85]

Social science research shows that for most men, and many women, work outside the home is a "central and defining characteristic of life. For such individuals, it is through the work role that life achieves its primary meaning and value."[86] The traditional work ethic places a high premium on individuals working hard to provide for their families. The ethic stigmatizes those who are not successful in their work efforts as lazy. This work ethic is important for all U.S. workers, including black workers. For example, one major study of working-class black men found that they held old-fashioned views of the importance of hard work.[87] Their work perspectives and family values were like those of whites who have been studied.

For nearly four centuries, white Americans have held the stereotype that they are superior in their work ethic and intelligence to African Americans. This general denial of African Americans' hard work, achievements, and intelligence is in effect a denial of their integrity and even their identity as human beings. It is not surprising that hostile white stereotypes and discriminatory practices—especially when they are commonplace and recurring in settings in which African Americans are seeking to make a living and provide for their families—often have a negative impact on blacks' personal, family, and community health.

In this book we describe and analyze the character and range of racial discrimination's continuing high costs by examining the experiences of some middle-class African American respondents who work in predominantly white employment settings. Our general research questions include the following: Is there a link between workplace and other types of discrimination and personal stress for African Americans? If so, what are the psychological and physical consequences of that racially related stress? In addition, what are the family and community consequences of that discrimination and its stress? And how do African Americans resist and counter this discrimination? Finally, what are the broader implications of these findings for questions of discrimination and hostile racial climates in U.S. workplaces and other important institutional settings?

More generally, we raise the issue of what the implications of the high cost of racism are for U.S. society as a whole. This country has indeed paid a heavy price in terms of the many human successes and achievements that have been blocked or destroyed by racism, to the loss of all Americans, and in the betrayal of the nation's often-asserted ideals of "liberty and justice for all." Ultimately, it is U.S. society as a whole that has paid, and that still pays, an extraordinarily heavy cost for the continuing high levels of discrimination against African Americans and other Americans of color.

2

The Psychological and Energy Costs of Contemporary Racism

I N CHAPTER 1 we underscored the point that historically Europeans generated worldwide expansion involving the development of colonial systems exploiting the land of indigenous peoples and the labor of enslaved Africans. This *external* colonialism often became *internal* colonialism when the control and exploitation of the non-European groups overseas passed on from whites in the home country to white immigrant groups and their descendants within the colonized countries. This describes what actually happened in the North America. First Europeans and later their descendants in America stole the land of Native Americans and the labor of African Americans.

More recently, during the 1960s, the perceptive critic of racial colonialism, Frantz Fanon, argued forcefully that the early and continuing processes of colonialism in Africa and elsewhere have had serious consequences for those exploited and oppressed. This racialized colonialism has inflicted serious psychological and physical stress on those colonized, both those initially colonized and their later descendants. One major reason for this is the constant barrage of racialized assaults by the colonial system on the personalities, lives, families, and communities of those it targets. Internal colonialism, with its many ideological interpretations and pressures, often makes those targeted for exploitation question their own abilities, understandings, and self-conceptions.[1] Writing in 1903 about the U.S. system of internal colonialism directed at African Americans, the pathbreaking African American scholar W. E. B. DuBois made a similar point: "But the facing of so vast a prejudice could not but bring the inevitable self-questioning, self-disparagement, and lowering of ideals which ever accompany repression and breed in an atmosphere of contempt and hate." DuBois also adds an important point about ongoing resistance by those targeted by white racism: "There are today no truer exponents of the pure human spirit of the Declaration of Independence than the American Negroes. . . . and the spiritual striving of the freedmen's sons is the travail of souls whose burden is almost beyond the measure of their strength, but who bear it in the name . . . of human opportunity."[2] In the past and the present, African Americans have had to fight against the negative conceptions of themselves that are constantly generated in the private presentations and public assertions of their many white oppressors. Today, we see this ongoing struggle, against racial oppression and for social justice, in the accounts of our respondents.

In recent years, as we saw in the previous chapter, numerous conservative analysts have asserted that there is much black "paranoia" about issues of racism. For example, one conservative journalist argues that middle-class African Americans move too quickly to see racism in their daily lives and, oddly enough, he further argues that black rage is a "dysfunctional aspect of black culture, a feature mainly of middle-class African American life," and that this rage represents "the frustration of pursuing unearned privileges" of affirmative action.[3] In effect, this conservative perspective suggests that African Americans themselves are mainly to blame for the anger, stress, and mental health problems that are linked to their personal histories in a racist system. The "blaming the victim" perspective is a common way many whites try to (mis)interpret ongoing racial oppression in the United States.

In contrast, those researchers who have actually interviewed African Americans and conducted other field research on racial discrimination have generally come to a much different conclusion. Their research suggests that rage and the so-called paranoia are often more or less healthy responses to constantly recurring experiences with racial discrimination. As the distinguished analyst bell hooks reminds us, black rage is "a potentially healthy, potentially healing response to oppression and exploitation."[4] Indeed, the attempt to colonize the minds of African Americans and others of color has long been a critical aspect of racism. hooks further notes: "To perpetuate and maintain white supremacy, white folks have colonized black Americans, and part of that colonizing process has been teaching us to repress our rage, to never make them the targets of any anger we feel about racism."[5] As for new action, she then suggests: "Progressive black activists must show how we take that rage and move it beyond fruitless scapegoating of any group, linking it instead to a passion for freedom and justice that illuminates, heals, and makes redemptive struggle possible."[6]

Similarly, the cultural mistrust that many African Americans have for white Americans involves a reasonable suspicion of whites, which is adopted by African Americans for survival and because they see the racist world accurately from their many unpleasant, discriminatory experiences at the hands of white Americans.[7] It is not at all abnormal for a black person to believe that numerous people are discriminating against him or her when in fact many whites actually are. Some researchers have used the term "racism reaction" to describe the normal, protective orientation that individual African Americans often take in their interaction with whites.[8] Indeed, some insightful training materials designed for health-care providers suggest that the latter should be fully familiar with this racism reaction in order to avoid misdiagnoses of black reactions to everyday discrimination as pathological.[9] Such precautions are very important. Although African Americans are generally less likely than whites to seek mental health care, those who do are more likely to be diagnosed with serious mental illness. Such diagnoses are still sometimes erroneous for racial reasons, and such faulty diagnoses can mean a serious social stigma—and, possibly, yet other serious consequences in terms of involuntary medication or institutional commitment.[10]

DISCRIMINATION, ANGER, AND RAGE

The African American philosopher Laurence Thomas has suggested that African Americans have perhaps not articulated the psychological pain they face as well as some other groups have: "My own view is that we did brilliantly up until about the '60s and then we lost it. I think the pain of racism really hasn't been fully articulated yet. We talk about various changes and all of that, but we've underestimated the psychological damage American slavery and its legacy has wrought upon the lives of Blacks in general."[11]

Variations in Stress: The Racial Factor

As we discussed previously, research on the contemporary workplace documents the harmful effects of work-related stress on the health of employees.[12] Although work is a primary source of stress for many workers, certain types of job stress are distinctive to the experiences of African Americans, and other Americans of color, and contribute to their physical and mental health challenges.[13] It is one thing to face the usual job stress and know that there are some measures one can take to decrease it. It is quite another matter to realize that the painful stress one faces is mainly because of the color of one's skin—and is thus largely beyond one's own control. Certain structural conditions and processes in workplaces and other societal settings—racial inequality, blocked opportunities, and other discrimination—are major generators of pain and distress, which can lead to or exacerbate physical and mental health problems. For example, one longitudinal research study has shown that African Americans who reported racial discrimination at one point in time were more likely to report high levels of psychological distress in another interview later on. Discrimination clearly has stressful consequences over time.[14]

Recent research accents several dimensions of the stress that affects the health of African Americans. Like many white Americans, some African Americans are susceptible to certain types of disease, propensities for illness that they inherited from their parents. Such a propensity, or the disease stemming from it, can cause much stress. In this regard, the relationship between stress and ill health for black Americans is much like that for white Americans. However, for black Americans, two other dimensions of health-related stress are linked to both past and present racism. One such dimension is that of interpersonal relationships at work and one's health. The discrimination faced by African Americans from their coworkers and employers often leads to increased, unhealthy stress. Whites may have negative encounters with other employees as well, but there is a major difference. For most whites, the negative encounters they typically have with fellow employees do not have explicitly racial overtones or racial consequences. The other critical dimension, the long-term consequences of racism-generated poverty or other lack of resources, involves even broader societal factors. For many African Americans, the lack of certain types of material assets or social-network resources can mean additional detrimental effects on their health. This added stress affects a much smaller proportion of whites. As a group, African Americans live with fewer socioeconomic resources, largely because of the long-term effects of slavery, legal segregation, and contemporary discrimination. As we noted in chapter 1, the average black family has only about a tenth of the wealth of the average white family. A relative lack of family wealth can mean considerably more financial worries, even for middle-class African Americans. This lack of resources thus contributes to the everyday stress that can generate pain, frustration, anger, and physical illness. Whites do not, on a structural and institutional level, encounter antiwhite racism or the long-term consequences of such racism. Not only do African Americans encounter the usual sources of stress that any person encounters, but they also face the structurally generated stress that stems from nearly four hundred years of racial oppression. For centuries, African Americans have been caught in economic, social, and political conditions that are harmful to their health.[15]

The Frequency of Anger and Rage

Commenting on the pervasive discrimination he faced in the workplace, the distinguished essayist and novelist James Baldwin once suggested that there is not a black person "alive who does not have rage in his blood— one has the choice, merely, of living with it consciously or surrendering to it. As for me, this fever has recurred in me, and does, and will until the day I die."[16] For most whites, it is likely hard to imagine living with this constant sense of justified rage. For many, if not most, African Americans, this is a recurring reality, and the only choice one has is to find personal or group-based ways to deal with it. Systemic racism has dealt African Americans a very hard hand to play.

In a now-classic study, psychiatrists William Grier and Price Cobbs examined the extent to which individual rage and depression among African Americans are shaped by discrimination. From clinical interviews with their own patients, they determined that black mistrust of whites is a very reasonable attitude, and one that is based on their many experiences with antiblack actions on the part of whites.[17] They concluded that the clinical treatment of enraged black Americans must take into account their experience with discrimination in many social settings, including workplaces, in order for psychological healing to take place. They note that black people "bear all they can and, if required, bear even more. But if they are black in present-day America they have been asked to shoulder too much. They have had all they can stand. They will be harried no more. Turning from their tormentors, they are filled with rage."[18] More recently, Cobbs has reiterated the point that rage against discrimination is reasonable and commonplace among African Americans, and for too many continues to be turned inward in a harmful fashion.[19] Thus, silent, all-consuming rage can lead to inner turmoil, emotional or social withdrawal, and numerous physical health problems.

African Americans working in, or traversing, historically white places commonly report pain, anguish, anger, and rage. These reactions may be immediately expressed in their words, the tone of their comments, or the character of their facial expressions. All of our focus group respondents indicated in one way or another that they suffer substantial and recurring stress and frustration in racially hostile workplaces or other societal settings. As one midwestern respondent put it, she knows her stress is linked to the workplace because her symptoms do *not* happen "on weekends or after five o'clock." The nine-to-five illnesses that stem from discrimination at work are commonplace and are often commented upon, or joked about, in African American families and communities.

As we have noted, there is a substantial literature that indicates that many workers suffer stress in dealing with employers, job requirements, pay levels, and other work-related issues.[20] However, in our interviews there is a general consensus that much life-damaging stress at work does not come from the performance of the job itself, but from racially hostile work environments. In our focus groups, we asked the respondents to discuss important questions such as, "Thinking about workplace discrimination by whites, have any of you suffered serious personal costs or pain because of the discrimination? Please give me a concrete example." In the discussions and commentaries about workplace matters, the respondents generally had in mind this and related questions about their reactions to everyday discrimination. Moreover, as we will see, their comments often included assessments of life experiences both inside and outside their workplaces.

We asked this more specific question: "How often do you get angry about the actions of white people?" One male focus group participant made this comment: "Well, I'm angry right now!" he said with a laugh. "I get *concerned* several times a week, concerned on some level. I may get angry once every week and a half. It's hard to try and quantify. It's not a great level of angry, but there's some concern." He then added a blunt commentary on how he deals with this anger about discriminatory white actions:

> I try to control it, but I don't try to muffle it. And I certainly don't
> ignore it. I try to develop a healthy approach to it, because what I
> really do understand is that it can destroy you, it can pervert your
> thinking. And it can make you the "nigger" that a lot of people want
> you to be, it can make you the stereotype. And we all have to fight
> that. I just think that I do my best to acknowledge that it is generated,
> and that it's natural. But that doesn't mean you just let it take its
> course. And I'm always in the process of trying to develop a better
> and healthier way of working through the inevitable anger about this
> situation. There's a price you pay in being sensitive and conscious.
> The irony of all of this is if you really were a "nigger," none of this
> would bother you, because you'd be a beast. Have you ever seen a
> dog really being angry about his condition? If you really were a beast,
> it wouldn't bother you. The problem is that . . . this treatment both-
> ers you most, because you definitively and clearly aren't what the
> world thinks you are.

Anger at constantly recurring racism is reasonable for sentient human beings. This man is very aware of the irony in the racist "beast" images of African Americans that are held by many whites. Nothing could be less true than these old white-racist images, for the frustration and pain felt because of white actions is often great. At the same time, this respondent realizes that to survive, one must find a way to control, yet not totally suppress, one's anger. It is likely that few whites must develop and frequently use the anger-management techniques that are more or less routinely developed by most African Americans over the course of their lives. Indeed, in a course recently taught by Karyn McKinney, a white college student realized and voiced this point—that blacks "probably know how to handle anger better than we do." Most whites probably cannot imagine dealing with such reasonable emotions of anger and rage at injustice over whole lifetimes.

Mistreatment that Causes Anger

African Americans face discrimination in an array of settings, including many different kinds of workplaces. Commenting on racially hostile or unsupportive workplaces, some focus group participants described general feelings of frustration and anger, while others emphasized specific incidents that generated such feelings. A common source of anger is whites' use of racist epithets and other derogatory references, which can trigger painful individual or collective memories. For example, one professional described her reaction to an incident with a white administrator:

> I have felt extremely upset, anger, rage, I guess you would call it. One incident that comes to mind happened in a social setting. I was with some, with my former boss and some coworkers and a man who ran, like, a federal program. And we were having dinner, and he made a comment, and he had been drinking *heavily*. And he referred to black people as "niggers." . . . I'm sitting—he's there, and I'm here. . . . And as soon as he said it, he looked in my face. And then he turned beet red, you know? And I said, "Excuse me, what did you say?" And he just couldn't say anything. And then my boss, my former boss, intervened and said, "Now, you know, move his glass, because he's had too much to drink." And you know just making all these excuses. So, of course, I got up and left. I said, "good night," and left. And the next morning, the man called me and apologized. . . . his excuse was that he had been drinking, you know. And I said, "Well [gives name], we don't get drunk and just say things that we

wouldn't otherwise say. You know, I don't get drunk and start speaking Spanish [group laughter]. This was already in you, you know, in order for it to come out. [Voices: Exactly. Yeah, yeah.] . . . I mean so, keep your apology, I'm not interested."

She then concluded with a comment on what she did with her anger:

I was so angered that I wanted to get him, you know? I was out to get him. I called his boss . . . who is black, and informed him of what happened. Because he was referring to his boss, actually. . . . And he [had] said, "Yeah, he's out with the other niggers."

This woman believed it was important that a fellow African American know that his white employee uses racist epithets to refer to blacks. While she describes her call to this other black man as her "out to get" the villain in her story, she also shows a concern for the larger black community.

Dealing with a similar problem, an administrative secretary relates an incident in which she had to explain the meaning of an old racial epithet to her white supervisor, who subsequently did nothing to reprimand the employee who used the term:

A white individual in my department was talking to me, and he referred to me as "Buckwheat." My supervisor, when I reported it to her, told me that she did not feel that I looked like "Buckwheat." Nor . . . did she understand what the term meant. Then she asked me to define it for her. She felt that [the term] was not derogatory. After I told her what it meant . . . she said "Well, you don't exemplify that, so I wouldn't worry about that." She also refused to talk to the individual.

Even today, some whites still use derogatory terms like "Buckwheat" and "Aunt Jemima" to put down and stigmatize black Americans. Recall, for example, the *Etter v. Veriflo Corporation* case discussed in chapter 1, in which three white judges on a California court decided that the recurring use of racist epithets like "Buckwheat" and "Jemima," directed at a black male employee, did not constitute serious discrimination. For nearly two centuries, the popular culture of ordinary white Americans—including the early minstrel shows of the mid-1800s and later radio and television since the 1920s—has been an important source of painful racist imaging of this type. Indeed, the term "Aunt Jemima" originally comes from an 1870s minstrel show, in which a white man, in blackface and dressed in women's clothes, sang a popular song. This name for African American women became widely known because of its later use as the name of a pancake mix—and eventually as a name on forty different products earning millions of dollars in revenues for the producing companies.[21] One analysis of the term "Buckwheat" suggests that whites originally called black Americans this derogatory name because blacks were thought to eat a lot of the grain buckwheat. Yet, the use of the term by whites since the 1930s stems mostly from the black child's name in the old "Our Gang" movie series and, most recently, from the name of a black comic character on *Saturday Night Live* in the 1980s.[22]

Why are these and other common racist epithets often an irritating and painful experience for African Americans? As mentioned in the introduction, one experienced African American psychologist once explained to Joe Feagin that, when he hears the epithet "nigger," in the back of his mind he often sees a black man hanging from a tree. This is not surprising, because he grew up in the segregation era when lynchings of black men were much more common than they are today. In this way, past experience informs and contextualizes present events. Indeed, the impact of racist epithets is often underestimated by outside, especially white, observers. Some whites have the audacity to counsel African Americans as to how they can or should simply ignore such comments. The psychologist further commented that his liberal white friends will sometimes tell him to "let go" of such racist comments from white bigots and quickly "move on." Thus, it appears that many whites believe that as long as one has a strong sense of self, or as long as one does not exemplify whatever racist remarks signify, such insults are "only words" and thus should not hurt or cause psychological damage. Such a perspective suggests that its advocates have not been the recipients of regular put-downs and questioning of one's worth. Most whites also do not seem to realize that it is not just the racial attacks on one's own person that a black person must face and process, but also the harmful attacks by whites that are experienced by, and held in the collective memories of, one's family and community. Memories of extensive experience with white racism have a major impact on one's feelings and understandings, as well as on the countering strategies at one's disposal.

Think, too, of the continuing reality of hostile attacks on African Americans across the country. Many violent attacks motivated by racist imaging and hatred are reported each year. The images of the worst of the attacks on African Americans are communicated, often repeatedly, in the mass media. Brutal lynchings of black Americans are *not* just a matter of the past. They still take place, as we saw in Jasper, Texas, in June of 1998. Revealing links to white supremacist groups, three white men seized James Byrd, Jr., tied him to the back of a pickup, and dragged him along a road until his body was dismembered.[23] Such attacks on African Americans are certainly much less common than in the recent past, but they do still take place, and they are not detached from the larger context of systemic racism in the United States—although most whites probably see them that way.

In addition, most African Americans know that white supremacist groups, such as the Ku Klux Klan, have participated in periodic violence against African Americans for more than a century. They know from experience that these groups are still operating across the United States, with little government intrusion on their terrorist plotting. Indeed, not long after this Texas lynching, there were copycat attacks on black men in at least two cities in other states—in Belleville, Illinois, and Slidell, Louisiana.[24] Doubtless, the Jasper lynching continues to have a lasting impact on many African Americans.[25] Recently, a black filmmaker, Marco Williams, and a white filmmaker, Whitney Dow, made a prize-winning documentary about the diverse reactions blacks and whites in the Jasper community had to this racialized crime. They found dramatically different reactions to the lynching in the two communities. From his interviews with whites in the town, the white filmmaker Dow came to view the town as dealing with a horrible racist event, yet one that is rare and isolated. In contrast, from his interviews with black townspeople, the black filmmaker came to see the brutally racist act as part of a larger and continuing story of racial oppression that persists to the present day. The black community has the experience to know that such events are not isolated, but rather form a continuum of racist events—ranging from nonviolent to extremely violent—that characterize the everyday lives of most African Americans.[26]

Individual and family memories of past discrimination, including recent racist events, compound the damage of everyday discrimination. Connections between hostile epithets and acts in the distant or recent past and those in the present are central aspects of individual and collective memories in black communities. Recall the focus groups in which we asked the respondents to discuss important questions such as: "Thinking about workplace discrimination by whites, have any of you suffered serious personal costs or pain because of the discrimination?" In one of the focus group discussions, a health care professional spoke about her anger over a traumatic workplace incident with a coworker. She partly attributed the hostility in their relationship to ongoing racial tensions in her white-dominated workplace:

> Most of the time you can do that [not get upset at racial hostility from whites], but it comes that point where you just can't. They have backed you into a corner. It's like a mouse, if you back him into a corner, he's going to come out. So, then you just explode. I had that happen on the job, and I hit this person. I physically, yes, I hit her. She's white, and she called me a "bitch." . . . That's why I hit her.
>
> She was abusive to the patients, and I had already had a conversation with her, with the supervisor. . . . She cursed me, and I'm looking at my supervisor who was her friend. . . . Both of them are white, and this was her friend. You know, they would go out to lunch together, whatever. She cursed me in the patient area, and I'm looking to my supervisor for some kind of response to her. Well, after she didn't say anything to her, then I cursed her back. And then I thought well, "Okay, this isn't cool, let me just get away from the situation." And I went [to] the medication room just to separate myself.

She then added this comment to complete the story:

> Well, that wasn't good enough for that person. She had to come where I was and ask me a question that she could have asked the patient. And I wouldn't respond to her. I said I'm not going to talk to her when she just cursed me. She just cursed me, what's the point? So, then she said, "Well, you bitch." When she said that, I just really lost it. . . . Well, when that happened of course your job flashes before your face. It's like, "God, I'm going to lose my job." Well, the supervisor had her back to us luckily. . . . I was angry with myself because I allowed this person to get me off my ground.

As can be seen here, many cases of antiblack hostility or harassment involve more than one brief encounter with a harassing white person. A sequence of events takes place over a period of time. In this case, the respondent is angry because of the pain the white attacks caused for her and also because she lost her temper over the situation. Such lashing out is rare for her, and most other African Americans, because it can mean the loss of one's job.

When this respondent finished her account in the focus group, one man added: "There's no one answer to a question [a racial situation] like that. Each situation warrants a different response. I think what helps us as being black now, we understand what these people think." One consequence of recurring racial harassment and other discrimination is the understanding that a black person typically, even necessarily, develops into the behavior of the white discriminators—an understanding leading to countering responses that usually have to be tailored for particular situations. This effort, and the consequent level of insight and understanding, is rarely required of whites.[27] Most whites are able to go to work without having to ponder deeply how to relate to others in their workplaces as one of just a few members of their own racial group because whites are ordinarily the substantial majority, if not the overwhelming majority, of employees. The informal and formal cultures of most U.S. workplaces are still white, and thus most whites are, without much personal adjustment, relatively comfortable there. Whites do not usually have to be bicultural in their workplaces. Not surprisingly, some recent research has linked the stress caused by the bicultural stance that African Americans and other racially oppressed people must take to their increased vulnerability to illnesses.[28]

An Impact Beyond the Individual

In another context, a black female supervisor in the South discussed the link between black rage and unfair promotion practices in workplaces:

> I think a lot of anger and rage comes in when we . . . feel like—like I have a friend, he's been with the company twenty years, and he didn't get a promotion. And he was well over-qualified. They gave it to a [white] guy who had been there only seven [years], and knows nothing. So, of course, I was kind of angry with the process, but it was because

he was the ex-boyfriend of the girl who was doing the promoting. So he was upset about it. But I told him, I felt like this: "They can only tell you 'no' so many times. Keep applying for that position."

Generally speaking, job satisfaction is rooted in how much employees' work contributes to their sense of control and self-esteem, in how much coworkers and supervisors are helpful in supporting one's work, and in whether rewards are truly meritocratic.[29] Employees, black and nonblack, have difficulty doing their best work when the conditions and rewards of employment are inequitable. Workers must be paid fairly and promoted equitably if employers expect them to do their best work. Recent research demonstrates that African Americans continue to receive lesser economic rewards than white Americans. This is true for middle-class individuals and African Americans as a group. Thus, the broad economic costs of being black include continuing disparities in income, wealth, and occupational position. In chapter 1, we noted the census data indicating that median black family income has hovered around 60 percent of white family income for decades. Black families also face poverty at a much greater rate than whites, while unemployment for black individuals is typically much higher than that of whites. Even middle-class African Americans generally have much less wealth, on the average, than their white counterparts.[30] One reason for this is continuing discrimination in the hiring and promotion processes of historically white workplaces.

In addition, as we see in numerous examples throughout this book, anger over racial mistreatment is more than a matter of what happens to an individual. Rage over racism is also fueled by what happens to friends and family members. Collective memories of the racism against black Americans as a group, as well as knowledge of specific discrimination against friends and relatives, can multiply racially related stress for individuals.[31] In recent years, several social scientists have researched collective and community memories. For example, Robert Bellah and his associates have noted that human communities "have a history" and "they are constituted by their past—for this reason we can speak of a real community as a 'community of memory,' one that does not forget its past."[32] These collective recollections are not always positive: "Remembering heritage involves accepting origins, including painful memories of prejudice and discrimination."[33]

For African Americans and other Americans of color, past and present discrimination perpetrated by white antagonists, as well as the responses to that oppression, are often inscribed in collective memory. The community passes along information from one generation to the next about how to deal with discrimination and the anger it causes. In one focus group, a nurse's assistant noted the importance of generational advice and collective memory: "Kindness will kill a person. My grandmother told me that so many times. 'Don't get upset. Don't fuss. Don't argue with them. Just smile at them.'" A male respondent in the group added, "That's true." Discrimination calls forth an expenditure of energy in developing countering responses, an issue we will return to in later chapters.

Accumulating experience with white racist practices often reaches into *thousands of minor and major incidents* by the time a black American reaches her or his sixties or seventies. This is not an exaggeration: Several of our African American informants and colleagues who spend much time in predominantly white settings have estimated that they face at least a hundred such incidents each year. Such long series of discriminatory events can have a major impact on the way one looks at the world. The accounts given throughout this book indicate how unexpected and severe the provocations of white-generated discrimination can be. The level and seriousness of black rage over racial animosity and discrimination were made clear by a retired professor interviewed in another study. Speaking to a question about the level of his anger toward whites because of everyday discrimination, on a scale from one to ten, this man replied:

> Ten! I think that there are many blacks whose anger is at that level. Mine has had time to grow over the years more and more and more until now I feel that my grasp on handling myself is tenuous. I think that now I would strike out to the point of killing, and not think anything about it. I really wouldn't care.[34]

After more than seven decades of living black in America, this otherwise mild-mannered professor, a prominent educator and researcher, is very angry over his own mistreatment at the hands of whites, as well as the mistreatment of his family, the young black people he knows, and African Americans generally. In his long interview, he is eloquent about how continuing discrimination over many decades has generated his anger at racist whites and his concern for the country's future.

As we have seen in our respondents' and other African Americans' accounts, anger at racism stems from particular social situations as well as a lifetime of experience with such events. These discriminatory situations are not isolated, but accumulate over one's life, in workplaces and other settings. Routinely, black workers' lives are disrupted by direct discrimination by white coworkers, supervisors, and employers in workplaces, as well as by various whites in other public settings such as malls, hotels, restaurants, classrooms, and voting precincts. Such encounters can become major life crises with a serious health impact similar to that of other crises such as the death of a loved one.[35] This impact is both psychological and physical.

DEPRESSION AND OTHER PSYCHOLOGICAL PROBLEMS

Stress in the Workplace: More Consequences

Researchers Mirowsky and Ross conclude that pain and distress can take two psychological forms: (1) depression, demoralization, and hopelessness, and (2) anxiety, fear, and worry.[36] In turn, these psychological reactions can have negative effects on physical health. Demoralization, depression, anxiety, and anger over everyday discrimination are to be expected under the circumstances faced by African Americans, but they are nonetheless unhealthy at the levels that many experience these feelings. In addition to older studies of black Americans such as that of Grier and Cobbs, more recent studies of Americans of color have found that experience with discrimination is linked to higher levels of stress and psychological suffering, including depression and lower levels of life satisfaction.[37] One analysis drawing on the National Study of Black Americans suggests that recent experiences with racial discrimination may be associated with "higher levels of chronic health problems, disability and psychological distress, and lower levels of happiness and life satisfaction."[38]

The African Americans in our focus groups and other interviews reported a variety of psychological problems that they view as linked, at least in part, to discrimination and related racial barriers in their workplaces. The psychological complaints range from moderate anxiety to depression severe enough to require medication or hospitalization. For example, an administrative assistant reported great mental anguish after unfair treatment at work:

> I had been in . . . my department for [some] years when . . . we had a major change in staff. We had gone from a white male boss who had just left, [to] a white female who had taken over in the position. I had seniority in the office as far as time, and had just received a promotion in the job, and had nothing but excellent, excellent performance evaluations. But when it came time to do the budget cuts, my position was offered as being ten percent cut. I was told that there was no way to avoid this position being cut. Being that at this time I was the only minority that was, that was in the office, it was devastating to me at the time because we tried to work it out.

Some observers might expect a black woman to fare better with a white female supervisor than a white male supervisor. Unfortunately, white women do not always feel a sense of gender unity that would lead them to be sure to treat black women fairly in making hiring and firing decisions. This respondent then described the resolution, which involved a black commissioner interceding for her:

> Because I was looking at a layoff . . . [he] basically went in and told this supervisor that, "With all these vacant positions that we have in this county, you *will* find her a job." I was told on a Friday, by the department they wanted to transfer me to, that I had to make a decision over the weekend and let them know by that following Monday whether I was going to accept this job, which was a six thousand dollar cut in pay . . . or go in the unemployment line. I had to help take care of two children, so I chose to go for the transfer. But . . . through all this, and the mental anguish that I went through, I was hospitalized for nine days. It was just devastating, because I saw it as *blatant discrimination.* . . . There was nothing they could go to in the file and find in terms of not performing or anything like that. And then the amount of time, [to] get basically kicked out the door is what happened. . . . But then, but not only the financial burden, but just the toll that it took. . . . I think the toll was *so* hurtful, because I saw it strictly as racial.

It appears that perpetrators disguise some racially linked mistreatment in employment settings in bureaucratic terms, as here in a reported budget cut. This woman's judgment of discrimination is not arbitrary but comes from past experience as the only minority person in her department. It is likely that her ability to read the situation is also grounded in past experiences—likely, hundreds of harassing and other discriminatory incidents—in a variety of settings. In many such cases of racial mistreatment, significant achievements are ignored and serious mental anguish and physical pain can result, even to the point of hospitalization.

Often a worker of color finds that she or he is one of few people, or even the only person, of her or his racial or ethnic background in a particular employment setting. This isolated status typically does not provide the social networking support that might alleviate some of the workplace stress. Variations in control and socioemotional support at work predict variations in psychological depression among workers.[39] In addition, being the only minority person (as some say, just the "only") at work can draw an inordinate amount of attention to one's job performance, and this attention may involve a stigmatizing token status. Moreover, black employees in many predominantly white work settings may feel pressure to prove that they were not hired only or mainly because of affirmative action—an assumption among many white employees. Such pressure can further accentuate the racialized stress they feel.[40]

A teacher discussed a situation in which her boss moved her to a different grade level with no notice, just before school started. This woman discovered later that she was moved in order to make room for a new and less experienced white teacher. She described the stress she underwent as a result of having to change so quickly:

> I was so upset I didn't know what to do. Just totally wiped out. I'm thinking about all of this stuff I've got to move. She promised that the janitors would help me move. Nobody helped me. People were almost in tears watching me move all of this stuff in a shopping cart. . . . And, it took me—that means I had to organize my stuff, move it, and get ready for another grade level and be ready to teach. . . . So I did my pre-planning; it almost killed me. . . . Nobody came to help me, but everybody was giving me sympathy. I had to go to the doctor. . . . and I had become hypertensive. But I felt myself, I

could hardly work, I was so upset. And I had gotten prayer, and was reading my scripture, and meditating.

There was no notice, and she did not get the assistance that was promised. We see here too some sources of the coping strategies, such as religion, that many African Americans use in dealing with the stress of everyday racism. When the moderator asked her if she had been hospitalized for hypertension, the woman answered:

> No, [the physician] put me on an antidepressant . . . in addition to the medication I needed to take—I'm glad you made me clarify that, helped me to clarify it, brother. I had to go on an antidepressant. I didn't take it very long. But that's how upset I was, had to see a physician. I was under his care for awhile. But, I mean, they brought these three white women on. . . . That's what irks me, when I hear about the white people attacking affirmative action, when it's worked in reverse, and it's still happening—to them. . . . Nobody hears about how they get hired and they're less qualified than we are. Nobody hears about how many times we're hired with *extra* qualifications, *more* than qualified, to do the same job that they're hired to do.

The impact of unfair treatment can be complex and extensive in its evolution and impact, involving pain, depression, and physical difficulties like increased hypertension, all at the same time. We also see the reality of many African American employees being *overqualified* for a job, an important issue we return to later.

Issues of Workplace Networking

Thinking along similar lines, an engineer spoke of a black coworker's experience of depression. His view, shared by other respondents, is that many African Americans are reluctant to seek assistance with psychological pain:

> But it's kind of more against black culture to go for any type of psychological . . . testing. . . . I had one friend who actually went to a depressive state . . . because he was the type of person who just tried to do the best he could at everything. And sometimes you just can't

do that, or do everything. So in this particular case, he went to the point where his body just collapsed, mentally. Where some people's bodies can collapse physically, his collapsed mentally. I personally didn't experience that, but I saw the pain that he went through. And likewise he's having racial-type things at his job, where his counterparts would get promoted at a certain level, where he would stay on a level below, after years. And he was as qualified—sometimes they get you in a position to think that you're not as qualified as the next person, where in reality you may be more qualified than the person that got promoted over you. But a promotion doesn't necessarily mean that this person does higher quality work. It means, sometimes that person knows how to network with the boss better than you do.

Discrimination at work includes getting passed over for promotions as well as discrimination at the entry level. Here again the suffering of one black person is communicated to and felt by others in his friendship network. Research shows that most African Americans rely heavily on informal social networks of friends and relatives for support in dealing with problems like racial discrimination. Thereby, the concerns of one individual are often known in detail by a larger friendship or family network.[41]

Some sociological analysts call social networking a type of "social capital," that is, a resource that stems from close relations among people. This social capital is "created when the relations among persons change in ways that facilitate action."[42] In most white-dominated workplaces, as the engineer suggests, whites have the most social-networking capital—capital that often facilitates their advance in an organization. Yet, African Americans, where possible, often develop their own social networks to counter discrimination, even if these networks are small or extend outside the workplace. We discuss the social capital of African Americans in other accounts over the next several chapters, and we return to the issue of countering and coping strategies for racial discrimination in chapters 5 and 6.

After the comment about whites' networking in the workplace, a woman in the group added that black employees usually have less time to socialize with the boss because they are often working extra hard to prove themselves as capable. The engineer agreed with her statement, then continued:

And if you're working, you can't network with the boss, and drink coffee with him, and tell him what kind of work and stuff that you're doing. Because you're actually out there in the trenches going to work. So it was not my personal case, but his particular case. He might have gone to a stage where he had such depression he had to actually take medication.

The idea about the qualifications of black and white employees is a theme that one finds in other accounts by black Americans of racial discrimination in the workplace, yet it receives little public and media attention. As reported by numerous African Americans in this and other studies, less qualified whites often get special consideration in competition with better-qualified people of color. Recall the woman above, who put this point accurately: "Nobody hears about how many times we're hired with *extra* qualifications, *more* than qualified, to do the same job that they're hired to do." The recurring white advantage— which is there whether or not whites meet a meritocratic standard—can create many psychological and physical health difficulties for African American employees.

Also critical here is the workplace networking theme suggested in previous comments and in later chapters. In the U.S. economy, many racial barriers are linked, directly or indirectly, to the white "good-ole-boy" networks, which are commonly at the core of workplaces and even of large business sectors.[43] In these critical social networks whites commonly restrict or exclude racial "outsiders" from the information flows and other resources that are critical for successful job or business performance.

THE HIGH ENERGY COSTS OF RACIAL DISCRIMINATION

Another major psychological cost of being mistreated in a racially hostile workplace can be a serious loss of personal energy, including the loss of motivation to work hard or to participate in various family and community activities. Recall from chapter 1 the black psychologist who commented about the energy loss suffered by those who are the daily targets of racial oppression: "Now a black person also has one hundred ergs; he uses fifty percent the same way a white man does, dealing with what the white man has [to deal with], so he has fifty percent left. But he uses twenty-five percent fighting being black, [with] all the problems being black and what it means."[44] The individual cost of dealing with discrimination is great, and one cannot accomplish as much as one might have when intellectual and physical energy is wasted in this way.

The loss of personal energy in dealing with persisting antiblack discrimination is more than an individual matter. An engineer made this clear in a focus group that was discussing the "eight whole hours of discrimination" they experience daily:

One of the things, though, that really has had an effect on my family personally was me having [less] time to really spend with my son. As far as reading him stories, talking, working with him, with his writing, and, all of that. And those things really, really hurt us, and it hurt my child, I think, in the long run, because he never had that really. . . . I know when the program was really, really running, some days I would come home and I would have such excruciating headaches and chest pains that I would just lay on the bed and put a cold compress on my head and just relax. Thank God, I got him through that period. . . . And by the time I come home, I'm so stressed out. And he runs up to me, and you know I give him a hug. But when you're so stressed out, you need just a little period of time, maybe an hour or so, just to unwind, just to relax, you know? . . . to just watch the news or something, to kind of unwind and everything. So it definitely affects [you] . . . and you know you're almost energy-less. . . . And then by the time you get home, you have your family. So, by the time you kind of unwind a little bit to get ready to go upstairs, you haven't handled responsibilities.

The pain of workplace mistreatment can have a domino effect, with chest pains and headaches being linked to a serious loss of personal energy. That, in turn, can mean far less energy to deal with important family matters, including raising children. The drain on personal strength caused by whites' discriminating at work can take a significant toll on the activities of black Americans in their individual and family lives well outside their places of employment.

In an important review of the literature, researchers Brown, Keith, and Jackson note that the constant threat of discrimination "may lead many African Americans to maintain a heightened state of anxiety and vigilance that has implications for mental health."[45] Constantly having to watch and counter discrimination takes a toll on mind and body. Thus, in one discussion, a government employee examined the energy exertion issue in another of its troubling aspects:

> One thing, too, is especially if you spend time documenting situations, that takes time: What was said, what did he say, what did I say, and what did I do? . . . That's time, too. I mean you're doing that because you never know what's going to jump out. [Moderator: Why do you feel it necessary to do that?] History. I mean, there were just certain things that [history] teaches you that you need to have some information [on] because that's really the only thing they [whites] understand. . . . Documents. When you start pulling out "This is mine, this is what was said, here, here, here," they understand that. [But if] you start talking off the top of your head . . . you have no credibility, you know what I'm saying? With us it always comes down to being above them. This is just like when we were talking about qualifications, you know, they can come in with less qualifications, but we always have to be maxed out. . . . And sometimes go beyond that.

A psychologist in the group put this issue into a long-term perspective: "That would seem like that's always been a factor, always has been a history of us having to prove ourselves, over and over again, with documentation, this and that, and I would like to . . . get to the point where *my* kids don't have to do that." Thus, the energy drain from white racism extends well beyond the extra effort necessary to prove oneself to those with racially prejudiced minds, because it often entails keeping documentation in order to prove one's accomplishments and counter the commonplace racial discrimination in many employment settings. In such documentation, each African American is often repeating what his or her predecessors had to do to protect against white discrimination. We return to this matter again in a later chapter on strategies for dealing with discrimination.

Note too the recurring sense of justice and fairness that is evident in many of these commentaries. African Americans are major carriers of the long tradition of liberty, freedom, justice, and fairness in the United States. They seek it out and call for it. Many try to get redress for the discrimination they encounter in their workplaces, yet the government agencies in charge of enforcing the U.S. civil rights laws generally do a weak job of enforcing them. So the effort of black employees to get redress there, or in the courts, requires the expenditure of yet more energy, typically to no avail. As we suggested in discussing the *Etter* case in chapter 1, all too often the U.S. "justice" system is really an "injustice" system. This legal system is white-controlled, and most whites in the system seem to have little understanding of the racial discrimination that targets Americans of color. Thus, many whites have little interest in rooting out that discrimination in its individual and institutional forms.

Moreover, to be good at what she or he does, a black worker usually must learn many things about coping with numerous ill-intentioned or hostile whites. As a general rule, this is not a requisite task for similarly situated white Americans. In another context, a female planner explained, "We have to keep learning things, you know; they need to do the same, they need to jump through the same hoops we have to jump through." In addition, the regular education of whites seems to be an imposed responsibility for many African Americans. A sheriff's deputy responded to a previous speaker's statement with this summary:

> And that's the same thing . . . we were talking about on the energy. Burning so much energy trying to educate these people that we qualify, you know? And I always said if you see a black doctor and a white doctor standing side by side, equal in status, that black man is *twice* as [good], because he had to work harder. . . . In every profession.

This is a point one often hears in interviews with African Americans.[46] It is well worth noting that the great achievements of so many African Americans have come in spite of, and on top of, the energy-sapping barriers of discrimination. One can only speculate about what most African Americans could really achieve—for themselves, their families, their communities, and the larger society—if they did not to have to waste so much energy contending with everyday racism.

CONCLUSION

As we have seen, the costs of white racism are extensive and difficult to fully describe or enumerate. They intrude into many areas of the lives of African Americans, as well as of many other Americans of color. They include a range of psychological costs. Central to these costs is a sense of separation or alienation from the core institutions of U.S. society. In the early twentieth century, in his pathbreaking *The Souls of Black Folk*, the ever-perceptive W. E. B. DuBois provided an eloquent description of the way in which African Americans are segregated from, and "veiled" from, the white world around them. The impact of being "others" and "outsiders" creates a kind of divided consciousness. A black person

> is a sort of seventh son, born with a veil, and gifted with second-sight in this American world—a world which yields him no true self-consciousness, but only lets him see himself through the revelation of the other world. It is a peculiar sensation, this double consciousness, this sense of always looking at one's self through the eyes of others, of measuring one's soul by the tape of a world that looks on in amused contempt and pity. One ever feels his two-ness—an American, a Negro; two souls, two thoughts, two unreconciled strivings; two warring ideals in one dark body, whose dogged strength alone keeps it from being torn asunder.[47]

Many African Americans still feel like outsiders in their own society. A recent research study of African American and Cuban American women asked them how they saw their identities. The majority of the black women felt that they were indeed "American," but that they were not seen that way by whites. Moreover, they felt that they as African Americans were economically and socially *excluded* from the mainstream. This was in contrast to the Cuban American women, almost all of whom had been in the United States for three generations or less. Most did not feel they were "American" and did not think whites saw them that way. Yet, these Cuban Americans felt strong feelings of *inclusion*, which increased with length of residence in the United States.[48]

Interestingly, in important ways African Americans as a group are among the most "American" of Americans. Most have nine to fifteen

generations of ancestors who have resided in North America. Most are *very* American in their ancestral mixtures as well. The majority has substantial ancestries going back not only to Africa but also to Europe and, in many cases, to Native American societies.

The sense of exclusion and alienation that most African Americans feel at some point, this sense of being unwelcome, is created by the recurring discriminatory practices of white (and sometimes other) Americans. This tragic and alienated sense comes from the negative reactions of whites in workplaces and in many other everyday settings such as stores, restaurants, schools, and various voluntary associations. When a black woman, man, or child enters a setting in which whites are the overwhelming majority and white norms are dominant, the "outsider" status is often felt in very perceptible and painful ways. Constantly being created and recreated as an outsider, and being excluded from full human recognition, usually has a profound impact. It often affects how African Americans see themselves, and affects their psychological and physical health.[49] At a minimum, they must develop an array of successful coping and contending strategies.

As we noted in chapter 1, modern social science has documented the serious impact that social dehumanization has on the physical and emotional health of human beings, whatever their racial or ethnic backgrounds. Racial oppression marginalizes and dehumanizes its targets. As we have demonstrated, for African Americans, this recurring degradation and discrimination have brought many heavy psychological burdens. It is their "dogged strength alone" that keeps African Americans "from being torn asunder" by these unjust racial burdens.

3

The Physical Health Consequences of Racism

RECENTLY, THE CENTERS FOR DISEASE CONTROL AND PREVENTION (CDC) released what seemed to be an optimistic portrait of the health of the nation. Examining data on disease and death rates for the previous decade, including major cancer rates, the CDC concluded that Americans as a group have gotten healthier. This good news was, however, paralleled by the continuing bad news: African Americans and other Americans of color had higher disease and death rates in almost every category than white Americans. Even the conservative head of the government's Department of Health and Human Services, Tommy Thompson, suggested that this differential "shows how far we still have to go" to "eliminate disparities in health among all population groups by 2010."[1]

STRIKING DIFFERENTIALS IN HEALTH STATISTICS

In no other area is the long-term impact of institutionalized racism so clear as in overall health and life expectancy statistics. Black American life expectancy is on average six years shorter than that of whites, and this disparity has not changed significantly in the past thirty years.[2] African

American men have the highest age-adjusted mortality rates of any major group, with 921 men dying, per 100,000, each year.[3] This rate is *60 percent* higher for black men than for white men. For African Americans under seventy years of age, 50 percent of excess deaths of men and 63 percent of excess deaths of women can be accounted for by cardiovascular disease, cancers, and problems resulting in infant mortality.[4] The black infant mortality rate is twice that of whites. In spite of popular contrary notions often fostered by the media, only 19 percent of excess male deaths and 6 percent of female excess deaths can be accounted for by homicide. Additionally, few excess deaths are related to distinctive genetic problems, such as sickle cell anemia.[5]

The most common chronic diseases are the same for blacks and whites, yet the rates of those diseases among blacks are greater. African Americans are disproportionately represented among people with coronary heart disease, strokes, and renal disease, and are more likely to have hypertension, high cholesterol, and diabetes. U.S. data indicate that African Americans are overrepresented in twelve of the fifteen major causes of death.[6] Black men have a 25 percent higher risk for cancer than other men.[7] As Clayton and Byrd note, "blacks have the highest age-adjusted cancer incidence and mortality rates of any racial and ethnic group within the United States."[8] Black men have higher rates of stroke than do other men in the population, and die from stroke at nearly twice the rate of other men. Diabetes is one-third more common among African Americans, as are various side effects that often accompany diabetes, such as blindness and heart disease. These data on the complications from diabetes suggest not only more health problems but also that African Americans are not receiving the same quality of health care as whites with that disease (see chapter 7). Moreover, black children who live in urban settings are at particular risk for lead poisoning, which affects more than 50 percent of them.[9] Lead and other poisoning, which often stems from poor quality housing and other environmental conditions, can cause numerous health problems.

Both social science research and medical research suggest that systemic racism affects the physical health of African Americans in at least three major ways. First, the everyday realities of systemic racism cause great psychological distress that, in turn, creates moderate-to-severe physical health problems for many people. Second, systemic racism works across many generations and transforms a lack of economic resources into a lack of access to quality housing and quality medical and health care for many people. Third, systemic racism keeps many African Americans from enjoying the same nondiscriminatory access to health care services or other facilities (for example, residential and recreational facilities) that can enhance physical health.

The Impact of Economic Inequality

In recent years, the economic status of African Americans has stagnated, and even declined in regard to some indicators, and this decline in economic well-being is often associated with their worsening health status.[10] However, we should reiterate that, for the most part, this economic situation is *not* the result of personal choices made by individual African Americans. The lesser economic position and resources of African Americans as a group are the *long term consequence* of the many forms of blatant, covert, and subtle discrimination that they and their recent and distant ancestors have faced—first under slavery, then under the regime of formal segregation (North and South), and now under a regime of informal discrimination that cuts across most U.S. organizations and institutions. As we discussed previously, a lack of income and wealth in one generation, such as that of parents or grandparents, often translates into more restricted educational and economic opportunities for children and grandchildren than for their more privileged white counterparts. In turn, more restricted opportunities for children and grandchildren often mean that, when they become adults, they too will have less access to the better-paying jobs and to better-quality health care, which is typically rationed by income in this society.

Racial discrimination continues to have many direct consequences for the psychological and physical health of African Americans.[11] Indeed, discrimination in the contemporary health care system is an important factor, an issue we examine in a later chapter. One study found that only 38 percent of black-white differentials in mortality were accounted for by socioeconomic status. And the racial disparity in infant mortality rates cannot be totally explained by socioeconomic status.[12] Such findings indicate the need to look at racial discrimination in its more immediate and situational forms, including discrimination in employment and health care settings.

Moreover, some studies have actually found higher mortality rates for African Americans with higher socioeconomic status.[13] Perhaps this latter finding means that the stress that contributes to poor physical health is higher for those African Americans who have more day-to-day contact with white employees, such as middle-class African American employees in formerly all-white, white-collar workplaces. White employees there may be more likely to resent, and thus to discriminate against, the black employees who are moving into these traditionally white workplaces.

Not in the Genes

Oft-repeated notions about genetic differences between racial groups cannot account for racial disparities in health. African Americans do not have a weak genetic background or some type of overall "genetic inferiority," a notion accented by many white supremacists. In her research, Camara Jones, an epidemiologist, found that African Americans have the *most* genetic diversity of any racially defined group. It may be the case that African Americans as a group have stronger immune systems than whites. In fact, black transplant patients run the highest risk of complications because their immune systems are so strong that their bodies are more likely to reject donated organs than those of whites.[14] In addition, the greater frequency of high blood pressure among African Americans has not been traced to genetic differences. In fact, the average blood pressure level of black Americans is similar to that of whites *until adulthood*, at which time the average blood pressure level increases faster with age for black Americans than for white Americans. Such data *strongly* suggest that the racial differential is *not* a matter of genetics or lifestyle. Instead, over the long-term, being a victim of racism has a detrimental cumulative impact on blood pressure and other physical conditions. Racial intrusions are constant over a black person's lifetime, and this can seriously affect physical health. Thus, in a study of black and white nurses, Jones found that a majority of black nurses are forced to think about racial matters at least daily, and many of them are constantly aware of their racialized status and treatment. These racist incursions likely contribute to stress that links to disease.[15]

Whether blatant, subtle, or covert, all types of discrimination impact the psychological and physical health of African Americans. One research study found that certain experiences of everyday discrimination (such as being insulted or harassed, receiving poor service, being treated with less courtesy or as if one is inferior or unintelligent) are more directly linked to poor physical health for African Americans than are incidents of major discrimination (like unfair hiring, firing, or job promotion practices, or threatening encounters with the police).[16] In addition, changes in the historical context are important in the history of the health of and health care for African Americans. For example, the 1960s civil rights movement brought about changes that have had a significant effect on the provision of health care for African Americans. Formerly segregated health care facilities were desegregated, and the number of black physicians and other health care providers increased under the newly desegregated conditions. This brought an improvement, compared to the segregated past, in the health care infrastructure for most black communities.[17]

SOME PHYSICAL HEALTH CONSEQUENCES OF EVERYDAY RACISM

Generally speaking, African Americans tend to report more physical health problems than people in most other racial or ethnic groups. In one national study of two thousand African Americans, when they were asked if they had health problems in the last month, only 35 percent of African Americans said they had none. The most common problems cited were high blood pressure, arthritis, and "nervous conditions."[18] As we see in the accounts of our respondents, African Americans often link certain physical health problems, at least to some degree, to the many pressures, strains, and stresses of everyday racism.

Problems with Sleep and General Illness

Assessing the impact of racism on their everyday lives, our respondents noted a broad range of effects on physical health. For example, a dental assistant made a connection between the stress of discrimination and several physical ailments:

> I don't think a lot of [people] realize that, when you're talking about ailments, you're talking about more colds, higher blood pressure, things like that, people don't relate that to your job. Like when you

come down with more colds, a lot of times, it's [racial] stress on your job. . . . [I was] in another job, and it seemed like the more stress I was under, it would make me feel worse. I would be sick, I would have more colds, I would want to sleep more, and basically it was related to my job, the pressure on my job. But I didn't put it that way, you know, a lot of times I would think if I was under stress, I wouldn't relate it to a cold. But a lot of times you get more colds when you're under more stress, and a lot of times, like the things that you're holding in, that you're not allowed to express on your job . . . [respondent trails off].

The pain of racially related stress on the job can translate into a weakening of the immune system, and thus to more colds and other diseases. It can also mean a general lack of energy and a feeling of malaise that may lead to excessive sleep. Here again we see the problem that comes from internalizing stress. Subtle and overt discrimination and the related blocked opportunities that our respondents face generate or aggravate psychological suffering as well as many physical health problems, such as colds, hypertension, chest pains, stomach problems, headaches, and insomnia.[19]

In one focus group, a psychologist practicing in the South related an account of stereotyping that had a significant impact on him:

I had an incident that happened not long ago, involving the Million Man March—my coworkers knew I was going to go. So, I'm all excited, and the time is getting near for me to go. And most of the staff I work [with] is white, you know, white women. And, you know, sometimes white folks don't get it. They don't understand that. Sometimes the things they say. . . . They're just, from another world, okay? So, we're sitting around, talking, and this one lady . . . says, "[His name], when you go, just be careful, you know, be careful. When you get to Washington be careful because there may be trouble." I said, "Trouble, there ain't going to be no trouble." And we all know that after the fact now, there was absolutely no trouble at the march. But that's the kind of thing that—it kind of bothered me that whole day—and I was kind of sleepless that night because of what she said, you know, and it's like those little things. [Woman in group: "She just *expected* it."]

Here the problem is being kept awake by stress from a stereotyped remark. Such incidents are commonplace in the black experience, and they may intrude on lives when least expected. Here the incident takes a subtle form coated in apparent concern for the respondent's welfare. Yet the assumption that black gatherings mean serious trouble causes him distress and sleeplessness.

Commonplace Headaches

Drawing on a review of the literature, researcher Jewelle Taylor Gibbs contends that the anger created in black men by discrimination frequently manifests itself in headaches and chronic fatigue, as well as in such psychological reactions as depression and anxiety.[20] In our study, a number of respondents spoke of severe headaches that they attribute to workplace stress, such as this social services coordinator who described headaches and other consequences in a group discussion of racially discriminatory work conditions:

> I was having severe headaches and chest pains. . . . It would be times when I would almost be in the office hyperventilating. And . . . it was just a lot of physical things happening to me. I would pull hair more, because, just the stress, you know? You just, you're trying to do so much, and collect your thoughts and do what needs to be done, and my hair had fallen out in the back of, the back of my hair, it just had fallen out! And, when I would talk to my beautician and other people about it, they said "It's just stress." And I knew I wasn't having any abnormal stress at home. There was just . . . no other area that, really, I had major concerns [about], so it had to be work. And the headaches were just, just terrible, just unbearable.

The stress from everyday racism at work can express itself in many forms, ranging from headaches and chest pains to hyperventilation and hair problems. The impact of racist practices at work is often more comprehensive and extensive than the uninformed observer might expect; the impact often extends beyond just one health problem to several aspects of a person's health. This respondent, like many other African Americans, thinks through her problem and tries examining alternative explanations, in this case with the help of other African Americans. Once again, we see the important and supportive social networking that is often embodied in personal relations in black communities.

After discussing her stress and physical problems, this woman offered some details on her problems with excessive white surveillance in her work setting:

> And it's also a psychological kind of ill, in that, well you know if people are constantly watching you. Everyday when I would get to the office, it was, it would be like, [white] people that were even on a lower level than me would have gone through my work, would have gone through my files trying to find things wrong, would even, to the point where if I was going to go on vacation, I would have to make sure that I clear everything off of my desk and locked up things to keep people from going in and going through my work to look for mistakes, and to look for problems, you know just to try to find something. . . . But it, it's just amazing the psychological ill that it does to you. And even though you know you're competent? People can do that so much to you . . . . They can get in meetings and try to show you up and make you look like you just don't know anything. And it is so many of them, you are outnumbered! Sometimes, you come out and lash out, and you almost validate what they're trying to say about you, because you feel outnumbered! . . . So, you, you begin to doubt yourself, you begin to psychologically feel somewhat incompetent. . . . So it can take a toll on you, and I think it takes more of a psychological toll on us than we even care to admit.

Here we see deeply into the interconnected character of modern discrimination and its diversified impact. Some discrimination takes the form of recurring racial harassment and excessive surveillance, and the impact can be serious for one's health in both psychological and physical terms. Not only are there the direct stresses and pains, but there is the questioning of abilities—which can, in its turn, create yet more problems for a person trying to perform well in the workplace. As several respondents note, the responses generated by racist acts—including lashing out, second-guessing, or loss of self-esteem—can themselves be used by whites to support yet more racial stereotyping or discrimination.

Similarly, one nurse in a focus group reported headaches brought on by the ongoing racial tensions at her place of employment:

> I would have this headache. And it would be for eight hours until I walked out the door and then it was like a weight was lifted off. . . . You know, you are always on the point because you don't know what's coming down because it was so many subtle things. You know little bitty things that this person in power—she would do or try to do until we had this blowout right in the hall. And she's yelling and screaming at me, and I was proud of myself because I took the high ground. I just totally ignored her and I walked away. And she's yelling, "[Name], don't you hear me talking to you?" I kept walking down the hall and I said, "No one is talking to me. Someone is screaming and I'm not going to respond to that." And I continued to walk down the hall. Because I know if I was to turn around and yell at her—which, that's the way that I felt—that . . . this is grounds for a termination.

African Americans frequently speak in these terms about racial conflict and tensions with white employees and their impact in their workplaces. Some refer to the "nine-to-five" headaches and other time-linked physical pains. For many such employees, the headaches and similar physical problems last only for the eight-hour workday and disappear once they are no longer faced with antagonistic white employees. This is the reality of "racialized space," in that such white-dominated places are often more comfortable, or less inhospitable, for white than black employees. In order to be comfortable—and for some, for life to be bearable—African Americans must leave these highly racialized spaces as soon as they can.

This nurse then continued by describing the confrontation she eventually had with the white woman:

> Until we got into a room with just she and I, then I let her have it. . . . I told her that I wasn't going to take that bullshit from her, just flat out. I said "I was looking for a job when I found this, and you and nobody else is going to talk to me that way. And if you're going to talk to me, you talk to me with respect. Before you are my supervisor, you're a woman. Just like I am. And you will treat [me] as such. And I will not

respond to that idiotic behavior that you're doing." And I just walked off. [Moderator: And she left you alone?] For that, for that evening. Then of course you're still [on] the point when you go in, every time you go in because you just don't know. And because out of, what was it, fifteen nurses there was only three blacks. . . . And they gave [the white nurses] the cream of the crop as far as you know. You got what no one else wanted. That's what you got. So, you know you had to be on the point for that sort of stuff. And that's why I was happy when they got rid of her.

Today, the negative racial attitudes of whites are commonly expressed in a recurring lack of respect, a disrespect that can be linked to a different management style and differential assignments for black employees, as in this case. Being black in the United States means constantly facing many types of racially related disrespect, as well as constantly being "on the point," that is, always being prepared to be called to question for actions taken in the workplace. Once again, in this case we see the willingness of some black professionals to confront those whites, including supervisors, who mistreat them. Such confrontations are often necessary, yet they still come at the price of great personal stress and potential illness. We examine the array of countering and fighting-back strategies in more detail in later chapters.

Throughout the commentaries in this chapter, several respondents mentioned the serious problem of headaches that stem from their relations with white employees in the workplace. In one group discussion, the moderator asked the participants about the causes of the headaches, and one health care professional noted the tension in her workplace:

You can feel the humiliation. You can feel the downgrading . . . because . . . it pours out of them. And you as a human, you know basically just through human instinct when someone [doesn't] like you. . . . You know, you know that. And no matter how subtle it tries to be or how covered up they try to do it, you know. Their actions can't be totally hidden. You know when someone doesn't care, is trying to make you miserable and trying to enrage you.

Like other African Americans, she has experienced so much of this practice that she has a good sensitivity to when whites are trying to be provocative. A technician in the same group commented about a white employee in her workplace who often caused problems and unnecessary stress when he was around. He would express his negative views very openly, saying, "Well, I don't like women. They're stupid. I don't like blacks, they're ignorant." She added that "everybody knew it." In such cases, the immediate cause of the tension is a matter of overt incidents of racism and sexism, which have been recurring in this workplace.

Women of color, as we noted in chapter 1, face both racist and sexist stereotyping and discrimination, which makes for a type of double burden. Yanick St. Jean and Joe Feagin have underscored this point: "Yet for black women racism and gendered racism remain widespread barriers. . . . Occupational ceilings, perceptions that they are incompetent, and excessive demands from whites are common. In work settings black women often lack mentorship, are intentionally isolated by whites, or are seen as unintelligent 'twofers' who hold their positions only because of some type of affirmative action."[21] In the case above, the technician indicates that racism and sexism are recurring. Other employees knew what was going on, yet apparently no one, including her white supervisor, intervened to stop the expressions of racial and sexual hostility. In other cases, as several respondents indicated, the racial or gender-related hostility of fellow employees does not take the form of overt comments, but rather is seen in the general attitude that they adopt. This attitude may be one of exclusion, condescension, or arrogance.

In these accounts, headaches are just one part of an often complex set of consequences that come from coping with hostile or unsupportive whites in employment settings with few black employees. The respondents' comments demonstrate that physical and psychological problems often go together. In numerous cases, as we noted previously and see in later chapters, workplace space is often racialized. A basic reason for this is that such places were, as a rule, originally created by, and are still largely controlled by, white employers and employees. Whites typically feel substantially in control of such spaces, and exert that control in several ways. When black employees are brought into such settings, especially in jobs where few black employees have preceded them, they are frequently forced to adapt and conform to the often-subtle white norms and ways of thinking, and in a more or less one-way fashion.

Hypertension and Heart Problems

Numerous recent research reports show that high blood pressure is a serious problem among black Americans. Black men, in particular, have high blood pressure at a rate four times that of white men. Socioeconomic status is associated with blood pressure and hypertension; as socioeconomic status decreases, average blood pressure increases. One study of 1,784 African Americans found that this relationship may be in part due to poorer nutrition for those with lower incomes—again a likely impact of the lower-income jobs that are linked to institutionalized racism.[22]

However, a number of research studies have also found that for hypertension, as well as certain other types of physical disease, socioeconomic status alone does not account for racial differences in illness rates.[23] Several research studies have suggested that stressful life events, such as encounters with discriminatory whites, are directly linked to higher levels of blood pressure.[24] One study, which controlled for age and weight, found that higher levels of discrimination were associated with higher blood pressure for African Americans.[25] In addition, research by Krieger and Sidney examined stress and blood pressure for nearly two thousand African Americans.[26] Eight in ten reported experiences with racial discrimination. When other factors were taken into account, working-class black women and men and middle-class black women who reported facing discrimination on three or more situational questions averaged higher blood pressure than those who reported facing discrimination in just one or two situations. They also had elevated blood pressure when compared to otherwise comparable whites. (Middle-class black men did not fit this pattern.) Interestingly, among working-class men and women, those respondents who reported no discrimination averaged higher levels of blood pressure than those who reported discrimination in three or more situations. One possible reason for this anomalous finding is that many of those reporting no discrimination are unwilling to verbalize their problems, thereby adding to their stress and the likelihood of having higher blood pressure. This suggestion is underscored by other data in this study, and in a previous study by Krieger, that show that black respondents who usually keep quiet about or accept unfair treatment are more likely to report hypertension problems than those who take action against unfair treatment.[27]

It would seem that those African Americans, both working- and middle-class, whose response style is to do something active about unfair treatment generally have lower blood pressure than those who accept it and keep it to themselves. This finding is supported by other research. One literature review discusses in some detail how researchers working on environmental stressors have found that suppressed hostility links to high blood pressure: *"Suppressed hostility* refers to a process of coping by inhibiting negative attitudes in situations where the person is the target of appraised noxious stimuli from some source of power. In objective terms, suppressing hostility to noxious stimuli involves avoidance of displaying hostile feelings to the unjustified attack and feeling that the display of hostile feelings should arouse guilt. They found evidence that a tendency to suppress angry feelings or, alternatively, to vent such feelings without much reflection were associated with higher blood pressures."[28]

Recall our discussion in chapter 1 of the work ethic of African Americans. Central to some white stereotyping is the notion that whites have a superior work ethic to darker-skinned Americans. The denial of black Americans' hard work and achievements is in effect a denial of their being full human beings. Ironically, however, African Americans must often *work harder* than whites to achieve their social positions or status. Some recent research links a pattern known as "John Henryism" with the higher blood pressure found among African Americans. John Henryism refers to attempts made by African Americans to respond to racial subordination by trying to control their environment through extra-intense commitments to hard work. These hard-work efforts amount to long-term, intensive contending with the many stressors associated with racial barriers. Sherman James and his colleagues have found that African Americans with a higher commitment to John Henryism are more likely to have high blood pressure.[29] In another study of physicians, attorneys, engineers, architects, professors, business executives, and accountants, the 71 percent who scored *high* on a test measuring to what degree a person believes that hard work leads to success also had generally higher blood pressure. These participants showed the high-effort coping that has come to be known as John Henryism. Conversely, only 36 percent of similarly successful white men reported the same intense, high-effort coping.[30] Presumably, similarly situated white men have not had to exert the same degree of effort to feel a sense of control over their surroundings in predominantly white (and often white male) work environments. These researchers suggest that John Henryism can cause short-term and long-run increases in blood pressure.

The character of the work arrangements can also make a difference. Recent research involving 726 African American men showed that the amount of job control and decision-making power they were allowed on their jobs was linked to the risk of hypertension. Those men who had more control over workplace decisions were much less likely to have hypertension.[31] As can be seen in several chapters of this book, many respondents allude to being excluded from decision-making in institutional settings such as workplaces. Attempting to respond to, or compensate for, this lack of control can lead to specific and serious health problems.

A number of our respondents detailed how hypertension is linked to racial stress. One health care professional commented on her reactions as she enters the driveway of her place of employment:

> That's when I got high blood pressure. And my doctor . . . I told him what my reaction, my body's reaction would be when I would go to this place of employment . . . which was a nursing home. When I turned into the driveway I got a major headache. I had this headache eight hours until I walked out that door leaving there. . . . I went to the doctor because the headaches had been so continuously. And he said, "[Her name], you need to find a job because you do not like where you work." And within myself I knew that was true. But also within myself I knew I had to have a job because I had children to take care of. But going through what I was going through wasn't really worth it because I was breaking my own self down. . . . It was constant intimidation, constant racism, but in a subtle way. You know, but enough whereas you were never comfortable.

Once again, we see how psychological stress is directly linked to at least two physical problems for the respondent, headaches and hypertension. Some well-meaning whites may tell their black friends who face such situations that they should simply leave the job. However, this is often difficult, for the targets of white discrimination may not be able to find such good-paying jobs elsewhere. They just have to endure the constant racism as part of the price of the job.

In reply to the moderator's question, "What were they doing to you that was so subtle?" this nurse replied:

> Okay, calling you down: "Did you go? Did you take care of this? Well, why can't we find this report?" Or one time . . . all of the checks in the place came but mine. Okay? And this happened after I witnessed a patient die due to inadequate care. And I made a statement, which I did mean, that if the wife asked me what happened, I would tell the truth. So therefore I was sent to another floor so I would never even have to see the wife when she came, okay. Then from that point on it was, "Well you didn't do this or you didn't do that." Knowing that I did, you know, I started actually having to make copies of things so if they call me, I could say "Well, why do I have a copy and you don't?" Like I said, everybody's check in the place came in the mail except mine. [They said,] "It was lost in the mail; it's nothing that we can do." This went on for two weeks until I took a stand: "I don't care if you have to go into petty cash; I want my money." And then I finally ended up on high blood pressure pills because for the longest, I tried to keep low. . . . I tried not to make waves. You know, it didn't work. I hurt me. I didn't hurt them. So, after that I no longer hurt me.

Again, the workplace is filled with the stress and pains of "constant intimidation" at the hands of white employees. For many black employees, the racially linked mistreatment is recurring and commonplace. The harassment and intimidation even forced her, like many other black employees in similar situations, to keep records showing that she had performed the tasks assigned. This record keeping cost her personal energy and doubtless created yet more stress. Note too that she reflects deeply on how she hurt herself by trying to go with the flow. Yet again, we also see an active response to racial harassment, by which she reduced her pain and, perhaps, some future mistreatment.

In one focus-group discussion of the impact of racial mistreatment, a secretary linked her experience with missed promotions to hypertension:

Well, I had an encounter probably about six months ago. And to me, it hurt me deeply. . . . I knew this was happening to me all the time. So . . . I had stood in prayer lines for prayer, you know, to help me ease my mind, and everything, to help me say the right thing, or go to the right, appropriate department, to get it started. And it was just hard, because I was real hurt, and sometimes I would just . . . cry about it. And it just got to me so bad, till I just went to administration. I just went to the head guy, because I said I'm tired of going to each individual talking about the problem, because it was getting no place. . . . I had applied for a promotion, and I had applied for this promotion twice. . . . And the first time, they gave it to another girl, which, they had let go because she was an alcoholic. . . . And then when this position opened up, some of her friends called her in for the position, and we both interviewed, and the supervisor, she talked like I was going to get the position. And, and she never called and told me that I didn't get it. And we was at a banquet one day, and you know, she had this girl with her, so I figured that she had gotten the position. And she said "Well, um, [name] did get the position, and I'm sorry, maybe something will open up regular." And they're supposed to hire people from within before they hire somebody from the outside. So I let that go by.

Bypassing her, they violated their own rules by going outside, an action that created pain for the respondent, who sought to alleviate it with tears and prayer. Then another woman in the focus group asked her, "She was white?" The secretary replied:

Yeah, she was white. . . . So another position come up. And she was working a weekend position. And I had applied for evening, because I was working nights, and I was wanting to get off of nights, because I was tired. I was getting stressed out and everything, and plus I was in a lot of pain, so I think I built up my blood pressure, really. So I went, I applied for another position, and I was the only one to apply for this position at this time. . . . And so it stayed in there for two months, and I kept calling, you know. I never did hear for an interview. I knew my references cleared; I knew it went through personnel. I went through my files and everything. And nothing ever happened. And so one of the other employees that worked there, she come and told me, she said, "Well, I was working at another place, and they called me and told me to come and apply for this position." And she was white.

Once again, the accumulation of psychological and physical costs from racial discrimination likely included increased blood pressure. Wanting to get off the night shift, this insightful respondent applied for yet another position, but did not get that position, which went to yet another white person.

After another woman in the group interposed, "Oh, no," this secretary continued the troubling account:

And I said, "They did what?" And so, you know, all this building up inside of me. So I went back to personnel, and I told him what was going on, and I just let him have it just the way she told it to me. And he said, "Well, um," he said "that's not right." He said, "you're here," and he said "um, we're going to call a meeting." . . . So I had got them together: My supervisor, the other supervisor that was on the other floor. And we [were] all supposed to meet the next week, and what they did within the meantime, they come up with a position for me to throw me off. But they had hired this other girl in the position from the outside. So, you know, that just goes to show you, they are prejudiced.

Like others among our respondents, she took action this time and confronted the personnel officer, who said he was setting up a meeting. However, the meeting did not happen, and another position appeared, which she had to take. This is a phenomenon that is reported by many African American workers. Some African Americans are placed in jobs that seem to be created for a minority employee, but these jobs are dead-end in terms of promotion or advancement.[32] This secretary still feels mistreated because she was better qualified than the white person:

I was, you know, the most qualified for the position, because I had been there fifteen years. I had been to college three and a half years, and I went to a technical institution. . . . And they [were] less qualified, but they were white, so they got the positions. [Another female voice:

"So, for me, what you're saying is that affirmative action is working as it always has worked: for them. On their side."] That's correct.

Later in the focus group interview, this secretary noted that she had to go to doctors for her hypertension—which she had not had to do before—because of the workplace problems:

I had to see several doctors because of the discrimination, and I went through a lot of stress. And then, my blood pressure, I had never had high blood pressure, and all of the sudden, it just went on the rise, and I couldn't control it. And . . . she [her supervisor] wanted me to perform the duties, you know, totally by myself, which it took like three, two or three people to do. And, she just wouldn't do it [hire more people] because I wanted this position, and she just wanted to see could I handle it. And I was just trying to prove to myself that I could. And basically, I got the worst end of it, because I'm being treated for high blood pressure now. But since then—the time that my doctor had told me to take off—and they had to fill in the position, and they saw what it was like. And now, they've hired several other people to help me with this position.

This account underscores the high level of pain and the loss of energy involved in contending with racial mistreatment. Using religion for solace, as well as speaking out, are some strategies used by African Americans in the daily struggle with racism. Although this woman noted that she finally received some medical help, the damage to her health had already been done.

Experiencing the Suffering of Others

In the focus groups, the physical suffering of other African Americans was sometimes cited as a cause of stress for a particular commentator. Those who suffer discrimination commonly share the burden with friends or family, thereby often creating a rippling of pain or anger across an extended network. Clearly, the impact of a particular discriminatory incident can be far more than it might initially appear to be, especially to an outside observer. Thus, in one focus group, an engineer explained how he empathized with a fellow employee who developed hypertension:

> I have a prime example of this, this has actually happened in our job. A particular [black] person in our, in the branch . . . was being discriminated against. The supervisor knew of it, and—what was happening, all our branch chiefs, they knew of it. And knew that the [white] supervisor was discriminating against this young lady. And, matter of fact, it drove this young lady to where now she's on high blood pressure medicine, and it really affected her. She wasn't getting promoted and all that. And the branch chief knew what was going on. But only, it was only attended to when the person actually had to go to our division chief, express her feelings. . . . [The] branch chief goes there and makes like he didn't know what was going on. . . . and he could see this person going through undue stress, didn't do nothing to try to, you know, clamp down on this supervisor and say "Well, you need to treat the person fairly," and things like this. And now, and so, once we got a, thank God, once we got a good division chief in there, that had feelings for people, and was concerned about this, that clamped down on this thing, that's the only time she got promoted and got any results. . . . But the thing is, is that this person went through all that, and now the person is on high blood [pressure medicine]—it affected her mentally and physically. . . . She went through all this undue stress, unnecessarily.

While several white supervisors knew about this problem of a blocked promotion for some time, no one took action, and the result, once again, was great stress and a physical health problem. The woman had to take action on her own. The engineer added a note about his own problems with a promotion:

> And not only that, I know a situation also where—this happened to me—where my immediate supervisor put in my paperwork to get promoted, and all of the sudden the branch chief lost my paperwork. Which really has cost me about a couple of thousands of dollars in the years . . . from my promotion being delayed. All of the sudden it just was missing. Not only that, I've heard it happened to a couple of more black people. . . . It's kind of, mighty funny that

the paperwork was lost, with all the minorities. That could of really, that really did affect their careers. . . . These slips-up keep happening systematically.

Such "slip-ups" in the workplace are common. Here we see how one respondent makes connections between his own negative experience with whites and that of another person. We hear the frustration in his voice, and his sense that these localized discriminatory actions are part of a systemic problem.

Other studies confirm that being hired is only the first hurdle, for African American employees also report recurring promotion problems in a variety of businesses.[33] For example, in the mid-1990s, some unexpected evidence of this problem surfaced on an audiotape made of Texaco executives discussing a lawsuit brought about by scores of black employees, some of whom asserted they had been passed over for promotion because they were black. Some white executives there did not take the discrimination complaints seriously. Black employees were termed "black jelly beans" who all agree with this "diversity thing" and who "seem to be stuck to the bottom of the bag." Some listening to the tape thought they heard the word "nigger" used, although this has been denied by those who were present.[34] In an affidavit filed with the lawsuit, a white manager in a midwestern office of Texaco reported to his boss, a senior executive in Texas, a discrimination complaint made by a black employee. His boss reportedly told the manager that he would "fire her black ass." When the manager pointed out that company policy protected her from dismissal, the senior executive said, "I guess we treat niggers differently down here."[35] Moreover, in 1996, the federal Equal Opportunity and Employment Commission found that Texaco had discriminated against black employees in promotions, and the company eventually agreed to a $176 million settlement with its black employees. This case gained notoriety because it was secretly tape-recorded. For once, all Americans who are not part of the corporate elite were privy to the way that white executives in power speak and act negatively in regard to African American employees. It would be naive to believe that this is a rare case of such discrimination; this is likely just one of the few cases where senior executives got caught and thus were held accountable.

Stomach Problems and Related Distress

According to several respondents, stress in the workplace also creates or contributes to certain intestinal problems. Contributing to a group discussion of racism at work, a female technician explained the intertwined nature of psychological and physical problems resulting from overt racial animosity and excessive surveillance:

> The psychological part and the physical part kind of go hand and hand. I can relate to actually having stomach problems, because the company that I work for, they was constantly watching, constantly badgering me about production, because I was in this type of position where quality was important, but quantity was always important, too. So you're constantly trying to push the work out, push the work out. And a lot of times, if you couldn't push it out so much per hour, per day, you'd have to do overtime. . . . And I have never been a sickly type person, and I had never had any problems with my stomach, but I actually did have to go to the doctor. And the doctor said I was having—they ran a test and he diagnosed it as gastrointestinal problems. And . . . depending on the amount of stress work would be in, I would actually have serious attacks, where I would really get, really feverish, high fever, and I would just get real, real sick. And they prescribed Tagamet . . . for me to take, but after taking that a couple of times, it made me really sick, and so, when I would have these gastrointestinal, these attacks, I would just kind of really have to go through it.

Providing interesting insight into the texture of everyday discrimination and its consequences, this woman notes the connection between her psychological well-being and physical health. She realizes that the "constant badgering" she faces in the workplace is directly linked to her illness, because she has not been a person who gets sick very often. She then described the range and depth of the recurring racial discrimination that she encountered in her place of employment:

> And a lot of times my job would just be so stressful, because I work for people that. . . . They were overt . . . not covert. . . . They'd just flat out let you know that they just didn't like black folks. . . . I worked

> with those kind of people. And even though I kind of enjoyed my work, I didn't enjoy those people, because they could make the situation really hard for me. . . . The people I worked for, they would get upset, because you knew your job well, you asked very little questions, and what you produced came out to be good work. And they would actually try to find . . . something wrong with [your work]. . . . They could come right behind me and try to pinpoint little, little small things, and find something wrong with it.

Serious gastrointestinal illness, including a fever, came into her life with this set of job experiences. In her account, she then noted how she tried to prepare for discrimination in advance: "It was very, very stressful, because every day you're constantly mentally trying to prepare yourself when you get out of the car in the morning and you go in, go into work, you're trying to prepare yourself, 'Well what do I have to face today?'" Though previously quite healthy, this woman became very ill substantially because of the racist actions of some white colleagues. Instead of going to work each day eager to take on new challenges, this woman faced each workday with a sense of dread and the need for preparation. One factor in the personal cost of discrimination is that which comes from this sense of having to be *constantly prepared* for what whites may do.

Another woman in our focus groups, a supervisor in the South, reported stomach problems that stemmed from the actions of a prejudiced white employee:

> But I was just so frustrated because she was . . . prejudiced, and she let it be known. And even though I confronted her on it, and any time she would say something to me, and I would tell her, I said "Look, if you can't deal with me on a professional level, then don't deal with me at all." And she was the type that, she would just do little things. And that just would annoy me. . . . And I never knew it then, and then I was reading a book one day, and it said don't let things bother you, because, you know, "physical breakdown." . . . I can't really say it's an ulcer, but I had stomach problems.

Here we have an openly disrespectful and prejudiced women who engages in racial harassment, the "little things" that led to illness for the respondent. This African American respondent attempts to disengage from the prejudiced coworker, and then seeks advice for dealing with the stress caused by these interactions in a book.

Continuing with the account, this respondent noted the ironic ending to the encounters. She first noted that the white woman was raised in the Deep South, then added:

> This is backwoods. So she was brought up that black people—you know to treat us like that. And I told her, I said, "Well, you can't treat—everybody's not the same, what if I treat all white people bad? You know, call you all kind of names and everything like that? That's not fair!" I said, "Because I could miss out on a good friend, or a good person." And it took some convincing, but what I did, I didn't step to her level. Because she would [say] little things—I would never get upset with her, but I always remained myself, because I didn't want her to think that she was getting next to me because once they figure that out, then they really start to pour it on.

One day her white antagonist got sick. The respondent continued:

> And all these white friends she had—she fainted on the second floor, and was laying down on the ground, now, and all these people walked over her and came back up and told me, they said, "Well you're the only one that can deal with her. You need to go down there and get her" [laughter in the focus group]. And I kid you not, they didn't even call security, and she was laying down on that floor when I got there. And she had been there—and I went down to her, I said, "[Name] are you all right?". . . She had a daughter, but her daughter's husband didn't like her, so she had no family. . . . When I got there she was laying on the floor, and I called security. They came and got her. I had to go with her to the emergency room. It took me all day at the emergency room with her. I had to get her admitted to a hospital. And then, after she got all this done, I was the only one calling her to see how she was doing, and she came and told me, she said, "You know what, all black people," she said "all blacks ain't bad, there's some of y'all . . . "

The respondent trailed off in her account as knowing laughter from the focus group filled the room. It is clear that physical ailments are only one aspect of such complex situations. A lot of energy is lost in making and implementing one's decision about interpersonal confrontations over racial matters.

Note too that this black woman acts as a Good Samaritan, showing understanding and forgiveness for a white employee. It is ironic how similar, in fact, this story is to the biblical Good Samaritan story. All the people that this white woman would expect to help her literally walk over her, just as those expected to help the fallen man are described as doing in the biblical tale. It is the one person she looks down upon, and probably least expects to help her, who provides care for her when she is ill. This black respondent was able to treat the prejudiced white woman with compassion despite how the woman had consistently treated her—the philosophy of returning hate with love that was advocated by Dr. Martin Luther King, Jr. It is our experience that many African Americans make such remarkable allowances for the whites who cause them trouble in their lives. Whites are often given the benefit of the doubt. Perhaps this is in part because many, if not most, African Americans make distinctions between whites in terms of the motivations behind their discriminatory behaviors. Contrary to what many whites believe, most African Americans do not see all whites as just one extreme type of "racist," a point to which we will return in later chapters. They often see the significant diversity in white Americans.

Several other respondents reported similar stomach problems that they attribute to workplace stress caused by racism. One medical professional discussed tensions with a supervisor that caused stomach problems:

> It was with a supervisor. . . . I think he felt that he was better than everybody. . . . It was like a tier: There was him. Then there was white males, then there was females, then there was a black female, then there was a Mexican guy, I think that he might have been below me. But even though I had done my job for a long time and was competent at it, he was constantly finding little things like, "if you are doing this, I want you to do something different." And then the way that I dealt with it; I told him that I couldn't stand it and that he made me sick to my stomach . . . [Moderator: You actually

confronted him?] Yeah. Sure. Yeah. Then I called his supervisor and told him that I didn't like the way he was treating me. So, he really didn't like that because, you know, people don't like for you to go over their heads. But I did it several times. . . . And then he said to me one day—and I probably should have filed a suit—his statement was, "I have a lot of energy and I'll use that against you." And then I said something and then his statement was. "If you don't like the way I treat you, maybe you should go to the NAACP," which was really the type of thing that you could file a suit [on] because I was the only black person that worked for him.

The racial hierarchy of U.S. society is on display in the white supervisor's attitude toward others in the workplace, with her and a Mexican American man at the bottom of the ladder. It is interesting to note the words that the supervisor used to threaten this woman—that he has "a lot of energy" to cause her harm. This man does not face discrimination on an everyday basis and so has not only more power, but also much more energy with which to cause trouble for this black woman. Because of her mistreatment, she would literally get sick to her stomach, a condition she then explained elsewhere in the discussion:

[T]his one supervisor used to make me feel like my stomach would get in knots when I saw him. But I handled it by telling him, "You make me sick to my stomach when [you] walk into the room." And it makes you feel better. . . . You know after you've done a particular job for ten or fifteen years, then you're capable of walking in in the morning, evaluating your work position, and deciding what needs to be done and doing it. . . . I mean naturally sometimes things are going to come up that might need to be changed. But he was constantly, whatever I decided to do that day, he had something else he wanted me to do. So, I went on midnights. That's how I ended up on midnights because he wasn't there then. But the initial costs to me, I felt, was monetary because when the company . . . didn't give me the opportunity to have a different job. . . . So, denying you access to certain jobs in the company for a long time cost me a lot of money. So as far [as] the health, I guess once he left . . . everybody was happy, and then the atmosphere changed.

For this woman, one supervisor caused her economic harm, stress, and physical discomfort. Eventually, his presence led her to have to change her work schedule to the night shift to avoid him. It is the insightful black worker who had to disrupt her life to accommodate a prejudiced white supervisor.

Clearly, blatant and aggressive racial discrimination in the workplace can create serious health problems for African Americans and other workers of color. In other cases, it is not the more aggressive type of discrimination that is the problem. Rather, it is what Joel Kovel has called "aversive racism," that is, the desire of whites to be away from, out of the presence of, black Americans.[36] This exclusionary behavior occurs inside and outside the workplace. Thus, one younger woman in a focus group, an administrative assistant in local government, described a situation in which exclusionary reactions caused her stress and stomach distress. When asked by the group moderator if she ever feels socially isolated as the only minority person in the workplace, she answered:

> I mean, you *are* isolated. . . . We were invited to a Christmas dinner just this past December. This was a county function, all of our employees were invited. We came over from [one] county to [another] county and I looked around the room, we were—I kept wondering, "Why are these ladies staring at me?" There was not another minority . . . in the whole room and . . . everybody was like, "Where did she come from?" And I was sitting there trying to eat my food, I got *such* indigestion, I could not eat, because it was like all eyes were upon me. I almost felt like they had never *seen* a black [laughter in the focus group] —and especially to be sitting and eating with one! It was like, do I have the plague?!

Aversive racism occurs often for black employees. It is part of the woodwork, the routine practices that African Americans face in and around their workplaces. This woman was frustrated by the reaction of whites to her presence at this holiday gathering. Although she can find the humor in the situation now, at the time her isolation and the stares of the whites caused her indigestion to such a degree that she was not able to enjoy the party. The party should have been a pleasant interlude for her. Additionally, such social gatherings are often occasions for making the types of connections and doing the informal networking in one's organization that eventually lead to promotions and raises. Yet she is not an intimate part of that critical networking situation. Indeed, this woman is not alone in this type of report. Many African Americans who spend any time in predominantly white social settings report such marginalizing or isolating treatment, including racially oriented stares.[37]

Why do so many whites react strongly to the bodies, the presence, of black women and men in traditionally white settings? One provocative suggestion is that many whites dislike black bodies because they project certain of their own deep fears onto them. According to Joel Kovel's analysis, when young whites are socialized, they consciously and unconsciously learn that the dark "otherness" of black Americans symbolizes degradation, danger, and the unknown—the common racist imagery dating back to at least the seventeenth century and still present in many white imaginings.[38]

DISCRIMINATION, STRESS, AND UNHEALTHY BEHAVIOR

Research shows that, for all Americans, a significant part of mortality is linked to certain types of unhealthy behavior. Many chronic illnesses can be prevented or alleviated with serious lifestyle changes, such as by discontinuing the use of alcohol or tobacco and by improving diet and increasing exercise. Although each individual has some control over lifestyle, there is a social dimension to healthy and unhealthy behavior. Thus, tobacco and alcohol use has become a more or less socially acceptable way of dealing with social stress, and studies show that the use of both increases during times of high stress for individuals. Not surprisingly, some African Americans turn to these substances for relief from the racially generated stress they feel inside and outside the workplace. In addition, alcohol and tobacco companies take advantage of this situation, intentionally or unintentionally, when they advertise more extensively in predominantly black communities and other communities of color.[39]

During one focus group, a nurse discussed the view that the heavy use of cigarettes or drugs is often linked to attempts to cope with the frustrations and pain of everyday racism:

> But you stuff that stuff inside, and it comes out in these kinds of ways. And we can sit down and talk to each other. And that pain, in

terms of it, they said that it can cause fibroids in women, that's why black women have a lot of fibroids. Because all of that pain gets stuffed inside. Or . . . that's why black men, you know, why is it that black men die so early? You know, if you take out the factors of drinking, and smoking, and why is it that black men die from heart disease or from, it's that stuffing inside of those subtle things that we, that we just, you know, that we can't say anything.

From her perspective, discrimination has many consequences. To ease the pain stemming from racial harassment and other discrimination, some people smoke or use alcohol excessively.

Overeating can also be a response to everyday stress, including that from racism. Obesity, a risk factor for high blood pressure and other health problems, occurs somewhat more frequently among black women than white women.[40] A recent study explored factors related to the weight control behavior of young black women. The women in this study, like many other black Americans, often had family histories that included chronic illness, such as hypertension and stroke, some of which are linked, at least in part, to diet. The study found that over half the women believed that various social stressors, including racist and sexist incidents, were a barrier to weight control. In addition to the stressors in educational pursuits, child care responsibilities, and financial and relationship concerns, the women discussed job-related stressors. One quarter explicitly discussed racism and sexism as adding to their stress and contributing to their overeating.[41] Some suggested that they and other African Americans sometimes overeat in order to cope with racially related stress in the workplace or other societal settings. One woman in this study reported on some of this stress: "I am in administration. And I am the alternate whenever the director, who is a white male, is not there. And so I have the supervisory position and it is an issue for some of the staff. I supervise all races and both sexes." She notes here that some whites had a problem with her being the supervisor. There was also the matter of priorities for the women in this study. Others asserted that weight management might not be as important to black women as to white women because "we have too many other things that we have to worry about," such as dealing with racism, coping with finances, and managing as single parents. As one respondent put it, "I mean survival is what our concern is, not being the right size or weight."[42]

CONCLUSION

The World Health Organization defines health as more than the absence of illness or disease. Instead, health is a basic human right and encompasses, in holistic fashion, the mental, physical, and social health of a human being. In this chapter, we see the many negative physical consequences for a person's health that stem from encounters with hostile whites across the workplaces and other institutional settings of this society. This physical illness ranges from chest pains and headaches to serious hypertension and gastrointestinal illness. It may well contribute to serious heart disease and cancer, given lifetimes of unremitting stress. It is often the case that these illnesses are aggravated by or flow out of continuing and recurring encounters with discrimination in this society, not just experience with one or two isolated incidents. A key factor in the ongoing damage that racial discrimination creates today is that it takes place again and again, in most areas of a black person's life, with no serious possibility of escape. Systemic racism guarantees that virtually all African Americans will face racial discrimination on a recurring basis over their entire lifetimes. The older one is, the more incidents of discrimination one has likely faced. This is the continuing legacy of what Supreme Court justice William O. Douglas once called "slavery unwilling to die."

African Americans learn to counter and contend with the many types of discrimination that are thrown into their life paths by an array of whites—indeed, as we see in their accounts, most often middle-class whites. These counterstrategies may involve withdrawing until another day, speaking out when this is difficult, keeping copious notes for a later day, or filing a timely lawsuit. We will return to these important issues in later chapters.

4

The Family and Community Costs of Racism

MOST AFRICAN AMERICANS see their families and communities as primary defenses against the daily assaults of racism. It is in these families that most black children first learn how to cope with racism. Additionally, the local black community often operates as extended kin. As they become adults, most black Americans seek support from others in their communities when they face increasing numbers of racist incidents in a variety of societal settings, including places of employment. As our respondents often note, the damage of a racially hostile workplace does not end at the workplace door. A black individual's experience with racial animosity and mistreatment is personally painful at the moment it happens, and also can have a cumulative and negative impact on other individuals, on one's family, and on one's community.

African American families and communities are negatively affected in many ways by continuing white-on-black racism. The black family has faced physical, ideological, and material assaults from whites for nearly four centuries. Over these centuries, family and community have been closely linked for African Americans, and for that reason the various white assaults on black families often have a significant impact on the larger black communities.

In this chapter we first address in some detail the continuing derogation of the African American family as pathological in academic literature and in related public policy literature. We do this in part because these literatures have been important in discussions of, and in the crafting of, government policies directed at African Americans. In addition, these literatures provide the most extensive discussions by researchers of what should be viewed as the impact of racism on black families and communities, although this is not the view of most mainstream analysts. Thus, we suggest a much more accurate perspective of African American families—one that places them within the larger social context of everyday racism. To make sense out of the difficult realities faced by African American families, one usually must dig beneath the surface—that is, much deeper than the commonplace superficial analyses of these families—in order to accurately examine their harsh historical and contemporary social contexts. This examination tells us something about African American families as well as about society at large. An in-depth dialectical approach, Bertell Ollman suggests, "helps us to see the present as a moment through which our society is passing, because it forces us to examine where it has come from and where it is heading."[1] Last, in this chapter we examine the present-day impacts of racism on African American families and communities, particularly as these are reflected in the experiences of middle-class African Americans.

THE LONG-TERM IDEOLOGICAL ASSAULT ON THE BLACK FAMILY

Most social science researchers view African American families as distinctive in certain characteristics when compared to similar white families. What is disputed is whether these differences are problematic. Rather than looking at African American families as simply *different* in certain ways from white families, most of the early literature and much recent literature addressing certain family forms found in black communities has described these family forms as more or less problematical or pathological.[2]

For example, an influential study by E. Franklin Frazier in 1957, *The Negro Family in the United States*, is generally regarded as the first extensive social science study to negatively characterize black families in a broad way as pathological: "The widespread disorganization of family life among Negroes has affected practically every phase of their community life and adjustments to the larger white world. Because of the absence of stability in family life, there is a lack of traditions. Life among a large portion of the urban Negro population is casual, precarious, and fragmentary."[3] This statement suggests the backward logic often employed by proponents of a pathological perspective on the black family. Frazier and similar commentators have missed a more important point: It is the attempt to adjust to a hostile white world, and the constant worry about making a living and supporting a family in such a hostile world, that actually *creates* great stress in black families. The illogic of the pathological perspective confuses cause and effect. It is that *surrounding white-controlled and racist world*, in the first instance, that is in fact pathological. And it is adaptations to the stress produced from life in a racist world that make it necessary for African Americans to sometimes create distinctive family forms and strategies in order to survive and thrive.

Perhaps the best-known example of this pathological-family viewpoint is the 1965 report by Daniel Patrick Moynihan, *The Negro Family: The Case for National Action*.[4] In this widely cited and influential government policy initiative, Moynihan writes about an allegedly distinctive pathology of black communities: "Obviously, not every instance of social pathology can be traced to the weakness of family structure. . . . Nonetheless, at the center of the tangle of pathology is the weakness of the family structure. Once or twice removed, it will be found to be the principal source of most of the aberrant, inadequate, or antisocial behavior that did not establish, but now serves to perpetuate the cycle of poverty and deprivation."[5] In this report, white society is all but absolved of contemporary responsibility for poverty, deprivation, and family stresses in black communities. This labeling of urban black communities as a "tangle of pathology" is commonplace and has been copied to the present day. According to many advocates of this pathology, the typical black family is matriarchal in character, has weak kinship ties, has "illegitimate" children, lacks mainstream values, and is present-oriented rather than future-oriented.[6] This group of factors is sometimes referred to as a "culture of poverty."[7] Thus defined, it can seem inevitable and somehow right to whites that African Americans are impoverished. Indeed, in recent decades, a number of studies have shown that many whites believe that blacks themselves are mainly responsible for their lack of economic opportunities and their economic disparities.[8]

A primary problem with the "culture of poverty" notion is that it confuses cause and result. While admitting that slavery and racism *began* the problems for the black family and community, those who adhere to this perspective believe that certain contemporary black family and community problems persist primarily because of an unhealthy black subculture. They do not recognize or admit that the original cause of stress on the black family, institutionalized racial oppression, is *still* the major and pervasive cause of much everyday stress for black families and communities today—and that the *results* of that stress include some of the adaptive characteristics often described in negative terms, or that are distorted in many analyses as supposed deviations from white family norms.

CONFRONTING AND COPING WITH RACISM: STRONG AND ADAPTIVE FAMILIES

Contrary to the common view of the pathology advocates, the African American family has long been characterized by strong kinship bonds and interaction. During slavery, one of the primary reasons that enslaved African Americans ran away was to return to their families. In fact, many who had escaped to freedom in the North again risked their lives to return South in the attempt to free their families.[9] After more than two centuries of colonial and U.S. slavery, during Reconstruction many African American families that had been separated by slaveholders began to regroup and re-create themselves. Although most of these newly freed black parents were struggling to feed their children, they often added to their families' innumerable "fictive kin"—the extended-family and non-kin children who were orphaned after slavery.[10] Similar family restructuring, and the care of extended family and "fictive kin," were seen again during the Great Depression of the 1930s.[11] These patterns of care and survival can still be seen in many African American families and communities today.

For several decades now, numerous scholars have shown that African American families and communities are remarkably adaptive and strong.

In seminal 1960s research, Andrew Billingsley found that the strengths of black families were much greater than their weaknesses, particularly considering that these strengths were developed as adaptations to extremely oppressive conditions.[12] In his pathbreaking 1971 book, Robert Hill effectively described in some detail the major strengths of black families. In the late 1990s, Hill revisited this assessment of the strengths of black families and found that, although these families faced new challenges, most of the strengths could still be found in them.[13] The first of these strengths of the African American family lies in its strong kinship bonds. Ever since African families struggled to survive and stay together as their family members were being sold off during slavery, African-origin families have fought against societal forces that have tried to tear them apart. Kinship bonds are exhibited in African American families, to take just a few examples, through the absorption of elderly family members, the creation of extended family networks, and the informal adoption of children.

Contrary to the "culture of poverty" thesis and commonplace white stereotyping, most members of black families exhibit a strong orientation toward work. Many studies show that whites and blacks are similarly oriented in their attitudes toward work.[14] Our data show that rather than working less hard than whites, most African Americans realize that they often must work *harder* than whites to achieve the same results. For example, a sheriff's deputy in one focus group put it this way: "And that's the same thing . . . we were talking about on the energy. Burning so much energy trying to educate these people, that we qualify, you know? And I always said if you see a black doctor and a white doctor standing side by side, equal in status, that black man is *twice* as [good], because he had to work harder. . . . In every profession."

Another strength of the black family is its adaptability in regard to family roles. Contrary to the popular notion that the black family is usually "matriarchal," even when there is a husband present, scholars have found that African American families are often more egalitarian than are white families. Because they are not as patriarchal as the traditional white family, black families thus appear to many (especially white) outsiders as part of a "matriarchal" family system.[15] Evidence of the adaptability of black families can also be seen when young women become mothers, in that the larger family is usually supportive. African American families are twice as likely as whites to take the children of premarital births into the homes of family or friends of the parents, and are *seven times less* likely than whites to put up these children for adoption.[16]

Another adaptation to unfavorable circumstances is a strong achievement orientation. Hill cites studies that show that lower-income blacks often have occupational aspirations higher than those of comparable lower-income whites, as well as greater educational aspirations.[17] Education is valued highly in the black family and community as one way to help overcome poverty and racism.

Another distinctive strength of African American families is their often strong religious orientation. This religious orientation contributes to cohesive black families, and has been used as a mechanism of survival for black communities from slavery through the 1960s civil rights movement to the present day.[18] As we discuss further in chapter 5, the church and spirituality can be a powerful tool for coping with discrimination. In fact, to address problems with stress, African Americans are more likely than are whites to turn to spiritual outlets, such as prayer, or informal community support networks than to formal psychological help.[19] Because many African Americans attend church regularly, the church services (and supportive church members) can serve in almost the same role as regular counseling therapy, to help bolster the person's defenses to face the environmental stressors that she or he may face in the coming week.[20]

Others have added to this list of strengths such group assets as "participation in kin-structured networks, elastic households, resilient children . . . and steadfast optimism."[21] One scholarly review has accented the black community's promotion of self-development. These include, first, the black helping tradition. Typically, a black community is centered in networks of mutual aid, which often involve the pooling of resources across extended families. In Robert Blauner's classic interview study, one black man recalled his communal upbringing: "We were dirt poor, but God we had a ball. My mother raised seven of us by herself, but we were one hell of a *family*. We took care of one another. . . .We weren't only raised by my mother and my grandmother. We were raised by anyone that saw us doing anything wrong. We were supervised by all the people in that little town."[22] In a recent interview study, a mother spoke of how she and her sister share family responsibilities: "I've tried to instill in my son how important family is. When he needs something, he knows to come to me or his father, I don't have any problem with that. He knows that my sister is there for him if anything were to happen to me. I would do the same for hers. It's just understood. . . . Even if times were not so hard, we'd be close this way. It's a matter of love, and it just so happens it takes care of our problems, too."[23] In addition to family, the majority of African Americans have other important informal networks. One review of the literature found that, when class and age were controlled, African Americans exceeded whites in regard to "church attendance, interaction with friends, enjoyment of clubs, and help from both friends and relatives."[24] This complex social reality contradicts the stereotyped notion held by many white Americans, including numerous researchers, that African Americans live in disorganized communities with weak organizations and inferior family values.

An ethic of prosocial behavior is typically held up as the ideal and is taught to children; this entails an attitude of cooperation and contribution to one's community. This helping tradition can be seen in the many black churches, mutual aid societies, fraternal orders, women's clubs, unions, orphanages, senior homes and hospitals, schools, protest groups, and other race-conscious organizations. Various grassroots efforts arise in black communities to extend the care-giving tradition. For example, in Indianapolis, there is a group called "One Hundred Black Men" that sits in on the editorial board meetings of local newspapers to push for fair coverage of young black men in the media.[25] In Detroit, there are youth leadership councils, formed to allow the ideas of youth to be heard in organizing programs for them. These are among the numerous groups of men active in black communities as mentors for young men.[26]

BLACK FAMILIES: THE CHALLENGE OF DIFFICULT ECONOMIC CONDITIONS

Some of the most difficult problems faced by black families stem from outside economic forces. Some of these economic forces have, unintentionally, a differential impact on African Americans, while other economic problems are created by government or private sector policies that intentionally, or at least knowingly, have a negative impact on African Americans. In other work, Feagin has distinguished between direct and indirect institutionalized discrimination. Direct institutionalized discrimination is that discrimination intentionally built into organizations and institutions by whites in order to have a significant negative impact on people in subordinate racial groups, especially African Americans. Examples include the intentional exclusion, blatant or subtle, of African Americans from traditionally white jobs and neighborhoods, discrimination that can still be found in some sectors of U.S. society. Indirect institutionalized discrimination involves the differential and negative treatment by whites of subordinate racial groups without that treatment being intentional in the present moment. This is oppressive and damaging discrimination, nonetheless, because it carries into the present the impact of the often blatant discrimination of the past. For example, intentional discrimination in the past often creates limited resources for the descendants of those so discriminated against, and current generations of groups once severely subordinated have less inherited wealth and other socioeconomic resources than do current generations of whites. This means that, today, the average African American typically does not have the same economic and educational resources and, thus, opportunities as the average white American. For example, as we noted in earlier chapters, the average black family today has about 60 percent of the income of the average white family—and only about a tenth of the average white family's wealth.[27]

Certainly, discriminatory and stressful economic conditions have generated a number of serious and continuing problems for African American families. As Harrison Smith underscores, "African American families are "affected by all the major social systems of our society, most notably economic, political, health care, welfare, housing, educational, criminal justice, military, transportation, communication, and religious systems. Clearly, the African American family's survival reflects its high degree of adaptability to the many vagaries of these systems and their many changes."[28] Serious family problems include some that are often underscored or exaggerated by the "pathology" advocates, such as those breadwinners who leave their families because they have no jobs or jobs that are degrading with very low wages. The stresses of unemployment and underemployment do indeed break up some families, thereby creating the much-noted single-parent families. However, what pathology advocates ignore, often intentionally, is that African Americans are often innovative and adaptive in solving these structurally created problems. While it is true that a large proportion of African American families are single-parent families, those who proclaim such data often ignore the critical larger social contexts. Thus, Toni Morrison has noted, "A single women who is raising children is not alone if she has a family."[29] Extended families often fill in to help raise the children and otherwise maintain the nuclear family.

In addition, many of the problems faced by single-parent families stem mainly, *not* from the absence of a second parent, but from the lack of decent-paying jobs, incomes, and housing—conditions resulting from the long-term effects of direct and indirect institutionalized discrimination.[30] The long history of racial oppression means that black workers today, as in the past, are more vulnerable to ups and downs and technological changes in the U.S. economy. Yet, the victim-blaming rhetoric is still common among many commentators who seek to deny the real reasons for the troubling economic problems of many African American workers and their families. Sociologist Sidney Willhelm has noted, "After centuries of abuse, the white majority repudiates the American minority for the very conditions it is itself to blame: poverty, ignorance, family disruption, filth, crime, disease, substandard housing, incompetence, lack of initiative."[31] Most of the causes of persisting economic problems lie in ongoing intentional discrimination or in structural types of indirect institutionalized discrimination.[32]

Moreover, after significant governmental efforts during the 1960s to improve the economic conditions of African Americans, by the end of that decade President Richard Nixon was dismantling many government programs that were helping black workers and their families achieve greater economic stability. Later Republican administrations, controlled by conservative white officials, have further cut government expenditures for programs to help modest-income workers and families.[33] Today, Social Security policies also discriminate against black families. The eligible age to retire with full Social Security benefits is being raised to older ages between the years 2000 and 2022, a policy that is not intentionally discriminatory. However, because African Americans have lower life expectancies than white Americans, this increasing retirement age for Social Security is adversely affecting them. A disproportionate number of black men will not live long enough to receive any returns on the Social Security taxes they paid. This negatively affects the families of these men.[34]

In addition, government housing policies have made it difficult for many African American families to obtain or maintain quality homes. First, the Federal Housing Administration (FHA) mortgage loan program that began in the 1930s promoted racial segregation in the suburbs until the 1960s, and contributed to "white flight" from cities and the extreme segregation of central-city black families.[35] Other policies, such as redlining, racial steering, and exclusionary zoning, although illegal, are still widely practiced, and keep black families from purchasing quality homes in many areas, or cause them to pay exorbitant prices.[36] In addition, because black families and their communities are closely linked, these discriminatory government programs have long interfered with the informal helping tradition in black communities.[37] And the lack of access to quality housing typically means less wealth and prosperity for later generations. For most white Americans, it is their housing equity that constitutes much of their family wealth, wealth that can be translated into educational advantages for children and grandchildren. These advantages are much less available to black children and grandchildren.

In addition, other government policies have adverse effects. Foster care and adoption policies often discriminate against African American children. They make it harder for black children to be adopted or make transracial adoption more likely.[38] Parents who apply to adopt must often meet rather stringent requirements; for example, they must often be (1) middle class, (2) a husband and wife, (3) wealthy enough to afford the agency fees, (4) childless, and (5) less than 55 years old.[39] The black parents most likely to be interested often do not meet some of these criteria. Thus, black children in foster care are more likely to remain in foster care longer, and are less likely than white children to be adopted. When they are adopted, they are often placed with white families inexperienced in contending with racism—which some analysts argue can be problematic for the child and the African American community as a whole.[40]

Often relatives take care of black children whose mothers are unable to do so. Government policies work against this tradition of care. When black grandmothers or other extended kin take in a child, they often do so at great sacrifice. Government policies are structured so that, since they are related to the child, these relatives receive about a third of the amount allotted to children placed in licensed group homes.[41] This is an example of how white policymakers attempt to force the black family into white middle-class norms and patterns. Rather than supporting an informal, community-based system of adoption and care, the white-dominated childcare system undermines it.[42] Not only are the costs of institutional racism felt by African American families, but some government systems set up to supposedly alleviate the symptoms of those costs cause further suffering by imposing white-centered family values on African American families and communities.

THE FAMILY COSTS OF RACISM: REPORTS FROM AFRICAN AMERICANS

The Burden of White People

Over the last few decades, numerous African American authors have noted the many impacts of racism on them, their families, and their communities. For example, the distinguished American novelist, Richard Wright, once described how his mother suffered repeated strokes throughout his youth. In his autobiography, *Black Boy*, he attributed this in part to the damage caused by the everyday stress that she faced in an openly and often viciously racist, white-controlled world.[43]

Similarly, the influential essayist and novelist James Baldwin wrote of the impact of the white-racist world on his father:

> [H]e was certainly the most bitter man I have ever met; yet it must be said that there was something else in him, buried in him. . . . He claimed to be proud of his blackness but it had also been the cause of much humiliation and it had fixed bleak boundaries to his life. He was not a young man when we were growing up and he had already suffered many kinds of ruin; in his outrageously demanding and protective way he loved his children, . . . and all these things sometime showed in his face when he tried, never to my knowledge with any success, to establish contact with any of us. When he took one of his children on his knee to play, the child always became fretful and began to cry; when he tried to help one of us with our homework the absolutely unabating tension which emanated from him caused our minds and our tongues to become paralyzed so that he, scarcely knowing why, flew into a rage, and the child, not knowing why, was punished.[44]

Tragically, this father tried to show affection to his children, but his level of tension was so high, because of the humiliations he faced from recurring racism, that he was often unable to communicate his feelings to his children effectively. It was only later in his life, after he moved away from home, that Baldwin came to fully realize the cause of his father's difficulties in connecting with his children:

> When he died I had been away from home for a little over a year. In that year I had had time to become aware of the meaning of all my father's bitter warnings, had discovered the secret of his proudly pursed lips and rigid carriage: I had discovered the *weight of white people* in the world. I saw that this had been for my ancestors and would now be for me an awful thing to live with and that the bitterness which had helped to kill my father could also kill me.[45]

For centuries, white racism has stressed and killed black bodies and souls.

Contemporary Accounts of Racism's Impact

Countless other African Americans have written about the harmful effects of racism on their families. In her recent and moving collection of journal entries, Toi Derricotte, an African American poet, has discussed the painful circumstances faced by her husband, her son, and herself when they moved into a predominantly white neighborhood. After looking unsuccessfully at eighty houses, she had to find their new home by herself, because she looks white. She discovered that when she brought her husband along to real estate offices, because he was "recognizably black," they suffered recurring discrimination, such as being shown houses only in all-black neighborhoods. She noted that she began her poignant journal entries "in the middle of a severe depression."[46]

Moreover, after moving to a prosperous, mostly white neighborhood, her family was excluded from the neighborhood club. This, coupled with other stressors, caused damage to the family:

> It's the loneliness I can't take, the way the house stuffs up with it like a head that can't breathe. The sun coming through the glass in the middle of the afternoon magnifies perfection. Everything's

right: . . . Am I dreaming they hate me? Am I dreaming the house, the block, the neighborhood? Is the whole world my evil dream?

My son comes home. I make all the right motions. I move the pots, my lips ask questions. I reassure. . . . It's the hardest when Bruce comes home, when part of me for an instant hopes, when I can almost touch the end of loneliness. . . . One time I even went back to Detroit, to my mother's house.[47]

Although this family had the income to purchase a home in an affluent white neighborhood, Derricotte is unable to enjoy her new surroundings because she had to worry about the racist reactions of her white neighbors. Later on, this loneliness and feeling of being hated, in a place where she should have been able to relax, began to affect her psychologically:

I creep downstairs to the basement when everyone is sleeping. It is two o'clock and I am so frightened of the darkness, . . . my whole body is cold. I go down on all fours like an animal, I put a pillow over my mouth so that I won't wake anybody, and I start to scream. . . . Bruce comes down in his tee shirt and jockey shorts. . . . He seems afraid to touch me. He speaks softly "Are you all right?" [Later]. . . I pick up a pencil and open my notebook. I can't think of anything to write, just little marks like chicken scratch. The only words that come are: "Like a tree in hostile soil."[48]

The tensions stemming from the racially hostile circumstances in which this family lived had begun to erode the couple's intimacy, and Derricotte felt alienated from her husband. Soon after, her journal records, "Bruce has agreed to see a marriage counselor. He doesn't want to, but he knows things are not going well between us."[49] In this same entry, she recounted an episode that showed that the stress of racism in the neighborhood was beginning to directly affect her husband as well:

Suddenly I heard a terrible sound from the dining room, like an animal gored in the heart. When I came into the room, he was screaming with his eyes forced shut and his teeth clenched. . . . He was shaking all over. "I just can't take it," he said. "I just can't!" I stood back in horror. I've only seen Bruce angry twice in ten years and never anything like this."[50]

In her journal Derricotte has also recounted her sense of guilt for moving her family into a predominantly white neighborhood in which they all experienced great anguish and pain. We see that the stress on one family member carries over to all—that the whole family often surrounds the one member and tries to comfort her or him, taking on some of the burden.

Researcher Susan Toliver interviewed 187 black corporate managers of Fortune 100 companies, as well as some of their spouses and children. These respondents noted numerous types of workplace stress. All answered "yes," emphatically, when asked if racism persists in corporate America. The managers felt isolated or excluded from social gatherings in their workplaces, and this kept them out of numerous informal networks that might help in getting promotions or securing other important corporate opportunities. Often, as in the case of Derricotte's family, African American corporate families live isolated lives as one of few black families (if not the only one) in a heavily white neighborhood. Highly qualified corporate employees, most in the study reported that they were better educated than the whites at their level, and all said they had more experience than the whites at their level. In addition, most reflected the "John Henryism" discussed in a previous chapter. These respondents reported working late at least four nights a week, probably because of the fact that we have noted before: Many black middle-class workers feel that they must work harder than whites to get and keep their jobs.[51] Working late takes away from time that could be spent with one's family. Yet everyone in the study affirmed the importance of the family in their lives. For example, one respondent stated, "Even if I don't need their support, it's extremely important to me to know that I can count on their support." Another, when asked how important the family is, said, "Critically important. The black family is one of our few institutions."[52]

Bringing frustrations home can have serious and negative effects on families and other close relationships. This impact includes the lack of energy that some of our respondents report for doing things with their children. Many black families are child-centered, and thus when a parent is unable to devote time and energy to her or his child, part of this important family dynamic is broken. Significantly, most of the fathers in the Toliver study said that, in spite of their long work hours, they spend three to five evenings a week with their children—helping them with homework, giving them baths, reading them bedtime stories, and engaging in similar activities. Yet, many also felt that work interfered with their spending as much time with children as they wanted to.[53]

Recall from a previous chapter the engineer who made clear the impact of the discrimination in the workplace on the energy he has to devote to his family:

> One of the things, though, that really has had an effect on my family personally was, me having [less] time to really spend with my son. As far as reading him stories, talking, working with him, with his writing, and, all of that. And those things really, really hurt us, and it hurt my child, I think, in the long run. . . . And he runs up to me, and you know I give him a hug, but when you're so stressed out, you need just a little period of time, maybe an hour or so, just to unwind, just to relax, you know? . . . . So it definitely affects [you] . . . and you know you're almost energy-less.

The pain of workplace mistreatment can have a domino effect, with chest pains and headaches being linked to a general loss of energy—and that, in turn, can mean less attention, at least some days, for important family needs. Clearly, the drain on personal strength caused by racial discrimination often takes some toll on the activities of many African Americans outside the workplace.

Even if a black mother or father is at home with her or his child, sometimes the racism experienced during the day detracts from the quality of interaction with children. The harmful effects of bringing discrimination home to one's family was elucidated by one mother, a social services administrator:

> So many times, after you've experienced an eight whole hours of discrimination, either directly or indirectly, it really doesn't put you in the mood to go home and read that wonderful bedtime story. . . . And that anger sometimes builds up, and you're not even aware that it's there—so the moment your spouse, or your child, if there

is anything that may seem like it was a belittling or demeaning, you're responding to them with a level of anger, even, that really is inappropriate for the situation.

Elsewhere, when asked if she has suffered health effects from the stress of workplace racism, she stated:

> I think I suffered health concerns, but probably never really followed up to actually go to a physician to be treated or anything. . . . About a year ago, I was just really on overload, because I had been promised so many things in order to do my job—I had been promised that I would get help, and I saw other people . . . who had similar jobs to me, I saw them getting help, with less and less responsibility, and then, I saw myself not getting the things that was promised to me, but yet having a job to do. And because of that, [I was] really just really stressed out. I gained weight; I forgot a lot of things that I needed to do for my family, and I was up night and day, trying to just keep the work afloat. I mean, I skipped lunch every day, stayed late, sometimes forgot to pick my daughter up when I was supposed to, so emotionally, there was a lot of costs to it. And I didn't see that my extra efforts were being appreciated, and I didn't see it getting me any closer to really even being able to really do my job effectively or for folks to really see that, "Oh, let us give her some help." . . . I just felt like I was being used, so emotionally it took a serious toll on me, and . . . while I didn't go to seek professional help, it was something that I had to deal with, sort out, and kind of get myself back on track.

Although this woman was working very hard and staying late, her superiors did not get her help nor did they reward her extra efforts.

Clearly, differential treatment and the consequent overworking caused her to be very stressed, and it reduced her intimate contacts with members of her family. And she regrets that. She reiterates how often she has had to deal with substantial amounts of stored-up anger over racism, and adds this final comment about its effects on her and her family:

> Well, a couple of times I totally forgot to pick my child up from school because I was so engrossed with trying to make sure that I do

this! . . . My daughter had gotten to the point during that year when I was under all that stress, till she would tell me four and five times, she would remind me, "Mom, I'm having this at school." And then she would get to school, and she would call me—one day she called me to remind me about something, I was supposed to pick her up, or something, and I just sat at my desk, and I just boo-hooed. I said, "My baby doesn't have any confidence in me anymore. . . . I'm really not there.". . . And that, really, that was really the beginning of me saying, "Look, nobody's going to do anything to get this on track for you; you got to get this on track for yourself." And then, sometimes you go home and you've held your peace so long, till the first hour that you walk in the door, you're still dealing with everything. You may even be dealing with it verbally. . . . And then, they have their own issues to deal with that day. And like, they just want to have dinner and relax, you know? So your family, inevitably I'd say, suffers.

Children may sometimes come to view parents negatively because of the contending the parents must do with racist whites outside the home. Moreover, it is not only relationships with one's children that can be affected by the tension of racism in the outside world, but also relationships with one's spouse, as is reflected in both this woman's words and the journal entries of Derricotte.

There are other family stresses as well. In the following quote from a field study by Bob Blauner, one black woman explained how black women's success in the corporate world is sometimes used, especially by whites, against black men. White male executives sometimes regard black female employees more favorably than they do similarly situated black male employees because the latter are seen as more competitive with and threatening to the white men. This, in turn, can affect black male-female relations at home:

And he [the black husband] has a competition kind of thing when he comes home, rather than resolving and salving and healing so you can go into the next day's battle. . . . In the black community, our men still see us as sort of an enemy. We've had to become aggressive to do things that our men couldn't do in the South, at a time they could not have stood up and still be alive. It made our men—shall I say the older guys above forty-five, forty-year bracket—very sensitive to the fact that we are a threat to them. They feel that there ought to be something that we can do "by acclamation" that will put them into a role they feel they rightfully belong in. They also resent us in that they feel the white males have used us to keep black males down.[54]

Whether a person recognizes the harmful affects of bringing home anger and resentment from the workplace to the extent that these women do, her or his struggles with discrimination can lead to a variety of suffering for others. We see this in the case of a child who is forgotten at school, of a spouse who wants to relax, or of a couple who has tension between them based on feelings about job competition.

A number of our respondents alluded to the fact that dealing with recurring racism at work can leave a person with a "short fuse"—and thus lead to misdirected anger in interactions within members of the family. A social services coordinator discussed this tension:

And it's really, you almost feel like you're backed up in a corner, so all of that psychological stuff going on, and the physical thing going on? It really [has] you really out of whack, so by the time you walk in your . . . house, [you're] just not in any physical shape to do anything. You just don't want to hear any noise, if your kids say anything to you, you're liable to blow up. . . . I think for a lot of African Americans, we probably could find ourselves somewhere undergoing counseling if we didn't know other ways to deal with that, if we could afford it, or if it wasn't something that was, like, you know, not acceptable in our culture?

This woman realizes that the stress of the workplace affects her both mentally and physically. She makes an insightful point not often mentioned in research literature: that perhaps one of the reasons African Americans have found alternative ways of coping with psychological problems is because they are not as able to afford formal counseling as are whites who encounter similar stress. The adaptability of the black family and community again is utilized to manage life crises that are exacerbated by structural inequality. Then she talks about her own efforts to deal with workplace denigration through her own type of "John Henryism":

And I consider myself a very strong person to deal with things—but psychologically, it was, it was just awful. I felt like, when I walked in that door, I did whatever I had to do for my family real quick. But I felt like if I wasn't working that night or getting up three o'clock in the morning, trying to get ahead, for the next day, I just felt like, "Gosh, they're going to think I'm incompetent, and they want proof." You know, that was the pressure that I had myself under. And then when I really took time to look at it logically and intellectually, what I realized was that I was already producing four times as much work and with better quality than anybody there. And they were peeping in at me while they're on their way to lunch! And they would [say], "Good night." It was almost like they were trying to like, drive the knife deeper. I would be there, they would go to lunch, they would socialize. I could hear them down the hall, laughing and having a good time. And I'm thinking now, "How can this be?!" So you begin to doubt yourself, you begin to psychologically feel somewhat incompetent. . . . So it can take a toll on you, and I think it takes more of a psychological toll on us than we even care to admit.

This woman realizes the psychological damage of stress and self-doubt that workplace discrimination has taken on her. And she also notes how this personal impact carries over to her neglecting interactions with members of her immediate family. In her extended account, she also mentions the fact that, like many other African Americans, she has often dealt with psychological stress through her church relationship rather than through formal therapeutic channels.

Sharing problems in dealing with white animosity and discrimination can create a domino effect of anguish and anger rippling across an extended group. Another result of using families as a resource to deal with the stress of racism can be troubled interpersonal relationships. It is often noted that black women are more likely than white women to become separated or divorced and less likely to remarry.[55] Nonetheless, the direct, negative impact of everyday racism on the difficulties faced by black families has *not* been featured in the mainstream literature on the so-called broken and disorganized black families.[56] Only a few studies have shown how racial discrimination in the workplace can lead to separated or divorced couples. For example, one study of black police officers found that those who felt that they had been penalized more because of their race, or that they were barred from assignments based on their race, were more likely to feel job strain. Consequently, they were more likely to have strain in their personal relationship, less couple interaction generally, and more divorce and separation.[57]

In our focus groups and in informal discussions with a number of other African American husbands and wives, we have found that many people explain in some detail how the stress of discrimination at work places an added burden on their relationships with their spouses. When husbands or wives are under great pressure and stress from the racist incidents in their predominantly white workplaces, their energy for, or willingness to interact with, their spouses when they come home is affected. They may wish to be secluded from family relationships, and perhaps just watch television for a long time in order to unwind for a while from the stress of dealing with whites in the workplace or other social settings. As we see in numerous commentaries in this book, many African Americans are aware of how this impacts the family, and they try to develop counter-strategies. In other cases, even these veterans of contending with racism do not realize fully just how that racism has negatively affected their intimate family relationships. In these cases, white racism has yet other negative, often energy-draining, effects on African American families.

For the family, another obvious consequence of workplace discrimination occurs when an important breadwinner is fired unfairly from his or her job because of discrimination, and then is not able to provide adequately for the family. Thus, one black man quoted in an earlier research study had worked for ten years as a school employee whose job it was to deal with the community. Although he was hired for his interpersonal skills and life experiences, after ten years on the job his employer decided to put some formal screening credentials into place for such community contact positions. Under this newly imposed standard, although he had personally moved up into the middle-class, his working-class demeanor and speech were no longer valued, and he was fired. At the time of his interview, he was preparing to sue to win back his job and was working a temporary job that paid a very low wage. He had also separated from his wife. In his interview, he spoke of the costs of this experience on his children:

I honestly believed and felt that I was put on this earth to help to work with kids, I really did. And I was good, I was damn good at my job to have, let's say, less education than probably anybody at that school. . . . I *am* angry. I'm very angry. Because what they did, they didn't do because I was not performing my job. They did [it] because I was a black man and I spoke out on what I believe and felt. If I hadda been one of their little henchmen to say "yes, no". . . . I would still be there. . . . They don't know what the hell they have put me through. I know I could have a job if it wasn't for them folks down there. They have shut off my livelihood. They don't know the suffering, not that I am absorbing, but my kids. . . . I don't know how many times I didn't have the money to pay the rent. They got food on their table when they come in, in the evening. Sometimes I don't have food here on my table for my kids.[58]

Damage is done to African American families because of workplace mistreatment along racial or racial-class lines. This man cannot feed his children adequately. He also notes that he has had to take his daughter out of college, thereby jeopardizing her ability to be economically successful in the future. And he has separated from his wife. His family has been torn apart by the racist actions of whites in his workplace. We see here the powerful domino effects on families of racist actions in yet another U.S. workplace.

THE IMPACT OF RACISM: THE BLACK COMMUNITY

The impact of discrimination and marginalization on individual African Americans carries over into an impact on local community organizations and activities. Black employees' lack of energy that stems from workplace discrimination can seriously affect their motivation to socialize outside the home and their energy to participate in various important community activities. The social services worker who discussed her family reported that she had withdrawn from activities in her community because of the drain on her energy caused by racial animosity at work. A teacher also described having to give up participation in community groups because of lack of energy:

At one point we had started a minority action committee which is still in existence, with the school district. And it's interesting, because it's very hard to get people after they've fought all day—in a sense, that have enough energy to come out and support an effort like that where it is needed. We know the racism is out there, we know we need to fight for our kids—that was the main thrust of it when we came together. We could see it happening in the schools everyday, particularly to our black boys. . . . And we endeavored to do something about it, but, as I was saying, we were just so drained, it just never got off the ground [speaking quietly]. Hopefully, somebody might.

Other participants echoed this sentiment, citing the impact of the energy loss on various community and church activities. Note here that there is both a personal and a community cost. Part of the personal price of racial discrimination is in not being able to do what one feels is necessary to feel fulfilled in life, which in this case includes meaningful interaction in and on behalf of important community groups and associations.

The spin-off effects of animosity and mistreatment in employment settings can be seen in yet other areas of the lives of these African Americans. Another respondent in a focus group sadly noted the negative impact on participation in church activities:

I have withdrawn from some of the things I was involved with at church that were very important to me, like dealing with the kids at church. Or we had an outreach ministry where we would go out into the low-income housing and we would share about our services, . . . and I was just so drained, like [another respondent] said, if we are all so drained, and we stop doing that, then we lose our connection. But I, physically, by the time I got home at the end of the day, I was just so tired. I didn't even feel like giving back to my community; I didn't feel like doing anything. And so I withdrew from church activities, to the point where I just really was not contributing anything. And it was pulling all that energy; I was exhausted from dealing with what I had to at work. And then whatever little bit was left went to my family, so there was nothing there to give.

The considerable impact of workplace racism is graphically described here, for even church activities become a challenge for this person. What energy there is left after struggles at work with racism is reserved for the family. These economically successful African Americans can be important role models in their local communities, but only if they have the energy to participate actively in churches and other community organizations. These accounts of withdrawal from, or lack of energy for, community activities are worth considering in the light of the many accomplishments of African Americans in organizing to improve both their own communities, in a variety of churches and other important local organizations, and also in working together in national organizations to improve the larger U.S. society. In spite of the great strain, pain, and energy loss stemming from individual and institutional racism, the majority of African Americans manage to strive, endure, and succeed in raising families and building communities. Being tired from the daily struggle against racism in the workplace, schools, and public accommodations has not stopped many African Americans from continuing to organize, a point we will accent in the conclusion that follows.

CONCLUSION: CREATING COMMUNITIES OF RESISTANCE

Dealing with the family and community impact of racism is a constant challenge for African Americans. The question of how to develop effective community strategies for development or change has been a recurring topic of concern and analysis for African American intellectuals and other leaders. For example, in a recently published conversation between noted African American intellectuals bell hooks and Cornell West, West discussed the continuing need for strong black "communities of resistance":

> Our struggles against a sense of nothingness and attempts to reduce us to nothing are ongoing. We confront regularly the question: "Where can I find a sense of home?" That sense of home can only be found in our construction of those communities of resistance bell [hooks] talks about and the solidarity we experience within them. Renewal comes through participating in community. That is the reason

so many folks continue to go to church. In religious experience they find a sense of renewal, a sense of home. In community one can feel that we are moving forward, that struggle can be sustained.[59]

West affirmed the African American value of renewal through community, of the locating of the self in community. His words highlight one of the ongoing problems for those among our respondents and other African Americans who are not able to find the time or energy to participate in community activities because of the profound and continuing effects of everyday racism: Many may be unable to find that renewal and thereby participate fully in community resistance, which is a constant danger for African Americans in white-racist society.

In the continuing conversation, bell hooks responded to West and discussed the interpersonal relationships generally within the African American community:

> The point of connection between Black women and men is that space of recognition and understanding, where we know one another so well, our histories, that we can take the bits and pieces, the fragments of who we are, and put them back together, re-member them. It is this joy of intellectual bonding, of working together to create liberatory theory of analysis that Black women and men can give one another, that Cornel and I give to each other. We are friends of one another's mind. We find a home with one another. It is that joy in community we celebrate and share with you this morning.[60]

Ideally, close friends and members of families use their collective knowledge and skills to take the pieces of a person—for example, after a person has been torn apart by discrimination in the workplace—and help put that individual back together again.

It is evident in the words of numerous respondents that interpersonal relationships, including family relationships, are sometimes jeopardized because one or both partners does not have much energy left at the end of a racially stressful day. Yet most seem to manage to overcome these huge challenges most of the time. Indeed, from their discussions of the energy-draining aspects of discrimination, one might wonder how

African Americans have developed vibrant community organizations and successful resistance movements over nearly four centuries now. Most African Americans persevere through the barriers and manage to overcome the constant "rain" of antiblack racism enough to stay centered in their life struggles and, remarkably, thrive.

Over the last two centuries of U.S. history, African Americans have managed to generate important community movements for social change, including the civil rights movement that overthrew legal segregation. In addition, African Americans have played an important role in trying to reform the U.S. health care system. Interestingly, after World War II some African Americans organized what has been called the "medical civil rights movement." This was an effort to gain fair and equal access to quality health care and was an important precursor to the larger civil rights movement of the 1960s.[61] Such efforts, as well as those expended to bring great success for the civil rights movement of the 1960s, required many African Americans to have a strong sense of who they were and possess the substantial energy necessary for this long struggle to bring about major societal change. Indeed, without these great efforts by many in African American communities, it is unlikely that the United States, and especially the southern United States, would have advanced as much economically and socially as it has in the intervening decades since the 1960s.

These organized efforts have not only liberated African Americans from legal segregation, but also the *country as a whole* from these enormous barriers to human progress. All Americans are the current beneficiaries of organized African American resistance to racial oppression. There is greater freedom in the U.S. today than there would have been without the civil rights movement of the 1960s. This is as true today as it has been in the past. Racism is a destructive force that ultimately affects all residents of this country. As the English poet John Donne said long ago, "Any man's death diminishes me, because I am involved in mankind; and therefore never send to know for whom the bell tolls; it tolls for thee."

5

Fighting and Managing Everyday Racism: An Array of Strategies

AFRICAN AMERICANS HAVE CREATED an impressive and innovative array of strategies that they use to resist or cope with the racial hostility and discrimination that regularly crashes into their lives. As a rule, African Americans learn effective strategies for fighting and coping with discrimination from parental instruction and from assessing their own experiences, as well as from hearing about the experiences of family members and friends. Thus, the experiences and learning of others, the *collective memory*, are critical resources for those who must deal with white racism throughout their lives. Painful experiences with discriminatory whites get imbedded in the memories of individuals as well as in collective memories of families, friends, local communities, and African Americans as a group.

Beyond drawing on the experiences of relatives and friends, African Americans have also learned many contending and coping lessons from accounts of the lives and struggles of African American leaders and heroes like Harriet Tubman, Frederick Douglass, Fannie Lou Hamer,

Martin Luther King, Jr., Malcolm X, and countless other African Americans who persevered under difficult life circumstances. These experiential accounts of dealing with white racism often provide models for contending with assaults by whites on one's dignity, livelihood, and, sometimes, one's very life. The strategies and coping skills are passed down through the generations as part of the valuable communal knowledge about contending with racism.

As we have seen in previous chapters, middle-class African Americans often find themselves in situations in which they must interact routinely with insensitive or discriminatory white coworkers. In such settings, out of necessity, most learn to be careful observers of white actions and behavior. For example, one of the country's leading philosophy professors, Kant scholar Adrian Piper, has written about how she sees an array of cues from whites that discrimination is about to crash into her life in a college setting: "The person looks at me with a fixed stare, her tension level visibly rising. Like a thermostat, when the tension reaches a certain level, the mechanism switches on: out comes some comment or action, often of an offensive personal nature, that attempts to locate me within the rigid confines of her stereotype of black people."[1] In many different social situations, not just in academia, African Americans face this type of white evaluation and response. As a result, it is common for African Americans to reflect deeply on the structure of their encounters with whites, in part as a way of crafting some countering and coping strategies. Many speak of reviewing such a situation carefully—by taking a second and third look—before judging it to be discriminatory. In this way, in a variety of situations and settings, African Americans often give whites the benefit of the doubt.

In order to succeed in such difficult workplaces, African Americans must find various ways to manage their frustration, pain, and anger, as well as counter other consequences of the discrimination they face. To that end, they use a variety of coping and contending strategies. In previous chapters, some respondents discussed methods of mentally or physically withdrawing from a hostile situation, while others verbally or physically confronted discriminatory whites. Sometimes they attribute whites' racist behavior to ignorance and choose to educate whites as a response to discrimination, which often gives them a sense of empowerment. Other times, they describe a "shield" they must put on each day in order to protect themselves as they traverse white institutions. Many discuss critical social networks—

in the family, community, and church—as important buffers against the harmful psychological and physical effects of everyday discrimination.

In many cases, one must withdraw from the discriminatory situation as a strategy of response. Yet, holding in one's emotions, as we have seen in previous chapters, is problematical if not unhealthy. Previous research indicates that a too-restrained response to anger over workplace problems can mean even more suffering because of feelings of impotence. These feelings can, in turn, contribute to stress-related illness. Coping with racism through avoidance can also be harmful to a person's satisfaction in life and self-esteem.[2] Numerous researchers have suggested that finding a socially viable way of openly expressing one's anger at oppression is much healthier than turning the anger inward.[3]

In addition, dealing with antiblack discrimination requires attention to situations and contexts. Most black Americans do not react to acts of discrimination with the same strategy every time. Instead, they often consider the situational context in which the questionable or discriminatory behavior arises, and assess the possible motivations of the white discriminators. Previous research has shown how spatial and temporal factors can be important in a black person's choice of a resistance or survival strategy.[4] Thus, in our interviews and in previous studies done by the authors, those interviewed have discussed the importance of "choosing one's battles" in confronting everyday discrimination. They indicate they do not have the personal energy to tackle each instance of discrimination openly or aggressively.[5]

REPERTOIRES OF RESPONSE TO EVERYDAY RACISM

Tailoring Responses to Situations

Generally speaking, middle-class black Americans have more resources to use in dealing with racist incidents than working-class black Americans; depending on the context, these middle-class resources may be more or less effective. A hospital executive in the Southwest discussed her contextual approach:

> It really depends on the situation. If it's something that doesn't push too much of a button that I think I'm angry, and therefore I express anger, then I may just leave the situation. I will divorce myself from

the situation, or I may make a joke. If it does cause so much anger at that moment, then I'm just going to blow up. I have never experienced a discriminatory situation where I just blew up. If anything it's been a name-calling type thing or something like that, so I just leave the scene. . . . I would say probably the most effective is to assertively stand up to the situation but not become threatening, unless you are totally and extremely provoked to do [so]. Or, you can take the passive approach and leave the scene. . . .To me, there's a difference between aggressiveness and assertiveness. Assertiveness to me is what your needs are, or what is wrong, how you want something to be, but in a very—let's say in a calmer fashion—and that's a win-win situation. Aggressiveness to me, is attacking and confronting, and you're not on an equal level with someone if you're above them, if you will. And then the passive means is by, is maybe by just divorcing yourself, or by being quiet, or ignoring the situation. So, to me, honestly, I don't believe there's any one way you can handle pressure.

This insightful commentary suggests the need for a repertoire of resistance. Like most African Americans, this woman has an array of tools she uses in countering various types of hostility and discrimination. Sometimes she chooses simply to ignore a racist situation, withdrawing from the discriminator. At other times she chooses to use humor to ridicule the situation or even the discriminator. Finally, although she says it has not happened yet, she allows for the possibility that a discriminatory situation could provoke her to be more aggressive. Clearly, a distinction can be made between more active and more passive forms of resistance to racial hostility and discrimination. Black Americans do not just passively cope with discrimination without standing up to the discriminator, nor do they always rush to actively confront white people who treat them unfairly. Various types of resistance are necessary and depend on the situation in a such a complex racist society as the United States.

Strategies for Everyday Racism:
Internal Coping and External Resistance

From the repertoire of possible responses to discrimination described by those African Americans we have interviewed, two general categories emerge. When faced with discrimination, our respondents report using (1) internal, spiritual, or cognitively-based coping skills and (2) behavioral, action-based resistance strategies. One professor highlighted these two types of responses:

> I use what, even if I do say it myself, is a smart approach that I've learned from years of experience, and listening to other people [dealing with discrimination with] wisdom and strength. I think there are two main goals that are important. The first is a more emotional, or spiritual, goal, which is not to be destroyed as a person. And then the other goal is, not more practical, but it's a more practically result-oriented, which is to get what it is that you're trying to get.

Generally speaking, internal responses to discrimination are more likely to be attitudinal and orientation-based mechanisms, while resistance strategies are action and behavioral responses. Most internal responses, such as trying not to internalize frustration, seem to be less about active resistance than about internal survival and coping; they do not involve an outward confrontation with the discriminator. Typically, behavioral strategies include responses in which a person overtly resists discrimination by dealing with or confronting the discriminator. This distinction is not clear-cut, for one can view the internal, protective coping mechanisms that keep discrimination from destroying a person as indeed a type of quiet resistance to racism. Any time a racially oppressed person refuses to let racism stop her or him, that too is an important form of opposition to racism.

The specific themes evident in the category of internal coping mechanisms are such strategies as cultivating a particular attitude about oneself and about oneself in a situation; developing specific attitudes toward whites; keeping control over oneself or over the situation and, conversely, recognizing the limits of one's control; engaging in spiritual or religious activities; and mentally withdrawing when a situation is too difficult.

INTERNALLY-FOCUSED COPING MECHANISMS

In workplaces and other important societal settings, African Americans sometimes choose to combat the substantial stress that discrimination causes them by using internally-directed coping mechanisms. Rather than, or in addition to, trying to change the attitudes or behavior of discriminatory whites, they adjust their own views or attitudes in order to shield themselves from some of the psychological and physical damage of recurring racism. Such internal strategies are frequently chosen when a person believes that it is futile to try to change the attitudes or behavior of the whites involved. This is especially true when a white person's behavior was apparently unintentional, or when no practical goal can be accomplished by actively confronting the discrimination.

It may also be necessary or useful to focus on changing one's reactions when the discriminatory behavior comes from one's immediate supervisor or employer, that is, when there is little hope of being able to change the behavior. This contrasts with discriminatory behavior that comes from a coworker, for which the target of discrimination might be able to appeal to a supervisor or other manager for redress. However, discrimination that is supported or ignored by higher-level supervisors can have an especially negative impact because the target of discrimination does not know where to turn for assistance, a point we have seen in earlier discussions. If higher-level supervisors do not act to end discriminatory actions by their subordinates, such inaction can accent the stress inflicted from discrimination.[6]

Being Prepared

There are a number of common sayings in this society along the lines of "always be prepared." Never was such a saying more appropriate than in regard to the repertoires of action needed to deal with racial mistreatment. Recall the technician quoted in chapter 3 who spoke of the gastrointestinal problems coming from workplace discrimination: "It was very, very stressful, because every day you're constantly mentally trying to prepare yourself when you get out of the car in the morning and you go in, go into work, you're trying to prepare yourself, 'Well what do I have to face today?'" Her strategy is one often used by African Americans to counter racial mistreatment. Similarly, a retired black teacher interviewed in a previous study eloquently contrasted her life with that of a white woman, who like her bathes and dresses before leaving the house. Unlike the white woman, however, she noted that she must put on her defensive "shield" just before she leaves. For many decades, she has had to prepare in advance for often unpredictable racist actions in the predominantly white worlds she traverses; she has developed an array of counterstrategies for whatever may happen.[7]

In one of our interviews, a self-employed business owner believes that since discrimination is a part of her life, she must prepare herself: "I face it all day, all the time, yes, in a way, I am [prepared]. Yeah, 'prepared' is a good word. Because if it just happens to come up, I've got something for it. It doesn't bother me anymore. I think that's when it stops bothering you, when you are prepared for it." Implicit in the idea of being prepared for antiblack actions is again a degree of acceptance of the sad fact, gleaned from previous experience, that this discrimination is likely to occur. This woman faces it "all day, all the time," and keeps her ways of dealing with it handy. Although we can admire the strength of character required to keep prepared for the daily assaults, we must also understand that this preparedness can come at a great personal cost. Over their lifetimes, African Americans must devote much valuable time and energy to protecting themselves against discrimination, discrimination that frequently blindsides its targets in a variety of societal settings. Indeed, one of the privileges of being white in the United States is that one does not usually have to waste time and energy on such racial matters.

Trying to Be Desensitized

Internal acceptance of the hard reality of racism, often with some resignation, is one tactic used to cope with it. When asked how often he gets angry about the actions of white people, one man who works in marketing answered this way:

> Not as much as I used to. I don't know if I can put any specific date and number on it; that's very difficult to do. It's very likely that we can be desensitized. I've been in the workforce now for quite a period of time dealing with this matter of not being totally accepted in professional America—in America, period. Like anything else, I think you become desensitized to it. You just deal with it. You don't pay as much attention to it today as you did yesterday.

Desensitization can be a positive force in dealing with a hostile workplace. When the interviewer asks if acceptance is the best way to handle discrimination, he added:

I think to maintain sanity, you must have a certain amount of acceptance. Certainly, there are just too numerous situations that you *cannot* do anything about. Some of those situations don't even involve you, but they're obvious to you. To try to handle all of the things that you see, I think would just be mind-boggling.

One must choose appropriate and effective coping strategies in order to maintain one's psychological health. Note that he alludes to the *collective* impact of witnessing discrimination against another person. Empathetic responses are common among people who have been through similar experiences. As we have also seen in discussions in previous chapters, when one person of color faces discrimination, often others who are aware of the situation vicariously experience it, a point that other respondents in this chapter make as well.

This man also makes reference to another theme that appears in many respondents' statements. This is the great frequency of racial discrimination in the everyday worlds—the "too numerous situations." This relates to our previous analysis of "woodwork" racism. Opinion surveys indicate that African Americans face large amounts of discrimination in their workplaces and in other areas of their lives. For example, a recent Gallup opinion poll asked black respondents if they had faced discrimination at work, dining out, shopping, with the police, or in public transportation during the last month. Some 45 percent reported discrimination in at least one area, including 70 percent of black men under the age of 35.[8] And these respondents were only reporting for just the last month! What would their candid reports for several years, or a lifetime, come out to be? In a previous study, Joe Feagin noted that a few African Americans had estimated how often they faced discrimination at the hands of whites over the course of a year. In one informal interview, a retired printer from a major northern city estimated that he faced at least 250 (blatant and subtle) incidents of discrimination annually—and that his estimate included only those he pays attention to. Thus, it seems probable that, over a long lifetime, many a black man or woman who has spent time in predominantly white institutions and areas will encounter *thousands* of acts of antiblack discrimination.[9]

This is a reality most whites do not want to face, and this white denial is a likely reason for the stereotyped white notion that African Americans "see racism under every rock." Yet what most whites miss, or do not want to understand, is that African Americans must try not to see, or not to attend to, much of the racism they encounter, if only to preserve their health. It seems that, to survive in this racist society, African Americans cannot pay too much attention to the racism that imposes itself routinely. They must become, to a varying extent, desensitized, for the health consequences of paying close attention to recurring discrimination is great.

To survive, black Americans must develop strategies *not* to see much of the discrimination they face, if only because attending to all such blatant and subtle discrimination would likely be a recipe for a mental breakdown. There is just too much of it in the rounds of everyday life. Feagin and Sikes summed this point up in an earlier work: "Much discrimination is overlooked if possible. There is much white hostility that blacks must ignore just to reduce the pain and to survive. If one can name racial discrimination something else, it may not hurt as much."[10]

Most African Americans, as well as other Americans of color, recognize the necessity of deciding which racially troubling situations to "try to handle" and which to ignore. Without making such choices, they would spend too much time and energy in the workplace or elsewhere dealing with everyday mistreatment. Indeed, significant time- and energy-management strategies are forced on those who are targets of recurring discrimination. Recall the comments of some respondents, who mentioned that one of their time-management difficulties caused by racism in the workplace is that they must spend time documenting the details of everyday activities in order to protect themselves from accusations of errors or incompetence. This is only one example of the wasted time that is spent dealing with racism, one involving a situation in which an African American employee feels she or he has no other choice.

Avoiding Internalization of Frustration, Anger, and Bitterness

In some cases, white coworkers or supervisors intentionally provoke black workers to see if they will react too strongly. In one of our focus groups, after a postal service manager spoke about handling his anger when he is poorly treated at work, a woman in the group added: "This is a set up. . . . You get into rage, they just say, 'See, that's why we didn't give it [a promotion] to her.'" The ability to hold in one's anger and control feelings is central to survival in a work world in which strong reactions to racial animosity can affect one's economic opportunities and success. African Americans often must check their emotions so as not to play into white stereotypes of being out of control.

One way that some African Americans deal with everyday racism is by internalizing much of the pain and anger. This response to discrimination is to hold it in. Recall from chapter 3 that recent research suggests that a pattern called "John Henryism" is associated with increased stress and health problems for African Americans. Many respond to discrimination by trying to increase control over their environment using extra-intense work efforts. This involves especially intensive internalized responses to environmental stressors. Research suggests that those with higher levels of this John Henryism are more likely to have high blood pressure than those who have more normal work commitments.[11] Also recall that some research on workplace and other environmental stressors indicates that suppressed hostility is one coping response in dealing with racism, but that it comes with a cost. Barbee Myers explains thus: "*Suppressed hostility refers to a process of coping by inhibiting negative attitudes in situations where the person is the target of appraised noxious stimuli from some source of power. . . .* This suppressed hostility pattern (anger-in) was found to be associated with elevated diastolic blood pressure for all men. The anger-in coping style was related to both higher blood pressure levels and the number of actual hypertensives in all groups except black low-stress men." Strategies like John Henryism and holding the anger in clearly have serious consequences. Myers has also suggested that a better coping strategy is "reflective coping," which is "a response pattern involving appropriate appraisal, constructive behavioral response, and vascular and neural deceleration." Research suggests that reflective coping is associated, albeit it moderately, with lower blood pressure and thus works better than the "anger-in and anger-out coping styles (collectively termed resentful coping)."[12]

Some of our respondents stress the importance of not letting discrimination take over their mental lives. For example, a female vice president of a chamber of commerce in a southwestern city commented, "I don't internalize it." And an engineer has also decided not to let rage have a negative affect on his health: "So you see, . . . those things make you upset . . . and the stress does make a difference, I think it probably takes five years off your life, to tell you the truth, if you let it get to you." An administrative secretary in the Midwest echoed this sentiment about how to deal with racially generated stress: "You learn how to deal with it. . . . You sit up there, and [you'll] be mad all day long and that's not good for you and you end up dead. I'm not dying from them. Until God gets ready to take me home. It ain't worth it."

A dentist who lives in the North spoke of an incident with his son. Although this experience occurred outside the workplace, he articulated a theme mentioned in other comments. When asked how he usually deals with discrimination, the dentist replied:

> My son and I were riding bicycles. . . . And we'd gotten off the bikes and we were drinking out of this water fountain, and this car pulled up, these white kids drove by. And they said, "Hey, nigger!" You know? . . . They never stopped, but they were just driving by slowly. And I said, "You're damn right I'm a 'nigger' and I'm proud of it!". . . you can't get bitter and have it consume you.

In this case a respondent openly claims the racial epithet and thereby tries to reduce its power to hurt him. He feels that this helps to keep him from becoming bitter, and internalizing bitterness can be personally destructive. He is asserting pride in his African American identity. There is a longstanding debate in African American communities over whether the intentional use of this painful, white-originated epithet by African Americans (such as by young people in their rap music)—as a term of endearment within the African American community or as a way of reducing its poisonous impact—actually does more harm than good, especially in the long run. Many African Americans would thus disagree with this respondent's innovative counter-response.

Yet most would likely agree with his continuing analysis. He further explained his reasons for protecting himself against anger over racial incidents, such as those that he encounters or those that he hears about:

> I get mad for the moment when I hear about it. It's not healthy to get angry, if you get bitter. That's not healthy because then they control you. Sure, I'm angry [mentions incidents that have angered him, like the killings of civil rights workers]. Some were brought to justice and

some weren't. Well, I'm angry. I'm angry at those that got away, but I turn it on and turn it off. I'm not so bitter that I'm going to go out and I'm going to be mean to somebody white today because of something that somebody else did. No.

Like other respondents, he notes that allowing whites to make him angry gives them too much control over his life. Note too the recognition of the cumulative dimension of racism, for he is angry about events that happened some decades back. One incident he has in mind involved the killing of two black and one white civil rights workers by white supremacists in Mississippi, apparently with the help of some law enforcement officials. Typically, the *collective memory* of past incidents of racism, both those suffered by the family and by the larger community, is passed along family and friendship networks and across the generations, and thus becomes a force into the present day.

Reflecting on counterstrategies that she has used, a woman who works in government administration in the South described how she tries "to never get upset. Not to let that rage consume you, and after, and it really takes a lot to be really thoughtful, and to get beyond that, and, and *try* to educate them. I, that's what I've found works for me. And it helps me not to go home and to have that just simmer in me—that I can just leave it." In this woman's statement, one notes the same ways of coping that many respondents have mentioned. It is important not to allow anger to completely take over to the point that it controls one's reactions, and it can be useful to try to educate some naïve white people regarding racism. In addition, as she notes, being able to disengage from a hostile setting can be an invaluable way to manage this stress. The fact that this woman's coping style is internal and cognitive in nature is apparent in that she says her attempt is to be "really thoughtful." In doing so, she seeks to move beyond an emotional response to a cognitively-based response.

Similarly, a woman broadcaster who works for a television station referred to the need to not become bitter. When asked how she copes with racial discrimination psychologically, she answered:

You mean coping with it? . . . You just, you go from day to day, and you wake up and you know you've got another day to face where, even with where I am now, I can still go into a restaurant and—little bitty things—and be seated by the kitchen. . . . Or I can go into a department store and there can be five people waiting to be waited on, and the salesgirl will invariably—and still, this still happens . . .— will invariably turn around and rather than saying, "Who's next?" will automatically go toward a person who is white. Oh, yeah, this still happens. And so, I can pull up in my Mercedes, you know, or I can walk into my $150,000 house, which I don't have all this, but I could do that, but when I left there, I'm still just another "nigger" to some people in this country. And I know that, and you recognize it, and you live with it and you tolerate it and you try not to let it get you paranoid, and you try not to let it make you bitter.

Even if a black person is middle- or upper-income, they are still treated with disdain and discrimination by many whites. Despite the claims of many neoconservative analysts, in the everyday lives of middle-class African Americans, one's racial position often trumps one's class position. If the hostility a person faces were considered in its total impact or reality, it might well be overwhelming. Like others, this woman tries to "go from day to day," and thereby counter to some degree the accumulating impact of discrimination.

Her statement contrasts with comments from many outside commentators about black "paranoia" regarding racism. We see this notion in the writings of such right-wing analysts as Dinesh D'Souza. Amazing enough, D'Souza calls the racist reality that African Americans face mostly an "imaginary racism." He argues, "The first dysfunctional aspect of black culture is racial paranoia—a reflexive tendency to blame racism for every failure, even those that are intensely personal."[13] In contrast, as the quotation from the respondent above clearly indicates, many if not most African Americans are conscious of the possibility of such paranoia—or of white stereotypes about that—and often take measures to combat such feelings and expressions.

Avoiding the Internalization of Negative Images

In a number of the respondents' commentaries in this and previous chapters, we see direct references or allusions to the need to fight commonplace white stereotypes of black Americans that are present in particular institutional settings or circulated by the media. For example, over several decades many whites have routinely asserted racist stereotypes of black Americans as intellectually or morally inferior to white Americans. Whites often denigrate black physical characteristics. Across society, this constant drumbeat of inferiority statements and theories creates difficult situations for black Americans and threatens to harm their health. Recent research studies have shown that those who substantially internalize some of the negative, white-racist views of African Americans are more likely to have problems with severe psychological distress, lowered self-esteem, and alcoholism than those who successfully fight this internalization. Research by social psychologist Claude Steele and his associates has shown that, when whites activate the stereotypes of inferiority in certain settings, they can affect the performance of young African Americans on education-related tasks. Thus, when tests similar to the Graduate Record Examination were presented to African American students as tests of "intellectual ability," they as a group did not perform as well as otherwise comparable white students. Yet, when the testing presentation did not mention the implicit stereotype of black intelligence, the black students performed as well as the white students. Steele terms this situation one of "stereotype threat," a commonplace situation in society that can cause anxiety or self-consciousness that interferes with educational or job performance.[14]

One aspect of white racism is the constant activation of these stereotypes for both young and older black Americans—an activation that must be countered by the array of strategies suggested by our respondents in this chapter and chapter 6. These include preparedness for stereotypical threats, learning to recognize them, and actively resisting their internalization. This is one of the less obvious aspects of everyday racism, and a cost of living in the United States that is not borne by white Americans.

Knowing One's Self

One way in which many African Americans cope with racial antipathy and discrimination is by shaping or changing their attitudes about themselves. Increasing self-knowledge is important, which may be accompanied by increased self-confidence. One entrepreneur expressed it this way:

Well, I guess one must know their own self first. And people will handle things differently. And I think a lot of it comes from your own upbringing and how you were raised, your family values that you carry with you throughout your life. . . . And again, if you have the vision to try and do something, to accomplish something that may be atypical of your sex or race, but if you have that vision nine out of ten times you're going to achieve it. So, the frustrations are going to come. I would say often times, if you understand yourself and how you respond to those frustrations, it may make you work even harder to achieve. So, I don't look at the frustration as, "dog-gone it, I'm just going to quit, fold up my tent and go home." Often times, my ego will say, "Well, you're going to have to fight harder for this, because it's not as easy as you may have initially thought, and that you may have to do more training, or whatever it is, more contacts with people, more reading, or whatever it may be, to get recognized by whatever achievement you have laid forth." So, the frustrations are just part of life, and some people eat, some people drink, some people overindulge in a lot of different things. If you do all of those things moderately, I think you can achieve it and with-stand the frustration.

This entrepreneur stresses the importance of knowing what one is capable of and how one tends to react. These things are, once again, learned in the critical context of families, indeed as "family values." Echoing respondents quoted in previous chapters, this woman also rec-ognizes that drinking or overindulgence can be problematical reactions to discrimination. We see the John Henry theme here as well: That because of discrimination, African Americans often compensate by working harder than their white peers to try to achieve the same rewards.

In addition to extra work efforts, African Americans frequently must go to great lengths to protect their self-conceptions and self-esteem. Parents usually bolster their children's self-esteem so that they, too, can withstand the racial blows that will be dealt in white society. This is an added family burden for black parents. In one in-depth exchange in a focus group, a nurse and a deputy sheriff spoke of the importance of self-con-fidence in fighting the harmful effects of recurring discrimination:

DEPUTY SHERIFF: Yeah. What you have to do to deal with that—first of all, you got to have it instilled within yourself that I [am] better than whatever any man, woman, boy or girl thinks about me [voices in group agree]. You've got to be so self-confident—in other words, you've got to be almost halfway cocky.

NURSE: But . . .you think about the people that you see every day, or with the—look at these kids and their parents—women, these women don't feel that way that we feel, you know?. . . They don't feel that cockiness, or—and what they do is they give it to their children.

DEPUTY SHERIFF: And they just, pass it on.

NURSE: They pass it on.

DEPUTY SHERIFF: They, they get—they're submissive to it.

NURSE: That's right. That's right.

DEPUTY SHERIFF: . . . and they just get trodden down.

These sharp-sighted respondents speak of the need for strong self-confidence. They have in mind both the way in which adults themselves must respond to racist indignities, and the way in which they as parents are forced to teach their children about such painful matters. Note, too, that these focus group participants lament the fact that some black parents do not have the self-esteem that is required to teach children. The conversation continues when the deputy sheriff comments in this manner: "But . . . what you've got to tell your kids, 'Child, you can do anything you want. You could be anything you want to be. And you got to really, you know, believe in this thing.' Because . . . white people, they ain't stopping! [laughter in the room]." Not only do parents need to tell children they can be anything, but they themselves must believe it. One of the challenges a black parent must face is negotiating how to tell a child that, while they have the *ability* to be anything, they live in a society that may *not allow* them to be anything they want to be. Thus, the common cliché, "you can be anything you want to be," takes on a different meaning for black children and adults than for white children and adults.

The deputy sheriff then showed how strong his own sense of self is. He added some biting commentary on how he handles incidents of derision from white coworkers:

They will tell you from day after day, every day goes by, about some sort of shortcoming. . . . Like, yesterday, we're at rifle training. The whole . . . rifle team went to [names place]. I'm the only [black] in the bunch. We get up there, and we [were] out there shooting, and they're making statements about, "[his name] go run through the woods!" [Other respondents react with sounds of dismay]. I said, "Well okay, I don't mind running through the woods—but I'm carrying my rifle, too!" You know. [Other respondents laugh]. Yeah. So, you know, they [are] making little statements that, you know, "Oh, you go running through the woods, we'll chase you!" "Fine! I ain't got no problem! But I'm going to have my three-twenty-three, and I'm going to be pumping back!" So . . . [I] lobbed it back, but see, if it had been some other person, maybe . . . they [would] get down and out, and they get depressed. . . . You know, you just have an answer for them.

He has learned several strategies to fight barbed or racist comments and actions, including those from fellow law enforcement officers. Singled out by white officers because of who he is, he has an answer for their comments and is able to keep his answer in the same apparently joking tone as the comments made to him. (Such comments could conceivably trigger memories of lynchings for black officers.) His white coworkers are likely unable to complain that he "overreacts" or is "too sensitive," because just as they are "just joking," so is he. This deputy sheriff understands the importance of not letting comments go by, and yet his replies are strategic and reflective in that he does not compromise his position by appearing to be "paranoid." As he later says, his white coworkers soon learn that if they "come at [him] all day, [they'd] better bring a lunch." Like previous respondents, this man highlights the fact that in order to have resources to constantly reply to the racism of fellow workers, something must be "built in yourself." Those who have strong self-esteem and poise are able to better withstand racist attacks in the workplace and elsewhere.

Finally, in this focus group discussion of the importance of self-esteem in coping with discrimination, a government administrator added, in the spirit of an old African proverb, that the whole community can play a vital role in supporting a child's self-esteem:

And I'd just like to add . . . to that, what [names another participant] said that, that some of these children's parents don't instill that. But it does not necessarily have to be a parent who—or relative, it can be anybody . . . out there in the community that helps develop that child's self-esteem. So, I mean, it can be children who come to church—building . . . that character from the church.

The recurring discrimination central to the U.S. system of racism operates to make families and communities, not just individuals, suffer when any member is discriminated against. For that reason, the community often takes some responsibility for raising children to cope with and resist discrimination. Thinking back to the last chapter, it is for this reason, among others, that it is particularly ironic and disheartening when racism damages the very African American institutions, families, and communities that have long served as supports against that racism.

Framing Attitudes about Whites

Not only do African Americans deal with everyday racism by shaping and honing their general outlook on life, they also consider whether developing certain views of whites might alleviate some of the harmful effects of this racism. Instead of only feeling the hostility and anger—which is, after all, a rather normal response to everyday racism—many try to modify these feelings into views that may be less harmful in their psychological or physical effects. Certain ways of viewing whites and what they do seem to reduce the stress that African Americans feel.

One way to do this is to find or accent the good people within a social, organizational, or community setting. A college-educated secretary for a government agency noted that one of her means of coping with racism is to realize that "they're not all like that." When asked if any whites have been helpful to her in achieving her goals, she stated:

Yeah, I have met some good white people out here who have kept me from becoming bitter because I realize that it's not just genetic, they're not all born that way, that there are some good people, and that they are capable of change. That's kept me from being bitter, because I've seen black people be so destroyed by racism in the sense that they become so bitter they can't function anymore.

By realizing that not every white person is the same, and that whites are capable of changing their racial attitudes, this respondent helps protect herself from bitterness. When the goal is to create a better life for oneself and one's family, one must realize the importance of not allowing racism to paralyze one's life. For some, believing that all whites are equally racist could cause them to give up altogether. Instead, if an African American can seek out and find white allies, that can restore that person's sense of faith in humanity and hope that, someday, the system of racism in the United States eventually might be destroyed. Hope for a better future is a central psychological defense for African Americans—a rather remarkable response given the heavy and continuing burden that is contemporary racism.

Framing White Acts as Ignorance

Another way to deal with white stereotyping and prejudice is to attribute some or much of it to ignorance rather than intentional antipathy and malevolence. For example, a respondent in the Midwest described an incident in which a young black man came to her workplace to donate items to the service organization for which she works. Her white boss asked the young man why he was donating, and he answered that he had grown up in the service organization, though in another location. The woman then concluded her account with this note: "And he [her boss] said, 'Oh, I will have to call him. I know the person who directs the organization down there. I'll have to tell him that you didn't end up in jail.' And the guy just, he's like, 'I don't . . . know quite how to take [that].' But he [her boss] says this all the time." Both African Americans who heard this comment perceived it the same way, as a stereotyped statement reflecting common white images of young black men as deviant or criminal. Although the woman recognizes her supervisor's comments as racially stereotypical, she tries to understand *why* he says these things: "I think that he just doesn't know any better. . . . I've come to grips with him, I've worked for him for many years. . . . I let him know that I don't like his comments and that they're inappropriate, but there's nothing I can do about it. But I just think he doesn't know any better." She attributes her supervisor's comments not to hostility, but to common ignorance. Again, we see how, contrary to what many whites believe, African Americans often give whites the benefit of the doubt for various prejudiced comments, rather than being quick to "play the race card" as numerous white commentators on racial issues assert. In another account, a young government worker in the Southeast accents a similar point: "But see, sometimes people do you like that. It was a girl at work, she . . . called me and another girl . . . a 'nigger' one day. And the other girl got mad—was very, was ready to fight. And this guy from Tennessee told me, he said, 'She was taught that. And it's her fault that she's too ignorant to go out and find different.'" Like the woman earlier, this young woman encountered racist comments in her workplace. She agrees that this can be attributed to the ignorance that comes from faulty parental upbringing.

African Americans sometimes deal with discrimination in workplace situations by finding ways to attribute the behavior of white coworkers to factors other than overt prejudice or stereotyping. Doubtless, this helps them continue to work with such whites on a daily basis. This response may help reduce the stress of everyday racism by attributing the problems to ignorance rather than overt racial hostility. For many African Americans, perhaps it is easier to believe that whites act cruelly by mistake or through ignorance than to believe that they do so with intentionally racist motivation and some knowledge of the harm that they are causing.

The insight of the next respondent, a college student, attests to the wisdom that many black Americans cultivate relatively early in their lives to handle racism. She discussed various ways that she has come to understand whites, which has helped her manage problems with racism:

> First I analyze it. I don't get irate. I never really go off on anybody. If it's something that I think I can address, I address it. But if it's something that's just so stupid, I take pity for the other person. I used to get real upset, and I'd go home and tell my mother and cry. But I realized that didn't solve the problem. That person was still doing the same thing they were doing, and if I get upset they're still going to do the same thing. So, I just feel sorry. And I get upset that they think that they're so much better. But otherwise, I just give someone a stupid

look, or just saying something like, "That was very uncalled for and that didn't look intelligent on your behalf." Or, if they can't understand something, I can try to explain, but that's the only way I can deal with it. I don't have the background to handle their problems. The only thing I could suggest is that you take the time to be more diverse, try accept diversity, that's the only thing that I can say.

She has learned through trial and error about white ignorance or lack of understanding and about how to cope with that. Even in her youth, she understood much about white behavior and developed a repertoire to deal with it. She places the locus of the problem of racism squarely at the feet of the whites who perpetuate it. One implication in the last part of her statement is that whites who do such things are sick and in need of professional help. She mentions that she does not have the background to give them that help, in effect disengaging from the situation. In an earlier part of the statement, she offers another possible explanation for racism on the part of whites—a lack of intelligence. Either way, this young woman clearly has found ways to understand and communicate that racism is a *white* problem. The depth of understanding that is required for dealing with pervasive white racism is remarkable when one reflects on it. Even those African Americans who are relatively young frequently have had to develop the "wisdom of Solomon" as part of the life tasks that are forced upon them by the mere color of their skin.

UNDERSTANDING THE POTENTIAL FOR CONTROL

Numerous respondents touched on or discussed more fully the importance of the degree of (or lack of) control they have over a discriminatory incident and the greater control they have in their reaction to it. These are important components of coping and resisting strategies. The following commentaries from respondents reveal different aspects of African Americans' using control over a situation as a coping mechanism. They realize that they do have some control in many interactions that involve racial discrimination. Yet, they also recognize that some discriminating situations are not under their control, and therefore cannot reasonably be construed to be their fault or their responsibility for elimination.

A self-employed designer who lives in the Southwest replied, when asked how often she gets angry at the actions of whites, this way:

Very seldom. Very seldom. I find it amusing. When I feel that I'm in control, I never get angry. And I am in control of every racial situation. I'm not the sick one, . . . and I've come up with little ways to handle these things when they come up. You know, what do you own that you can stand to part with? It's going to be mine if you keep it up, that kind of thing. . . . I'm in control, I don't get mad anymore.

Anger is a reasonable response to many discriminatory interactions with white Americans, so one must be prepared to forestall or deal with such a reaction. Realizing that racist whites are the problem, this woman tries to stay in control and handle discrimination by making it clear to those who would mistreat her that doing so carries with it a significant cost *for them.*

A young man who works in law school administration discussed issues of control and responsibility with his own slant:

I don't get angry very often at all. I get very frustrated. There are occasions where I've been angry [at] blatant racism. But usually my anger is in balance by the same thing that I mentioned before, the fact that we tend to not do enough for ourselves. When people lie down in the middle of the street, someone lies down, someone's going to come and walk right over them. So if we're going to lie down, people are going to take advantage of us. And I never lie down, you know. I do my best to not to put myself in a position where anyone can do something to me. So if they *would*, it would definitely be very obvious, very blatant, and I would make *sure* that it was very obvious and very blatant. We have a lot of things that are set in place these days so that we can sort of take care of those kinds of actions, so it keeps people from doing what they maybe would want to do. But it protects me at the same time. So, again, I have a hard time getting angry at racism because if, I mean, food is there so we eat. If there's a lot of food there, we eat a lot. And if there's a lot of opportunity for people to discriminate against us, they're going to.

We have *some* control over those opportunities, we need to minimize
them as much as possible. . . . And I don't like to get angry, I like to
act instead.

In his view, African Americans must take some action and responsibility to prevent or to counter everyday discrimination. There are ways to
shape or engineer many situations so that the antiblack discrimination
there is exposed for all to see, to make what may be somewhat hidden
very apparent. Recognizing that African Americans do not have full control over discriminatory incidents, he still marshals what control he can.
Again, we see the high level of thought and preparation—the wasted
energy and creativity—that must go into being ready to deal with the discrimination that crosses one's path on any given day. In effect, African
Americans must become experts on discriminatory behavior as well as
strategies for dealing with that behavior whenever it appears over the
course of one's life. This man deals with discrimination by taking it as a
given, and from there he works to find to what extent he has control over
the opportunities for that discrimination.

Also central to coping with antiblack discrimination is realizing that
one does not have complete control over when or whether one faces
that discrimination. An executive at a chamber of commerce in the
Southwest discussed where her control ends. When she is asked how
she handles discrimination, she answered that she will call a friend and,
in addition, not blame the victim, noting that "the thing that works for
me is, I know it's not me." The attribution of whites' motives is very
important in the coping-with-racism skills of African Americans. Realizing
that what is happening to her has whites as the fundamental problem,
she is able to keep from internalizing the incident and blaming the victim, that is, herself.

SPIRITUAL SURVIVAL SKILLS

From the early days of enslavement, through the 1960s civil rights movement, to the present, spirituality and the black church have served an
important role in helping African Americans cope internally with, and
externally resist, oppression. A probing article in the influential magazine

Black Enterprise gave several suggestions for coping with work-related stress. These included seeking professional help, a response that studies show black Americans use much less frequently than white Americans.[15] Notably, this article also offers a suggestion for coping with stress that would most likely not appear in the white-oriented business magazines such as *Forbes* or *Fortune*. It suggests prayer, meditation, and reliance on "a higher force within us."[16]

In our research here and elsewhere, numerous African Americans discuss spirituality as important in coping with and resisting white antipathy and discrimination. After discussing the point that no matter how well off she is, she is still viewed as inferior by some whites (in a commentary earlier in this chapter), a woman broadcaster approached the issue with some gentle questioning:

> And I know that, and you recognize it, and you live with it, and you tolerate it, and you try not to let it get you paranoid, and you try not to let it make you bitter. But sometimes it does, and you question, and particularly if you're a Christian person like I am. You know, I've got a list of questions that if I ever meet our Maker face-to-face, racism is at the top of my list. I do not understand racism in this country. I do not understand why someone would look at me without knowing who I am or what I've got or how intelligent I am or how bright I am or how witty I am or whatever, would look at me and automatically start making some assumptions because I'm a person of color. I don't understand that, and I don't think I ever will.

Clearly, for African Americans, everyday racism—especially antiblack stereotyping and prejudice—makes little or no sense, in terms of either reason or religion. Because of her Christian affiliation and beliefs, she knows that she may not understand racism until she is able to meet her Maker. For many African Americans, belief in God and an afterlife has long made dealing with the nonsense of white racism somewhat, or a lot, easier.

An older minister also spoke of spirituality as a tool for managing everyday discrimination. When asked how often he gets angry about the discriminatory actions of whites, he answered: "Well, to be utterly frank with you, I have to quote a scripture, and I know that doesn't mean too much because you can quote it out of context. Paul says, 'Be angry and sin not.' But as you grow older, you mellow. I don't get as angry as I used to, but I used to get terribly angry every time I found *any* semblance of discrimination." Today, his religious beliefs help keep him from becoming as angry as he might otherwise, or as he used to, become. With a lot of experience, and the development of a religious framing, he has mellowed in regard to the angry response that discrimination provokes.

These comments indicate a major set of religious responses to racism that are common in black communities. Religion has long been central to the African American strategy for dealing with the great strains and pressures of everyday life, going back into the earliest days of enslavement. Sometimes religion is used for solace and internal strength, and other times it is used to buttress open protest. For centuries religious gatherings and religious leaders have been central to organized protests against antiblack racism. The nonviolent civil disobedience movement from the 1950s to the 1970s, led by prominent minister-leaders like Dr. Martin Luther King, Jr. among many others, had a religious foundation.

Another respondent, a nursing professor, also suggested that aging and the accompanying experience have had an effect on her responses to discrimination:

> The older I get, the less angry I get, but the more responsive I get when I do get a little rise in blood pressure. There's so many other things in life, that I can't be angry about the situations that occur. . . . And I don't take everything that happens to me as necessarily discrimination or racially motivated. Sometimes it's more because I'm a female than because I'm black, okay? And one of the things that I do with that is I point out the situation, and I do some exploring. Example: three weeks ago I was in Washington, D.C. . . . [respondent then relates incident regarding receiving an inferior hotel room location]. So, those kinds of issues. Had I felt that strongly about—after one night—about being in that room I would have asked for a change; had I not received one, I would have asked to see the manager. But I do take more time to process incidences. And those that just simply slap me in the face as being racist, I respond to; others, life's too short.

Although, as an older and experienced person, she gets angry less often, her body still reacts negatively to the anger she does feel. The effects of racism may be particularly bad for older African Americans, for on the average they have more cumulative experience with racism, and their bodies may be less able to handle the physical stress.

It is also important to note that, like some other female respondents cited in this book, this respondent mentions that some negative things that happen to her are not a matter of racism, but rather of sexism. For African American women, encounters with whites often involve the double burden of *gendered racism*.[17] She also notes another point that others have cited as well—that before responding to the incident, she does some processing and reflecting. At a minimum, racism generates reflection and assessment of such painful life events.

CONCLUSION

Clearly, these African Americans have developed psychological mechanisms and other strategies, some rather elaborate, to deal with the many overt and hidden injuries of being black in America. Although some have devised what appear to be healthy coping mechanisms, for others, dealing with racism often entails ignoring or swallowing a great deal of justified anger, which can be unhealthy for body and mind. Even so, the character of the social situations in which they find themselves may force such a reaction on them.

Many researchers have observed that, given the amount of societal stress imposed on African Americans, one would expect them to exhibit higher rates of mental illness than they do.[18] How do we explain this lesser rate of mental illness? Some analysts suggest that African Americans as a group may be more flexible in coping with stress than whites.[19] Thus, some call for more research on the resilience and coping skills that black Americans use to protect their mental health from a variety of racist attacks.[20] To this end, a few researchers have suggested using a stress-and-adaptation paradigm in mental health research—one that emphasizes environmental as well as personality factors in seeking the cause of African Americans' mental health problems, and one that focuses on their distinctive coping and resistance skills.[21] Any such study should begin by noting the complex repertoire of coping and resistance resources that are used by African Americans to deal with racism.

In this chapter, we reviewed coping skills that are internally-oriented. Sometimes, in order to deal with discrimination they face in the workplace and elsewhere, it becomes evident to African Americans that overtly confronting the discriminating white person would be counterproductive. In such cases, a person frequently manages the strain caused by the discrimination by dealing with it internally instead, that is, cognitively or attitudinally. For example, several of our respondents mentioned the need for preparedness, for being ready for whatever racial discrimination they might face from day to day. This requires an expenditure of energy not required of white Americans. Others discussed the necessity of having self-esteem that is strong enough to withstand the many blows of recurring discrimination. Although one might not expect black respondents to discuss changing how they think and feel about whites as a way of coping with discrimination, many of them did note that as a critical strategy. In addition, they alluded to the need to recognize that there are nondiscriminatory whites in their communities who can be allies to people of color, and to the coping benefits that realizing this fact can sometimes bring. Some also stated that understanding that many whites behave in discriminatory ways not intentionally, but out of ignorance, can help one to cope with that behavior.

In discussions of coping and contending with racism, control was an issue often cited by respondents in our interviews. Interestingly, this control over certain events and incidents with whites was discussed from two perspectives: that black people should recognize that they have control over what happens to them, but should also recognize the *limits* of their control. Specifically, numerous respondents felt that they themselves could control how much they allowed anger over discrimination to affect their lives.

Finally, in comparison with comparable whites, African Americans have not as often sought out formal psychological and counseling help for their everyday stress. Instead, they have most often relied on family, community, or religious support. Thus, it is not surprising that our respondents referred to prayer, going to church services, or visiting a minister as ways of coping with the strain and worry caused by everyday racism.

Since slavery, the black church and black spirituality have held a major place in African American life, one that has been central to individual and community survival. Our respondents' words make it clear that this is still true for many African Americans today.

In addition to these strategies, sometimes respondents discussed the most internal of all coping mechanisms: They simply withdraw, mentally, into themselves. Although withdrawal can be an effective method of dealing with racial hostility or discrimination temporarily, some research shows that, over the long term, it can have damaging effects to one's health, and externally-oriented coping skills are likely healthier. In the next chapter, we explore the more external, action-oriented resistance strategies discussed by our respondents.

6

Combating Racism: Active Behavioral Strategies

DEALING WITH EVERYDAY RACISM is more than a matter of managing internal concerns and crises. It is often a matter of intervening actively in immediate situations, and dealing directly with those whites who are the perpetrators of the discrimination. In encounters with whites who are discriminating, African Americans often engage in direct and external action. After evaluating an incident to make a judgment about the motivation and goals of the whites involved, they may decide that the situation needs to be dealt with internally, and also that it requires an active engagement with or response to the white discriminator or discriminators.

In our focus groups and other interviews, numerous respondents explained a range of active strategies they use for dealing with racial discrimination in particular social settings. These action strategies include direct verbal or physical confrontation, going through formal organization channels, using humor, maintaining a utilitarian focus, and relying on the support of others. These strategies may also include physically withdrawing from a difficult situation to "fight another day."

STRATEGIES OF DIRECT CONFRONTATION

Verbal Confrontation

Numerous respondents noted that often the best response to discrimination is to directly and firmly confront the white person who has caused the problem. Frequently, this involves a verbal confrontation. For many respondents, this is a key strategy for handling racial discrimination. For example, when asked how she deals with discrimination, a young hospital executive answered, "I would think, to me, the most effective way of dealing with it is assertively making some comment." Here she uses the word "assertively," not "aggressively." For African Americans, it is difficult to maintain a position of assertiveness without being accused of too-aggressive behavior by whites—an old white stereotype of African Americans.

A number of the respondents offered examples of the verbal replies and retorts they use in resisting discriminatory treatment. In one focus group, a government administrator described a situation many African Americans face as consumers: "They won't put money in your hand. [Male voice: 'Yeah.'] They lay in on the counter. . . . And depending upon how bad I want it, I may just tell them to give my money back. Keep your, your items." What is the motivation in white minds for refusing to touch a black hand? Apparently, for many whites there is a notion that somehow black skin is dirty or contaminating. Confronting this and other strange responses from white Americans requires the development of a variety of coping and contending strategies. For this African American, the strategy sometimes includes a strong response, one that is costly in an economic sense for the white person involved.

Putting Whites on the Defensive

During his interview, a law professor discussed how he uses confrontational strategies when a white person is trying to thwart his efforts. Asked if this is how he avoids wasting energy on fighting discrimination, he answered:

> Yeah, that's my goal. And I'm often able to put it into practice. I mean, there are some times when it just happens, and I say, well, "god-damn it, I'm tired of being decent; I'm tired of being wiser, I'm tired of being bigger, and better, and rising above the situation. Maybe I ought to just stay down here and fuss and argue and fight." And there are days when

you want to do just that, just curse them out, just tell them, "Hey, you're not fooling me, I know that this is racism, it's just bigotry, and that's all it is." And sometimes, I want to do what Eddie Murphy did in one of his movies, just to confront them and say, "Is this a racial thing? Is it because I'm black?" And sometimes it embarrasses them.

This professor then related an incident in which a female sales clerk refused his check:

And people were looking, and she said, "Oh, well, we're just not able to take checks," and all that. And I said, "Oh, that's all right, I understand." And I said it with the kind of English and the kind of dignity that she would think should be reserved for whites, and I said it in the most logistic voice I had. I said, "I understand *exceedingly well*." I said it just that way. . . . And that's my point, there's so much wrapped up in the approach that I have. It allows me to get practical results. I understand the larger issues. It also lowers my stress. . . . You can tell I've thought about this. I've thought about it a lot.

Middle-class African Americans frequently report that store clerks will not take their checks, or will scrutinize them more carefully, but do not take such actions for whites who come to the counter. Indeed, white clerks will often take checks from seedily-dressed whites, but not from well-dressed, middle-class African Americans. In this case, a law professor found a way to embarrass those whites who discriminate in this way. He shows that he is aware of the likely motivation of the white discriminator. He makes a concerted effort to make the discriminator feel uncomfortable, to put that person on the defensive. Once again, we see that African Americans have to spend a *great* amount of time and energy in dealing with, and thinking about, everyday discrimination.

Another woman discussed an experience with a white clerk that shows a similar type of audacity:

I just had an incident happen maybe, you know, around about four o'clock today. [Voices in focus group: Oh, my goodness. Oh, Lord.] I had went to [a fast food restaurant] to get some chicken. And, you know, we went through the drive-through, and we ordered everything, and then . . . she gave us back our change, and she dropped a dollar, you know, and it flew out the window somewhere. And she said, "Oh, you're going to have to get your money." I say, "Oh, no, you're going to give me another dollar." I said, "I'm not getting out of my car to get nothing. . . ." '

And so, she told somebody else. Well, she was a white girl. And she had a black girl to come outside the [restaurant], and go around there and pick up that dollar. . . . Just because I told her I wouldn't go around there and pick it up.

After the clerk's disrespect, this woman asserts herself by demanding another dollar. To compound matters, the white employee makes a black employee come outside to find the dollar. Most African Americans have likely dealt with a range of incidents involving disrespect from white store employees, and thus have thought about specific counterstrategies for such situations.

Our respondents also discussed other types of assertive reactions in their workplaces. For example, one well-educated respondent, who works in administration, explained her understanding of the importance of selectivity in choosing which white people she allows to be close to her:

I mean, [whites] have this idea of black females and what we should be doing, as opposed to what we *are* doing. And many of them think they want to buddy up with me, and I'm not the buddy type. I've told this many times to many people, that it is just not me. And they go to my supervisor and they ask what am I mad about, what's the problem? And . . . when my supervisor comes to me, and asks me about that, I said, "Well, you need to tell them they need to come talk to me. If they want to know what my problem is, [speaking louder] *if I have a problem*, they need to come and ask me. And, if they're not willing to do that, then obviously it's not important enough to them to find out why." And I said, "But between you and me . . . I have a right to keep anybody at a distance that I don't want in my circle. . . . I don't want them in my circle" . . . and I told him, "because I think they're racists."

While our respondents generally recognize that not all whites are intentionally racist, this woman focuses on another aspect of this matter: That some white people will be painfully racist, and thus it is important to be selective in interpersonal associations. Being able to distinguish between white allies and white enemies is an important coping-with-racism technique.

Interestingly, in our classes and at lectures we give around the country, whites sometimes indicate that they are afraid to discuss racial issues with black acquaintances or fellow workers—indeed some are afraid to interact much with black acquaintances—out of fear of being called "a racist." What these whites fail to understand is that most African Americans are fully capable of distinguishing between levels of white-racist inclinations and practice—between overtly racist, subtly racist, and antiracist whites. Judging from the hundreds of interviews with African Americans that we have conducted or supervised, as well as other research studies with which we are familiar, most African Americans do not make the assumption that all whites are equally racist or that all whites should be reacted to in the same way. Indeed, in our experience many African Americans will go *out of their way* to give whites the benefit of the doubt or to be supportive of a white person who is honestly trying to understand their own personal racism or that of the larger society.

Instructing Whites on How to Behave

Many African Americans report, in our data as well as in other research studies, that they periodically spend a significant amount of time in teaching whites about a variety of racial matters, including how to behave and act in regard to African Americans. For example, a senior planner in one focus group described a complex incident of mistreatment and the subsequent discussion and protest:

> I was visiting [a town in the Southwest], and I have a friend of mine . . . who's Puerto Rican, and he and I drove to L.A. together. He had relatives there, and I have relatives there. . . . And, we stopped in some little town in [names state] to eat, to get some gas, and to just, you know, eat. . . . [Respondent then discusses waiting a long time to be helped in the restaurant.] So it's like, "what is taking so long?" So finally the guy who was cooking asked [the waitress], "Have you waited on these people?" And she said, "Oh, I'm not going to wait on them." [Female voice in focus group: "Ooo." Second female voice: "She *said* it?"] Yes! And, by this time, my friend . . . jumps up, and had

a fit, I mean . . . he just cussed the woman out, and you know . . . [Female voice: That's what my sister would've done, that's how she handles it.] . . . I said, "Wait . . . just calm down, you know," I said. "This woman is out of her mind." So, the guy who was behind the counter, I guess he was really the manager or something, he was really upset, he came out and said, "What's the problem? . . . What have they done that you're refusing to wait on them?" "Well, I don't, I don't believe in interracial couples," and this, that, and the other . . . and I just said, "You know, not that it's any of your business, but for your information, we are *friends*. . . . It's not your business, but I just want you to know, we are *not* an interracial couple. You know, and even if we are, we deserve the same respect and services that any-body else should get. . . . And it's not up to *you* to decide who gets fed and who doesn't, because of who they're married to. Or who they're with. . . ." And we just left. . . . [Female voice: But "racism doesn't exist anymore."] So they say.

While her Latino companion reacted strongly to the white waitress's racist actions, this respondent suggested that the white woman must be "out of her mind." Her response suggests the mental pathology of racist attitudes. For some centuries now, African Americans have underscored this woman's point that racism is a white-generated problem. An understand-ing of that fact often has a certain liberating effect for African Americans. This respondent also corrects the common assumption that when two peo-ple of different racial or ethnic groups, and of the opposite sex, are together, that involvement must be sexual. Such an assumption may be rooted in the old racist notion that African American women (and men) are over-sexed.[1]

Given that her Puerto Rican friend was apparently lighter in skin color, this assumption may also be linked to the white supremacist place-ment of whites at the top of a hierarchy in terms of physical beauty and appeal. Because of this placement, many whites believe that blacks often seek to become sexually involved with people whose skin color is lighter than their own—and preferably with whites. Thus, from this white-racist point of view, any interracial interaction involving blacks and lighter-skinned people likely has sexual involvement as its purpose. This view also feeds white fears of interracial rape, which are usually ungrounded in reality, according to the crime statistics (most rapists of whites are white). Moreover, similar white-racist fears have contributed to violence against black men (such as in lynchings) for more than a century now.

Note too that this woman's verbal resistance does more than deny a romantic interracial relationship. Had this been her only response, it might have been perceived as an affirmation of the waitress's racist view, as suggesting that interracial relationships are something to be ashamed of. Instead, this woman strongly asserts the view that even if they were an interracial couple, they should be waited on. In doing so, she takes a broader stand against racism.

There are yet other confrontational or assertive strategies used by African Americans to deal with recurring white actions that are discriminatory. Some are more active than others. There is, thus, an array of cautioning and teaching strategies. For example, a prominent black intellectual and *New York Times* journalist, Brent Staples, has explained how he whistles Vivaldi in order to appear nonthreatening to whites on the street.[2] A more assertive teaching strategy is indicated by African American philosopher, Laurence Thomas. He has noted that often, when a white woman grabs her purse when he comes near, "I grab my bags right back so that she can see that maybe I'm worried about her. I think that these small social ways of interacting make all the difference in the world."[3]

PROTESTING THROUGH FORMAL CHANNELS

"Shopping While Black"

When verbal responses to a white person practicing discrimination are ineffective, those facing the mistreatment may seek redress by going through formal organizational channels, such as seeking out higher management or filing a lawsuit. African Americans face serious problems with discrimination in many different types of societal settings. A recent national opinion survey asked African American respondents if in the last month they had experienced discrimination at work, in dining out and shopping, in dealing with the police, and in public transportation. Some 45 percent had faced discrimination in at least one area, including most men under the age of 35.[4] In this particular survey, many people reported discrimination in public accommodations. Among our respondents, a nursing professor, who lives in a southwestern city, related an incident in which she was ignored for some time while waiting for service at a grocery store in which she had shopped for some years. After two white female clerks served an older white woman, they then kept this black woman waiting. After some time, the respondent asked for help, to which a white clerk replied, "I didn't see you." The respondent then took more assertive action:

> I immediately asked to see the manager. *Again* being one of the few African Americans in this particular area, the manager knew me. He'd known that I'd shopped there for eight or nine years. He asked what my problem was. I explained, at the same time asking for the address of district headquarters for [the grocery store's] company. He said, "I can't tell you the address, but I can give you the telephone number." He handled my return, and I accepted the telephone number from him, went home, called the number, asked for the contact person and the address. I immediately got my computer on; I sent them a letter—one to headquarters and one to the district. I received a telephone call within a week and [they] followed up with a letter of apology, telling me that this person was no longer employed. My issue there was not only blatant racism, but the kind of person that was put in a job where you have to be a people person.

The fact that the disrespectful clerk deals with the public is viewed as particularly problematical, and the respondent formally complains to higher management about her treatment. Because this white person deals with the public, she will most likely have another opportunity to mistreat people of color. This respondent shows a real concern for the collective good and a sense of a responsibility to the larger community.

In the same interview, the interviewer asked this: "You had mentioned, for instance, about the two instances at the store and the bank, and you respond by pointing it out, writing a letter, contacting the people who you feel are in charge. Is that generally the way that you've found to be an effective way?" The nursing professor answered the question forcefully:

> That's the way I handle the situation almost always. Part of the reason is you can express anger at the time that the incident occurs. You can let the person know that you recognize what's going on. You can let their supervisor know what's going on, but often that's as far as it goes. And I rationalize [it] like this, if they did it to me and it's obvious

that I'm reasonably articulate and reasonably assertive and intelligent, and I look reasonably presentable all the time, that they will do it to another person who they assess to have less status. Okay. Because if they do it to me, they'll do it to them. So that sets up a pattern. Now, other people may leave in anger or react differently; I make the choice to put my feelings in writing. And I think that that has—when you send a letter to the person that you're aiming them at and you send a carbon copy to headquarters—that means money and that means consumer reaction. Consequently, that gets attention.

It is likely unnerving for a white person who believes they can get away with ignoring or talking down to an African American customer to be put on the spot, especially in front of coworkers, other customers, or the boss. For this woman, there is a sense of satisfaction in being able to confront racism when it happens. Following up with a letter to the company is often an effective weapon of resistance, since negative consumer reactions can threaten a company financially. She believes that it is important for her to speak out publicly, and realizes that if she—a middle-class, educated African American woman—faces discrimination, so must other African Americans who do not have her resources. Contrary to some misconceptions, most middle-class African Americans have not "forgotten where they came from," but use their social and economic resources to help the situation of all black Americans. Additionally, the fact that something positive resulted from her action will likely become part of the collective memory among those close to her about successful fighting-back strategies to use against racially contoured mistreatment in retail stores and similar social settings. Recall from chapter 5 that the collective memory of African American families and communities has long been a resource for dealing with the painful experiences of everyday racism.

By dealing with racism in public, when it happens, this woman also has an impact on numerous other whites. Not only was the white woman apparently fired for her behavior forever impacted, but so was the store manager, the white customers witnessing the scene, and the white personnel who received her call and letter at the home office. These people will perhaps learn a valuable lesson from seeing this black woman's courage in standing up to her mistreatment, and from witnessing the company's response to the discriminatory action of its employee.

Calling Whites to Account at Work: Other Examples

Most of the settings we examine in this book are workplaces. Negative encounters with whites in these employment settings frequently call forth strategies similar to those just examined. In one focus group, a woman employed in government administration explained how she handles workplace racism that is, as she puts it, both "subtle and blatant." For her, white women often cause more problems than white men:

> They like to try to circumvent me, and go through other people to talk to me. And the most recent case is . . . about a week ago. And the white female, she had a problem with the way we were structured at one of the county commission meetings. And, as opposed to talking to me about making a change, she went to my supervisor. And of course, he doesn't deal with stuff like that, it's like, you know, "[Respondent's name], you need to handle this." So, I called her, but she wasn't there, and I left a message on her recorder, and I was thorough and clear and polite when I made the comment.

She continued the account for the focus group, noting that the white woman did not call her back, then added: "And I was really very nice to her, and I think she was really surprised, but I was nice. . . . Even though you know a person is racist, there still is a way to handle people like that and still—because you still got to get the job done." When this administrator realized that a white coworker was going over her head, as happened regularly with various white women in her workplace, she first tried to contact the woman by phone. She continued her story for the group by describing that when her call was ignored, she communicated to this woman more directly that she cannot act that way. After years of dealing with white coworkers, this woman knows how to get practical results without angering people that she has to work with in the future. This is a utilitarian approach to workplace racism that other respondents also discussed, and we review these matters in more depth later in this chapter.

This woman noted some problems with certain white women whom she believes are used to being able to have their own way in such matters. She then explained to the moderator and the focus group that sometimes she keeps documentation of events at work in order to be prepared to pursue formal avenues of complaint if necessary:

The white men are really different because, I think, I'm a double-whammy for them. . . . [Another voice in focus group: "Yes, you are."] . . . I'm a black person, and I'm a woman. And many of these men are in this "good ole boys" school. . . . So they bring that way of thinking to the business place also. . . . And sometimes, you make the phone calls, and people don't call you back in a day or two. You know, you're not sure whether it's because you're a woman, because you're black, whether you guess that they don't have time, or whatever. But when it happens repeatedly, there is this red light that comes on that something is wrong. And I started thinking about ways to deal with people like that. I mean, [if] people don't call me back, I do, and I start writing stuff down. Start documenting stuff, sending them a copy, sending him a copy.

This respondent has several different strategies for surviving in a predominantly white workplace. She has not only learned how to interact with white coworkers who attempt to bypass her authority, but also has realized that it is important to document her efforts in doing her job. As an African American and a woman, she realizes that she might lose in a situation where it was her word against that of a white person. Again, an African American employee must expend extra energy and time that white coworkers do not have to expend in order to protect herself. This is one of the broad costs of continuing racism for African Americans—the constant feeling of having to protect one's livelihood through backup and documentation. Most whites do not experience a recurring feeling that their word will not be taken at face value because of their skin color. They have not often had to provide proof of what they say and do in the workplace. For many African Americans, they not only must work hard in their job, but also must increase their work effort by compiling evidence showing that they actually did the work they say they did.

Another woman respondent, who works in a government setting, discussed how she has dealt formally with recent racist comments in her workplace:

I think what's surprising to me is that in the work atmosphere that I'm in right now—which is an . . . office that is about 98.5 percent Caucasian, and about 95 percent white males—[we] had an incident that just happened about three weeks ago, that involved actually a civil rights complaint that was filed by my immediate supervisor. But it involved a comment that was made, a racial overtone, that involved me. At a breakfast social, it was allegedly said that (being that at most gatherings . . . I am the only minority, male or female), and the comment that was allegedly made [was] . . . , "So you're going to sit with the white folks today." And this was said by a white female. He [her boss] did not hear the comment, but her immediate supervisor was sitting next to her, and the next morning it was reported to my boss what was said. The follow-up comment to that was "Because the table won't be black and white until [names respondent] sits down." . . . I also serve in the capacity, in my position, as intake officer for civil rights complaints. So I am the one that actually had to do the investigation. And a lot of people asked why I did it. Well, I didn't file the complaint; my boss did. I did not hear the comment. I did go to the female that said it and told her, "You can be assured that I didn't [hear it], because if I had, you would have heard an added response."

The setting is a very white workplace, like many such government workplaces across the United States. This respondent's supervisor considered the comment racially derogatory and filed a civil rights complaint on his own. Note, too, that the respondent emphasized that, had she heard the disrespectful comment, she would have verbally responded, which suggests that she has had to deal with racially derogatory or insensitive comments before. In such predominantly white social settings, whites often make racially derogatory or insensitive comments to people of color. A similar example is the repetition by whites of the common phrase "you people" when referring to black people. In our interviews and discussions with African Americans, they have reported such comments as a recurring source of irritation. They cannot comprehend why whites do not see that such a phrase—which implies a homogenous group of nameless, faceless, one-dimensional people set off from whites—is offensive.

In many settings, African Americans have to take these racially derogatory remarks without comment, but that was not the case in this government setting. The respondent continued with the account of what happened subsequently after her required investigation:

I did the investigation. I interviewed eight people who, it was believed, were close enough to her to possibly have heard the comment. I was surprised to find out that so many thought that the comment was not racial. My boss filed it as a civil rights complaint based on racial comment, even though it was denied. She admitted saying the comment to him about . . . "sitting with the white folks." She denied having said, she denied to me of having said the comment about *me*. What was surprising, though, is her boss said that she heard it, three people said that they heard it, but on tape, I could not get these people to *admit* that they heard it. Now I did not have to record the investigations, but being the environment that it was, I felt it necessary to record it.

This latter statement suggests a problem encountered often by people of color in a white workplace: It may be difficult to get whites to break ranks publicly in support of a black person's account of racially generated mistreatment. Because a black person's word would likely be doubted against a white person's, she is obliged to make an extra effort to document the events. Also, because of white solidarity, assertive African Americans and other employees of color may become labeled as "troublemakers" by the white majority in the workplace.

This respondent continued, explaining the outcome of the situation:

And so, it went on, and then one person said that it was not a "derogatory" racial comment. It was not "malicious intent." Maybe it was not, but when I asked . . . her, "If you had seen it on paper, what kind of comment is it, just the words in print, what does it say to anybody?" "It was just a figure of speech," was the comment. And, at any rate, I was told, and this is where I guess it took a twist, I was told the ultimate decision was to be made by the chief judge as to the disciplinary action. I was under the impression, or made to believe that it was going to be very, very strong disciplinary action which could lead up to dismissal. He called us all together. She cried through the entire . . . setting of where we all came together. She apologized, and when it was time for him to make the decision, he said, . . . "I hope that you will never make this statement again." My boss had wanted at least a letter of reprimand in the file to stay. . . . Nothing was done, basically he said, "I consider the case closed." So, even, all this time, it was leading up to something was going to be done, *again*. So . . .[Another voice: Swept under.] swept under. And I think it was mainly because—I didn't file the complaint. I told the chief judge, "If I filed a complaint for every time I heard a racial comment, there would no rainforest, because there would be no trees." Because black folks just deal with it [Other voices in group, "Right, ummhmm."] . . . every day.

After all the time and energy this woman put into investigating this incident, the white woman at fault was only gently reprimanded, and no record was made of her behavior. Using humor to describe how many complaints she would make if she herself were formally to protest every racist incident, she highlights the point made by so many respondents: African Americans must choose their battles when resisting discrimination or many would expend energy that they need for work, family, and community involvement.

USING HUMOR TO FIGHT EVERYDAY RACISM

The Value of Humor

Since the days of slavery, African Americans have found ways to resist white domination using humor, irony, and sarcasm. These are useful strategies of everyday resistance and have some advantages over more in-your-face strategies. Responding to hostility with humor allows one to use wit to mock discriminators typically without as much personal risk as more direct strategies might involve. Such strategies were particularly important when African Americans were enslaved or legally segregated in settings in which resistance was often punished with violence.[5]

Even today, when African Americans are forced to submit to unfair and discriminatory white decisions in workplaces and other settings, humor can be an effective means of resistance, as well as of maintaining self-esteem. Using humor to respond to racist actions can allow one to feel better by holding the high moral ground in a difficult situation. Several respondents described incidents in which they responded to mistreatment by whites with some humor. Consider this woman's response to mistreatment by a store clerk that she read as racially motivated:

This happened fairly recently . . . here in good old [names city]. And I have a sweet tooth, and I go to [a doughnut shop] whenever I have a chance like we all do. . . . I stopped by there, and as I waited and this—and I think she was a student—but anyway, I walked in, and she was standing to the counter. And I went over to the other side, and [we] spent at least thirty seconds just looking at one another. She didn't say, "May I help you?" uh, "How're you doing?" or anything. We just looked. So finally I said, "Um, may I help you?" And I said, "Yes, thank you very much, you know what I'd love to have? I'd love to have one of those doughnuts . . . ," and you know, I was just, carrying on a conversation with myself [laughter in the focus group], because that's what, that's what she *should've* said. And then asked her for, how much . . . and she's slamming doors. . . . I mean she really had a real bad attitude. But I had hoped, and actually, I hope she had gotten the point in terms of what I was trying to get her to see. [Female voice: "Yeah, I like that."]

African Americans report this type of mistreatment in a variety of stores. Whites will often ignore black customers and withhold service or, if there is a line of people, the white clerk will call on a white person standing behind a black person who is first in line. In addition, black customers are often followed around in stores because white clerks stereotype black customers as likely shoplifters.[6] Clearly, this is not the genuinely helpful attention that a black consumer hopes to receive when entering a business establishment. Ironically, some attentiveness by white clerks in stores is actually not intended to offer assistance, but rather constitutes a prodding to leave the store.

In this case, when the white clerk ignored her, this black woman modeled the appropriate customer-service behavior by carrying on a conversation with herself. In the focus group, she then continued: "I came back, I think it was the next week, maybe a couple of days later, to get my doughnuts. And she was at the counter. And, really, she said, 'May I help you?' And I think, I don't know whether she thought about it, that light came on, or whatever, but . . . she was very pleasant, smiling or whatever." After facing discrimination and related mistreatment, one can only hope that the chosen response will work effectively and change the white person's future behavior. In this case, a black woman was able to see how a white salesperson's behavior changed, and feel that she may have had a role in that change. She finished her story by noting that the situation she encountered with the salesperson is a common one.

A man in the focus group continued the discussion of the use of humor as a resistance strategy against racial mistreatment at the hands of whites:

> I use humor, like the example she gave with the doughnuts, you know? Because, I think, that's my style. I use that as a way to show them that you just can't keep on thinking that kind of way, you know. So I use humor to relieve the tension. I don't want to get all upset and angry and get headaches and stuff like that, because I've been through that. And this way I find it easier for me to deal with, using humor, to educate them and it works. Sometimes it works.

This man also uses humor to counter and educate whites who think in stereotypical ways, and he also recognizes the health benefits of this form of resistance. He is able to relieve some of the strain that instead could be linked to health problems. Indeed, the stress-alleviating benefits of humor are well-documented in medical literature.[7]

Laughing at Racism

A college counselor who lives on the West Coast specifically alluded to the survival benefits of laughing at encounters with everyday racism. She discussed how her family deals with the problem: "We've been able to talk about something that was quite serious, but we've been able to make light of it. Well, not to make light of it, but to laugh at it, at how bad something really is, just turn it over." This woman recognizes the necessity of dealing with discrimination in order to protect her health, and has found that humor is an effective way to do so. Her statement also highlights the tradition of group support in the African American community. She and her friends and family laugh at these things *together*. Throughout the interviews and focus group conversations, the participants explicitly stated their understanding of the linkage between discrimination and the related stress and physical illness.

A professor who has worked for politicians described her initial reaction to the type of backhanded compliments middle-class African Americans often receive:

> There are all kinds of tasks that people in the political arena have to do, and a lot of writing is required. And all of us on the governor's

staff had to write speeches for the governor and all the rest. And I was pretty successful at performing those tasks. And quite often there would be a roundabout, sort of backhanded compliment, like, "Oh! Well, how'd you learn to write a good speech like that?" You know, it would be almost as if, "We don't expect that of you." And I'm sure that that was sort of subtle racism, you know, that was there. So there were those kinds of things. And . . . you learn not to let that kind of comment get next to you, because if it does it can undo you [laughs]. [Interviewer: I was going to say, how does that feeling hit you initially?] Well, you know, you feel a bit of rage. You think, "This is outrageous. Who is this person, saying this to me, who probably has trouble writing a sentence" [laughs]. I mean, what is this? And you *do* have that feeling, you know. But, as I said, you can't let it overtake you.

This is a type of assault on self-esteem that is often reported by African American employees in historically white workplaces.[8] This woman's first reaction to her colleagues' low expectations of her abilities is one of outrage. Yet she realizes that she should not allow the feeling of anger to remain with no outlet. Indeed, she even laughs as she retells what is doubtless a painful account for her. The conversation continued with another question from the interviewer, "And how did you not let it get to you?"

Well, I think learning to laugh at some of that is very good. If you've listened to *any* big-city politician—you're probably too young to appreciate this—but Mayor Daley in Chicago, there's a book that's been put out called "Daleyisms" because he murdered the English language so atrociously. That, if you analyzed any sentence that he spoke, you would think, "Gee, I wonder if that sentence had a subject or a predicate or anything else." But he was in charge of the city, you know.

This woman here redirects her anger with a humorous critique of the weak English-language abilities of some successful whites. In doing so, she is able to regard with humor and a sense of irony the sometimes loose connection between being articulate or "correct" in the English language and being successful.

She continued by elaborating on the balance required of African Americans in dealing with workplace racism and related issues: "So that you learned how to just have some sort of a sense of humor about those things, and also you balanced off of the people who would make those kinds of comments, or the people who are genuinely *not* making judgments like that. So that I think it's a combination of having some of both present." Here again is an example of using multiple strategies to cope with and resist racism. This respondent uses humor to resist discrimination, and she also is careful to note that not all of her white coworkers share in the negative stereotyping. As we mentioned previously, many of our respondents typically make a distinction among whites based on what they consider the motivation of their behavior to be. In most interactions with whites they, contrary to commonplace white notions, do not jump quickly to judgments but usually consider carefully what the motivation behind the discriminating act might be. Only after doing that do they usually choose how to name the behavior—and respond to what is, in their estimation, subtly or overtly discriminatory behavior.

TAKING A UTILITARIAN ORIENTATION TO EVERYDAY RACISM

As we have seen in several previous accounts, one way African Americans have found to deal with everyday discrimination is focusing on immediate and utilitarian goals. Realizing that discrimination can serve as a distraction that keeps them from attaining their personal goals, such as career aspirations, these African Americans direct their energy toward handling workplace frustration in ways that help achieve their goals. In his interview, for example, a law professor described how this process works for him in dealing with obviously differential treatment by whites in the justice system:

> When I was a lawyer with the [names federal agency], I had to go and try cases all across the country. Often it would require going into the [white] clerk's office where the records were kept, or a hearing with the [white] judge himself. And in many of these instances, the people would try to steer you wrong and thwart you from carrying out your functions. Obviously, having a temper doesn't help. You might have a right to be mad; it might be understandable that you'd get angry. So, what I often do is be persistent, but do it with dignity, and do it with good taste, and I'd be very well-mannered, but that shouldn't be mistaken for being docile, because I wouldn't give up. I'd be polite. I'd say, "Well, your honor, no, obviously, we have a constitutional right to

question these witnesses. It's clear; it's in the rules; and it's supported by the cases in the law. We would, with all due respect to the court, like to proceed and exercise our constitutional right." In the clerk's offices of the courts where the records were, if I needed to see the records, I'd often have a clerk say, "Well, I'm sorry, but you're not able to see them." And I'd say, "Well, I'm legal counsel on this case, and we are entitled, if I should come back a little later on when it's more convenient, good, but I will come back. I do need to see these documents."

A first step in taking action against discrimination is recognizing that one has every right to be upset at whites who practice it, whether it is blatant or subtle mistreatment. In many cases, as here, the racialized mistreatment takes the form of a "runaround" in which whites try delaying or deflecting actions that they hope will force the black person to give up. Today, one of the most common types of discrimination faced by African Americans, in most institutions, is this runaround.

This lawyer is rightfully angry at white attempts to thwart his work but persists while maintaining his dignity. He continued:

It's important not to allow yourself to be maneuvered into a situation where you don't get the results, where you're able to be written off, or carried off, as the "beast" that you're considered to be. You don't want to let yourself be maneuvered into that. One has to exercise the level of control that allows you to not be pushed into retaliating in a physical or emotional way. Because that way, what happens is that, they think you're a "nigger," and then you act like one. So, I'm very conscious of avoiding that. I'm conscious of the fact that it doesn't yield any results. I'm also conscious of the fact that that's where the loss will be. I also realize that I need to get things done that I need to have done.

Stereotyping African Americans leads whites to expect behavior that is less-than-human, even beast-like. Like another respondent quoted in chapter 2, this man is aware that, despite his accomplishments, if he responds to discrimination in a physical or emotional manner, he likely will be dismissed, or worse. In many cases, reacting in a physical or emotional way, however legitimate, would not allow African Americans to reach their personal goals, and they will suffer a loss, a point we return to below.

While anger is a reasonable, legitimate response, it is frequently submerged in favor of a more practical reaction. This lawyer finished his well-considered statement in this way:

So, I engage in a process of negotiating with them, and it's smart actually, only it's even more accepted. It's even more wise for people who are throwing out racism. It's strong, but it's acceptable. It's strong, and it's wise. And I guess that what happens is that one of the things you have to do when you adopt an approach like that is reconcile the fact that you haven't been able just to lash out and attack. And the best way I've been able to do it is to say to myself, "What you're doing here is one, getting results, and you're getting results with at least a minimum level of difficulty and a sense of having protected yourself. And also, you're brushing aside a lot of evil and a lot of ugliness, and you're not wasting a lot of your energy attacking the evil." So, you're spending more of your energy moving out of the way, or gently jousting with it, but keeping your eye on things. And I've had to deal with that in a number of instances, but through having the wisdom, and having a sense of determination, I've been able to move through a lot of situations on a day to day basis.

This lawyer and law professor carefully described the benefits of a cautious, measured approach to combating everyday racism. Because he remains in control, his response always signals personal strength. He protects himself by ensuring that he completes his work, yet still allows himself some active resistance to mistreatment. He realizes the energy that might be wasted in fighting discrimination too aggressively, so instead he "jousts" with it. His extensive experience is honed into operational wisdom. His discussion brings to mind the metaphor used in certain martial arts, in which one expends little energy to overcome an opponent, instead using the opponent's own energy against him to win the encounter.

Another respondent, a self-employed political consultant, also approached discrimination with a utilitarian perspective, as we see in this reply to a question asking if she feels "that anger is wrong":

I sure don't. No, but at one time, I used to, you know, just let it go. [Interviewer: How often do you get angry about the actions of white people?] I don't get angry any more. I figure I don't have time to get angry any more. Because see, when you're angry, you can't think. See, this is about being able to be composed and strategize and implement. That's why I think we're so successful in what we do. Now occasionally [name of a coworker] will get angry; see, I don't have time for that.

Although anger often is justified, this woman believes that allowing herself to become angry inhibits her ability to think clearly, and also absorbs valuable time. From this carefully considered perspective, being able to set her reasonable anger aside allows her to be more successful than she might otherwise be. She has realized the energy-sapping aspect of discrimination and is now fighting it with a utilitarian approach.

PHYSICAL WITHDRAWAL

Avoiding the Office

As we discussed earlier, African Americans must sometimes mentally withdraw from racially hostile or discriminatory situations in order to protect themselves from more serious harm. Periodically, the hostility or discrimination faced by African Americans in predominantly white workplaces and other social settings forces the response of physical withdrawal, which also provokes stress and other undesired pain. One woman, working in corporate administrative services in the Midwest, noted her response to racial and sexual harassment: "The way I deal with it is I try to stay out of the office as much as I can. . . . Even outsiders who come in the office, they can sense the air is tight . . . and it's all because of our boss. And it's not just racial harassment; it's sexual harassment." Several female respondents described how racial marginalization at work was amplified by the sexist behavior of white male coworkers and supervisors. Racial and sexual harassment at work often places a "double burden" on black women.[9] In one study of the obstacles faced by African American women in higher education, an administrator is quoted as saying, "Racism and sexism are inherent so I ignore them. My obstacle is that I am assertive and I say what I feel. This doesn't fit into the old white boy system."[10] Once again, a combination of strategies—ignoring some cases, being assertive at other times—designed to contend with racial barriers in the workplace is a successful approach. Note, too, the recurring sense that racism and sexism are part of the "woodwork" of everyday life.

The ultimate withdrawal is to quit one's stressful job. In another interview, a woman who works as a college advisor described racially related stress, and why she quit her previous job in a department store over blatant discrimination:

When the black customers would come into the store to possibly return merchandise, and maybe not have a receipt to accompany that purchase, they were asked. . . . "Do you think you could go home and find it [the receipt]? Well, when was it purchased?" They were denied adequate assistance. But when the white people would come into the store, it was like, "Oh, well, can I credit it to your [store credit account] or Visa?" . . . It was always, with the black person, it's like, "Well, where did you buy it? Well, take it back to the store that you bought it from," although you can take any of that merchandise to any store, because that's policy. . . . I was just amazed by the kind of things that would occur. And that's a reason why I no longer work there, because I could no longer work for a company that discriminated against my race. . . . They did it blatantly and they really didn't care.

Whatever the source of stress at work, its consequences can be serious. What is noteworthy about racial stress is that it generally comes on top of the other frustrations in the workplace. Note, too, that this woman's frustration and anger were generated by what was happening, not to herself, but to other African Americans. In her case, physical withdrawal from the discriminatory situation was economically costly, as well as personally stressful. Recall a point we made previously about African Americans and other people of color who are usually forced to adjust to workplaces that will not change much (or at all) to accommodate them. This is an extreme example of such an employment situation. Sometimes a workplace is so hostile to African Americans, so unwilling to accommodate them, that it drives them out altogether.

The Trials of Young People

For many young people, college or university settings are in effect their main, everyday "workplaces." Predominantly white colleges and universities place some of the same pressures on black students that predominantly white work environments impose on black adults. In the following account, a male college student described physically withdrawing from a discriminatory incident in a university cafeteria:

> [There was] a white girl and myself and a lot of people behind me, and [at] the counter there was a black lady and another white lady. So the black lady told the white lady that, "O.K. you take one person and I'll take the other person," so the black lady took the girl because she was ahead of me, so when the black lady was serving the girl, the black lady instructed the white lady to serve me. The white lady said she's closed, but then I said, "I have been standing in line, and whereas the other girl, she had been standing in front of me, she had been served by the black lady so why can't you serve me when I have been standing in line?" And she says she's closed so I got mad and [walked] off. Then, I don't know, for some reason I turned around. And when I turned around another girl went back into the line, and she was white and this lady served the girl. So I mean I was just so mad I just walked out of the dining hall and I went and told my friends and they were saying that "You should've reported her to whoever the supervisor was." Then I said, "Nah, it's not worth it. It's not worth the pain at all."

The racially differential treatment was clear here, yet apparently no one protested how the white employee treated the African American student. It is important to note that this young man has learned that he must decide which battles are "worth the pain" of confrontation, and which are not. He is faced with such agonizing choices because of the color of his skin, a racialized agony that is not visited upon white students in similar situations. Expending energy resisting each incident of discrimination would likely subtract from the energy a student has to pursue his or her education.

DRAWING ON THE SUPPORT OF OTHERS

The Lack of Formal Support and Redress

Although their specific strategies for dealing with racist encounters differ, there is a general consensus among our respondents that the pain, frustration, and anger generated by racial stereotyping and discrimination in workplaces and other institutional settings must be dealt with by black people themselves. They can expect little, if any, support from whites.

Thus, a nurse described the lack of concern for problems of antiblack racism shown by white supervisors at work:

> I think that most supervisors, managers, [the] higher echelon knows about racism in the workplace. And I think some of them leave it up to lower managers to do something about it even when they discuss it, and some of them just leave it, period. And then some have diversity groups . . . or seminars or things. . . . But racism is so prevalent I just think that it's going to be hard to get rid of.

In most U.S. workplaces, the formal organization is important to an employee's successful performance of her or his work. The higher-level managers of a government agency or company are part of its formal hierarchy and are in the position to punish workplace discrimination, or to "wink at" it and allow it to continue. The discrimination that individual workers face is even more difficult when it is ignored, or ineffectively dealt with, by higher management. Everyday discrimination that is ignored—or only dealt with in a general way by brief "diversity" workshops—by higher-level management can be especially negative in its effects, since the black target of such action or inaction has no where to turn for redress. In our interviews with African American employees, the respondents have periodically noted a negative consequence of racial discrimination at the workplace—white supervisors and managers often will not stop the actions of lower-level discriminators. Most workers orient their actions to signals from higher management, who usually set the general tone for a workplace, and punished behavior tends to be reduced or eliminated.[11]

Finding Other Social Capital: The Family Network

Here we can reiterate a point made in earlier chapters about informal networks among black Americans. Because of this commonplace lack of support from white peers or management in dealing with discrimination, African Americans use other social support networks to fight discrimination. Those who are targets of discrimination frequently share their accounts of these experiences with family and friends in order to lighten the heavy and recurring burden. Research shows that most African

Americans especially rely on informal social networks for emotional support; as a result, the racial concerns of one individual are often assessed, and known in detail, by a larger support network of friends and relatives.[12] As we discussed previously, some analysts call this "social capital," that is, the resource that stems from close relations among people, from having important social networks. This capital is "created when the relations among persons change in ways that facilitate action." In addition, the "function identified by the concept social capital is the value of those aspects of social structure to actors, as resources that can be used by the actors to realize their interests."[13] Even groups with limited economic resources have the social resources of their own relatives and friends.

African Americans rely on their families, other relatives, friends, and certain community institutions, such as local church groups, as part of their coping mechanism for dealing with recurrent discrimination at work and elsewhere. Several researchers have pointed out that, because racism is often institutionalized and systemic, seeking social support from relatives and friends may be one of the few ways that those who are targeted by discrimination have of handling or contending with institutional racism.[14] If a black person is unable to point to a specific person who is the perpetrator of a racial barrier, but feels the institutionalized woodwork racism in her or his workplace or other social setting, then responses such as verbal confrontation or going through formal channels may be impractical. In such situations, regular communication and commiseration with friends and relatives may one of the remaining strategies for dealing with the pain and frustration of everyday discrimination. We return to the importance of this point in the last chapter, which is about healthcare institutions.

Interestingly, one recent study suggests that black women may rely on social support more as a coping or resistance strategy than black men.[15] In our individual and group interviews, however, we found that both men and women repeatedly underscore the critical sources of social support found in families and groups of close friends. One teacher commented on bringing the stress of racism home with her: "I think I bring it home with me, I do. But, I have a good partner here, who listens. . . . and, you know, I tell him all the problems, when it's happened. And I get feedback from him. And I get it all out, and that, I think that's good." Similarly, a male respondent in the Southeast said his wife was his major source of support in dealing with stress from racial animosity:

I'd say oftentimes I've brought it home. Because I don't share that stuff with my work group, but I can share it with my wife. And she'll listen and give me appropriate feedback, and help me get through that. And you know I get the bike out, and I'll ride, or take the kids and go somewhere, or take me a good, hot, steamy shower. And get a back rub, or something [others in group chuckle]. And that kind of thing. Settle for that!

Numerous respondents indicate that they tell their families and friends about discriminatory events in employment and other settings. These accounts spread both the knowledge essential to dealing with discrimination and the pain that accompanies such responses through informal social networks and local communities, which are often extensive. Note, also, that in the case above, this man cited physical exercise as an effective way to cope with everyday racism, a common strategy that many people use for a variety of personal and social strains.

In a recent volume of writings by young African Americans on racial issues, one young woman away at college wrote the following letter to her sister, who is under psychiatric care:

Hi Jessica,

I spoke with a dean outside of my department today. I told him about that incident with my professor. . . . I was answering a question he had put to the class when he interrupted me. Attempting to test my newly acquired middle-class and professional skills, I continued, "As I was saying . . ." then, "If you would just let me finish." But the man was determined not to let me finish.

People keep telling me that I should forget the whole incident. The idea is foreign to me. . . . How are you getting along with Dr. Sully? What are sessions with her like? Is there anyone else in your ward you can talk to? Any people of color? Any Black folk? College grads? . . .

It's so different to work within a system (me with a dean & you, a psychiatrist) especially when such systems ignored us for umpteen years. I'll always wonder why our teachers, coaches, and church members ignored the scars and even the tears on some days. But those days are over, Jes. . . . You're not another patient in the system, you're a woman in my heart.[16]

These sisters grew up together in an abusive family situation and were each other's only form of support. The letter shows both the importance of support from relatives in dealing with racism and, once again, the way that personal energy must be wasted to deal with this racism by proceeding through formal protest channels, as in the case of the student going to her dean. The struggle against energy loss affects the lives of young and old African Americans.

Socializing Children to Deal with Racism

Families are of course very important in the socialization of black children to deal with the racism in everyday life. Several of our respondents mentioned how their families of origin raised them to recognize and deal with a range of racial hostility and discrimination. Clearly, family members recommend a variety of counterstrategies. Thus, in a focus group, one secretary described her family as "very supportive," although her father and mother used different strategies: "My father is more like, 'Maybe you should ignore it and turn the other cheek,' where my mom is like, 'Report it.'" Another woman, a purchasing agent, added to this line of discussion with the comment that her family had "told us different stories that have happened to them, so we can distinguish between what is and what is not [racism]. . . . They give you an example of subtle prejudice and racism." Providing accounts of past discrimination, and passing them down the generations, has been very important in the processes through which African Americans have long dealt with the ways in which systemic discrimination interferes with their everyday lives.

In these interviews, as well as in other studies that we and others have conducted, African American parents underscore the importance of preparing their children, typically at an early age, for dealing with the racist actions of white Americans and with the consequent torments and frustrations of such actions. This is a difficult parental responsibility that is not faced by most white parents.[17] One recent study noted a difficulty for African American parents in socializing their children to cope with and succeed in U.S. society lies in the fact that one parental task "is to incorporate dominant societal values that insidiously devalue their group."[18] This study also found that, while these parents realize that racial derogation and mistreatment add stress to children's lives, parents must balance the need to prepare children for that challenge with the danger of overwhelming or overprotecting their children. In order to be sure not to overprotect their children, for example, the parents in this study had to struggle with the decision as to when to intervene by going to see their children's teachers when the children had suffered racist insults or other antiblack discrimination.

Other research studies have found that most African American parents have already told their two- and three-year-old children that they are black, and often some of what this means—a first step in racial socialization. Parents use several strategies to prepare their children for the racial hostility and discrimination they will face at the hands of white Americans in the outside world. By the time the children are older, they have usually had extensive lessons in "Racism 101." One recent study found that almost all black parents with children aged nine to seventeen had talked with their children about racism issues. Some two-thirds of the parents had given their children instructions on how to respond effectively to verbal racial insults. The most frequent instruction that these parents gave to their children was to respond to racial insults by telling someone else about the insults. Half of the respondents told their children to take action, such as by replying verbally to the children who insulted them.[19]

Some parents also teach their children coping strategies through personal demonstration. One effective teaching mechanism has been called "proactive problem solving," by which children participate with their parents in coming up with ways to manage negative experiences. Parents thus recount fictional or personal narratives as models for triumphing over white-generated racism. Other parents use a type of inoculation strategy. This involves telling their children some things that will be used by whites to challenge their beliefs about themselves and their group or culture, and then giving them arguments and refutations against those white challenges.[20] Such strategies work against the internalization of negative imagery that is a threat to the health of African Americans of all ages.

Research studies have found some general things to be true about effective parental teaching about racism. First, the strategies for managing racial discrimination are usually more effective when children themselves participate in creating them. Second, the strategies parents teach their children for resisting and coping with discrimination do not need to specifically address the content of each event or episode. Generic strategies are often quite successful. Finally, researchers have found that personally supportive messages alone—for example, reassuring messages telling a child that, contrary to what society may tell her, she is valuable—will most likely have a modest effect. Children need to be taught not only these internal and defensive strategies, but also more assertive, external tactics that make them feel that they have some control over their world—that is, that they have a sense of self-efficacy. Studies also show that parents who themselves feel a greater sense of self-efficacy in dealing with discrimination are better able to teach their children self-efficacy and to handle racial attacks assertively.[21]

In addition, a few research studies of specifically middle-class families explore the particular challenges that these parents sometimes face in preparing their children for countering racism. A significant number of black middle-class children have grown up surrounded by white middle-class children. Because of this, some of the black children—at least those who are younger or who have not yet encountered the overt types of racism—may come to believe they will be fully accepted in the larger white society. Thus, their parents, who are well aware of continuing racism in the school and in the larger society, must prepare their children to cope with the racism that some children may find hard to believe exists because of their relative lack of experience.[22]

In our interviews, a dentist attributed an ability to control anger to his father's early instruction: "My attitude basically stems from my parents, my father. He told me, years ago, that you can't go through life being bitter. I'm not the kind of person who, you know, you kick me and you slap me and I'll smile at you. No, you slap me; I'm going to slap you back. But I'm not going to be ruled by other people. I learned at an early age to always be in control." Rejecting bitterness, he draws on his father's attitude about standing up for oneself. Similarly, a middle-aged female entrepreneur spoke of her family upbringing as an important source of strength for dealing with racial difficulties. In reply to an interviewer's question, "Where does that kind of strength come from?" she answered:

> Well, you know, I mentioned earlier that it gets back to how you were raised. And I was raised in [a northeastern city] in a sort of lower middle-class interracial community. We all fought, slept, went to school, went to church together, and I really didn't know too much about segregation at that time. And I had a brother, he was older, and I tried to

do everything he did, so therefore I became a tomboy. So, being competitive was part of my upbringing. . . . So, the competitiveness value was developed in our household. . . . But that made me have a belief that I can do, and not be sidetracked by all of the external obstacles in this world. So, that's generally how it started.

Relying on Black Acquaintances

Friends and acquaintances also provide important social capital for many African Americans. When asked if family or friends have helped him deal with the frustrations of discrimination, a young businessperson who lives in the Southwest highlighted the importance of *community* support:

> They're very supportive. I think everyone has experienced some sort of racism, especially if you're an African American, so it kind of helps to talk to someone else who's been involved in something. My personality is I try to turn it around and make it lighthearted. You know, "Can we talk about it?" And just laugh about it now because there's no reason to get all stressed out about it if it's already happened, if there's nothing you can do about it. Just forget about it and move on.

Discussion and communication with other African Americans, both friends and acquaintances, in one's local community can be very helpful. Like other's respondents we have cited previously, this man also suggests that downplaying what happens can be useful.

Those who have shared the experience of dealing with racial barriers and active discrimination are in the best position to support each other. Since African Americans discuss incidents that they have encountered with their friends, they may, in this fashion, be able to help prepare one another for future frustrations at the hands of whites. In doing so, as in the case of relatives, the cumulative harm of racism may be partially countered by the collective knowledge of coping and resistance that is passed along. In an article in a leading academic journal, "Black Scholars Recall Racism from Their Undergraduate Years," several black intellectuals shared their experiences with racist incidents and the ways that they had learned to counter them. The dean of historians on U.S. racial history, John Hope Franklin, described his reaction to a racist incident in Nashville during his first year at

Fisk university: "From that day until I graduated, I very seldom went to Nashville, and when I did I never went *alone*." His painful experience taught him the value of social support from acquaintances and friends.[23]

Exchanging strategies is critical to survival in a racially hostile world, for people of all ages. African Americans and other Americans of color help each another be vigilant in resisting racism, and they assist one other in devising effective and appropriate responses. Thus, in his interview, a male college student spoke of the need for social support in organizational settings:

> Coming into [a northeastern state university], one thing that I would have loved to have happen was to have more relations with black professors and with the courses that I have to take. I consider it a sort of negative to not have that guided factor out there teaching you. Some of them—if you just know somebody up there that went through struggles and tension and pain, and he is actually teaching you. And if [you] can see a black sister or a black brother out there teaching you, it would just make me want to try harder.

Many major colleges and universities in the U.S. are predominantly white in their student body as well as in the makeup of their faculty.[24] African American students in predominantly white universities often lack the full range of social support from fellow students or faculty members that other students can receive. Thus, they often lack good mentors, have a minority status in terms of numbers, and face recurring racial discrimination and subtle racial barriers. Many rely on the support of other African American students, or on friends and relatives back home, in coping with and resisting racial mistreatment in university settings. Many choose to group with other African Americans, such as by forming or joining black organizations, thereby causing white students or administrators to criticize them for "self-segregation."[25] African American students thus face a catch-22 situation, for the strategies that they use to cope with on-campus discrimination are frequently misrecognized or resented by white students and faculty.

CONCLUSION

The novelist and essayist James Baldwin once probed this terrain of African American responses to racism, noting that:

People who cannot suffer can never grow up, can never discover who they are. That man who is forced each day to snatch his manhood, his identity, out of the fire of human cruelty that rages to destroy it knows, if he survives his effort, and even if he does not survive it, something about himself and human life that no school on earth—and, indeed, no church—can teach. . . . If one is continually surviving the worst that life can bring, one eventually ceases to be controlled by a fear of what life can bring; whatever it brings must be borne.[26]

In this chapter we see a range of behavioral strategies for fighting back against racial discrimination and related social barriers. These responses range from physical withdrawal to direct confrontation to humor and sarcasm. Different situations call for different contending and coping strategies. Whatever the strategy, by surviving and countering human cruelty, most black men and women become very knowledgeable and mature about social interaction with whites, and often cease to be significantly controlled by the bitterness or fearfulness that can come from dealing with everyday racism.

Most of our respondents are middle-class adults and have more social and economic resources that some other African Americans. They are aware of their greater empowerment. In one focus group conversation, a respondent underscored this point:

I think that we're some empowered people sitting around the table, and so we can do that. I think that there's a lot of people that don't feel that they have the power to do that. There's a lot of African Americans who don't feel that they have the power. I've seen it in the kids . . . [Another female voice: "That's true."] I've seen it in the workplaces. They don't [feel powerful], and so that rage just builds up. I see it in black men. They don't feel that they have the power. [Female voice: "And older people."] And old people. They really don't. And that's, I think the issue that really needs to be spoken to. We can do it because we've made up in our minds that we're going to educate them. But what about those people that really have not, you know, are not feeling this strength and energy? What about those, those *kids* that I see everyday? . . . You see, a lot of people, I think a lot of our people end up in jail or dead because they don't have the tools that we're talking about, that we use to deal with it.

There is general agreement among the participants in this focus group that middle-class African Americans have a larger responsibility to their communities. They often have more socioeconomic resources and educational (or legal) skills to deal with white racism than do many others, including young African Americans. The implication is spelled out: Middle-class African Americans must take an active role in helping empower other African Americans in dealing with the impact of everyday racism. Many comments in this book show that these middle-class respondents are well aware of this responsibility, and often choose the strategies that they use to deal with discrimination with this in mind. Sometimes, when they could just ignore a racist incident to conserve personal energy, or could deal with a racist incident in a way that would benefit only themselves, these black Americans instead choose to deal with the incident with an approach that smoothes the way for others who may not have the resources to deal with such incidents as effectively. The point is to take the action that benefits the larger community.

Although middle-class African Americans frequently have more tools than other African Americans to deal effectively with the racial discrimination they face, they by no means face little discrimination. Discrimination at the hands of whites—discrimination that is subtle and blatant—is far from being a thing of the past. Educated and successful African Americans and other people of color must regularly contend with assaults on their dignity that most whites cannot imagine. Moreover, these last two chapters dispel the popular white notion that African Americans and many other people of color react in a uniformly confrontational way to most discriminatory incidents that they encounter. On the contrary, our respondents show that they have a large box full of tools that they use to cope with and fight against racism in the social worlds that still surround them and their families.

7

Racism and the U.S. Health Care System

IN 1787 THE ELITE MEN who created the U.S. Constitution added this preamble to their work: "We, the people of the United States, in order to form a more perfect union, establish justice, insure domestic tranquility, provide for the common defense, promote the general welfare, and secure the blessings of liberty to ourselves and our posterity, do ordain and establish this Constitution for the United States of America." These men were all white and mostly well-off citizens of the new nation that they were creating. Although they announced that they were speaking for the "people of the United States," they, of course, did not, for these men of property actually represented only a small proportion of the population. There were no women, African Americans, Native Americans, or poor white men among them. A majority of them were slaveholders, had owned slaves, or were merchants and investors who had made a substantial income off the commercial trade centered around slave trading, slave plantations, or slave-produced products.

While these elite white men did announce some very important democratic ideals for the new country—including the asserted goal of promoting general welfare and establishing justice—they actually created a *highly unjust* social system that worked to promote, most effectively, the welfare of white men like them. For much of its first century, the new nation was riddled with extreme injustices, including the state-sanctioned actions taking Indian lives and lands, and the enslavement of African Americans. The burdensome legacies of these early injustices have persisted to the present day.

THE CONTINUING IMPORTANCE OF WHITE RACISM

In recent decades a number of analysts and commentators have tried to argue that there is a "declining significance of race" in the United States. Some have also argued that the troubled situation of African Americans is becoming more of an issue of class than of race. Some commentators even make the extreme argument that we are viewing the "end of racism" in the United States today. Clearly, our research data flatly contradict the notions that racial oppression is being eradicated and that racial discrimination is now being replaced by class discrimination. While racial and class (and gender) factors do interact in the etiologies of health problems for many African Americans, our interviews with numerous relatively affluent African Americans demonstrate that racial discrimination *alone* creates many serious personal health, family, and community problems. A racialized society exists because racial discrimination is practiced, rewarded, or overlooked by whites within most institutional settings, such as historically white workplaces. Our data and that of other recent studies show that discrimination targeting African Americans and other Americans of color is still commonplace in a variety of institutions, including government and private workplaces.

Much research on racial matters in the United States focuses on the attitudes of those who discriminate rather than on the pain, anguish, and suffering daily inflicted on the targets of discrimination. We focus here on African Americans as the targets of white-generated discrimination and oppression, but much of what we have to say applies to other groups, such as Latino, Asian, and Native Americans, as well.

The Broken Covenant: The Many Costs of Racism

In his widely read book *The Rage of a Privileged Class*, African American journalist Ellis Cose began his analysis with this comment: "Despite its very evident prosperity, much of America's black middle class is in excruciating pain. And that distress—although most of the country does not see it—illuminates a serious American problem: the problem of the broken covenant, of the pact ensuring that if you work hard, get a good education, and play by the rules, you will be allowed to advance and achieve to the limits of your ability."[1] Yet middle-class African Americans who play by all of the rules are generally not allowed to achieve to their *full* potential. Instead, they confront racial barriers and blockades throughout their lives—lives that may indeed be cut short by these obstacles.

Recall that the World Health Organization defines human health as a condition of full physical, mental, and social well-being. Health is thus much more than the absence of disease and infirmity, for it includes positive well-being and the active possession of basic human rights.[2] Attaining this well-being is made difficult by the continuing reality of widespread discrimination. Widespread and recurring white discrimination in many institutional settings wastes human beings and their resources, and it usually restricts, dehumanizes, or marginalizes its targets, to the point of making normal lives difficult. Indeed, this everyday racism is so dehumanizing that in discussing it many African Americans make reference to what they term the "slavemaster mentality" of discriminating whites, and to "feeling like a slave" in white workplaces. The legacy of slavery means that current racial oppression is in effect "slavery unwilling to die," as Supreme Court justice, William O. Douglas, once put it.[3] Many of the "badges" and effects of slavery can be seen in the long history of legal segregation as well as in continuing patterns of informal discrimination. If we are to begin to understand fully the physical and psychological suffering that black Americans endure at the hands of white Americans, we must look closely at the character and impact of the discriminatory workplaces and other institutional settings, particularly as they are experienced regularly by African Americans.

The testimony of African Americans demonstrates that this pain and suffering takes many forms. The negative impact of racial animosity and discrimination includes a sense of threat at work, challenges to self-esteem, rage at mistreatment, depression, and other psychological and physical health problems. Racial animosity and discrimination also require, usually at a very early age, the development of a range of protective and fighting-back tactics. The psychological impact of everyday racism is accentuated by yet other negative consequences. Racialized stress in workplaces and other institutional settings frequently generates or aggravates a range of physical health problems. Most of our respondents recognize the threat that everyday racism brings to their psychological and physical health, and most try hard to counter it and its many consequences. Not surprisingly in light of the data from our interviews with African Americans, a growing public health literature indicates that there are wide disparities in the physical health of white Americans and African Americans, as well as in access to quality health care services.

The Community Impact

The damage of racism extends well beyond its effect on individuals. As we saw in chapter 4, some social scientists and many popular commentators have written much in recent years about the social and other problems faced by black families and communities. It is frequently the case that such discussions, particularly those of white analysts, focus on "broken" or "disorganized" black families, and the responsibility for this social disorganization is typically placed on black Americans. It is alleged that they do not maintain their families and communities "properly" and do not adhere to certain mainstream (usually white) values. Such analyses are problematic because they are often stereotypical in their assessments of such things as the "work ethic" and "family problems" of African Americans.

In assessing these "problems" black families and communities face, more thoughtful commentators probe the important impact of the U.S. economy—for example, its failure to provide enough jobs, or government job training, for those who seek to work.[4] Yet, to our knowledge, *nowhere* in the contemporary social science literature is there a serious and extended discussion of the key points made by our respondents about the direct and harsh effects of everyday racism on their personal health and on their families, associations, and communities. As we have suggested, the centuries-long era of racial oppression has over several generations reduced the energy available to African Americans to build stronger and better families and communities. We need to be clear on this: While most African Americans have indeed managed to build strong families and communities in spite of recurring racism, they have often done this by exerting *super-human efforts* that may take a toll on their lives in yet other ways—such as on their personal health, on their life expectancies, and on their ability to maximize contributions to their communities or the larger society. Over the course of this book, we have seen that the cost of racial animosity and discrimination to individuals, families, and communities is much higher than most social science and popular commentators, especially those who are white, have heretofore recognized.

In addition, we should add, the high costs of antiblack racism extend to the larger society, a point our respondents often noted. Because African Americans are still subjected to widespread discrimination in the workplace and many other social settings—and thus to a societal division of labor not based on merit but racial characteristics—U.S. society does not match the ideal of "organic solidarity" with a division of labor premised mainly on personal ability and merit.[5] The French sociologist Emile Durkheim's analyses of organic solidarity in the late nineteenth century, as well as similar analyses in recent research, suggest that a workplace that is fragmented socially and unsupportive for many workers has negative effects on the workers' health and productivity. Moreover, a society whose many workplaces are fragmented in this way, and hierarchical along racial lines, has questionable viability for the long-term.

RACISM IN THE U.S. MEDICAL CARE SYSTEM: THE HISTORICAL BACKGROUND

Naming the Problem

In spring 2002 a long report titled, "Unequal Treatment: Confronting Racial and Ethnic Disparities in Health Care," was released by the distinguished National Academy of Science's Institute of Medicine, an organization that assists Congress on health matters. The report concluded that African Americans and other Americans of color do *not* receive the same quality of health care as white Americans, even when their incomes and insurance coverage *are similar*. This study examined many research studies on the higher disease and death rates faced by Americans of color. As a *New York Times* summary put it, the distinguished national study found that Americans of color "were less likely to be given appropriate medications for heart disease, or to undergo bypass surgery, and are less likely to receive kidney dialysis or transplants than whites."[6] Americans of color were also less likely to receive the better treatment for HIV infections than whites. Yet, they were *more* likely to get less sophisticated treatment for certain procedures, such as amputations of arms or legs. The report explains the racial differentials and cites problems in patient-doctor communication, including the lack of trust that many Americans of color have in white doctors. It also notes the major problem of a lack of health care facilities in many communities of color.[7] Interestingly, even this mostly white institute suggested, on the basis of reviewing many research studies, that racism of various types—including racial stereotyping on the part of physicians—was a likely factor in the formation of racial differentials in health care.

Clearly, the pervasive racism that has characterized the United States for centuries has had a negative impact on the health of African Americans. Given this reality, it is not surprising that many African Americans have sought help in the health care system. However, when they have turned to white health care practitioners, those who are supposedly oriented to the health and well being of all human beings, they have too often encountered yet more racial animosity and discrimination.

Some Historical Background

For several centuries, the treatment of African Americans by white health care practitioners has often been very inadequate, if not exclusionary or openly hostile. This mistreatment has generally been conducted on a foundation of stereotypical notions.[8] Oddly enough, in mental health terminology of the nineteenth century, enslaved African Americans who disobeyed their slavemasters or ran away were sometimes described as having a special mental illness (for example, "drapetomania" for their inclination to run away). After the Civil War, some white health practitioners went so far as to argue that what they thought was an increase in mental illness among African Americans was caused by a supposed loss of the "civilizing benefits" of white-controlled slavery.[9] Moreover, since the early 1900s, white physicians and other health practitioners have periodically viewed African Americans in stereotypical terms as promiscuous, emotionally or criminally volatile, childlike, or unintelligent.[10]

There is a lot of oddball stereotyping in the mental health analyses written by white physicians and other analysts between the late 1800s and the mid-1900s. Some such analyses actually asserted that African Americans lacked the psychological complexity to become depressed, given their "inferior" psyches.[11] And in the 1960s, when much research turned to cultural, rather than biological, explanations for racial differences in mental health, some researchers and physicians adopted the view that the more African Americans became culturally integrated into the core society, the more they would come to share certain mental problems like depression, which is "the white man's malady."[12]

Over the last century or two, the physical and psychological characteristics of African Americans have received much attention from white medical practitioners and researchers. As recently as the 1950s, some mainstream white physicians and researchers, writing in distinguished medical journals, made arguments that one now finds mainly in white supremacist publications. For example, in 1953 in the journal *Anesthesiology*, Dr. Mary F. Poe, head of the department of anesthesiology at the University of Tennessee, wrote about what she called the "peculiar liability of the Negro to sudden death under anesthesia." This white doctor concluded, "No real rapport can be established with the Negro patient. . . . The Negro's *primitive* reaction to life accounts for the high proportion of wounds of violence in this race. His tendency to procrastinate and to delay in seeking medical treatment for any disease which does not involve pain is a fundamental factor in the mortality of various surgical diseases."[13] Here she is accepting without data stereotypical images of African Americans as "primitive," as well as their alleged "tendencies" in regard to procrastination, and she does not consider that some procrastination might well be because of racial hostility and discrimination faced by blacks from those in the medical profession.

Poe also concluded that the statistical fact that African Americans faced greater problems with cardiovascular diseases than whites resulted from the fact that the "cardiovascular system of the Negro is *inferior* to that of the white race."[14] This medical leader further argued that there is much evidence that the nervous system of African Americans is different "in many respects from that of the white race." In these views, she is developing stereotypes about the physical characteristics and anatomy of African Americans. In her conclusion, she adds that the "Negro is particularly susceptible to apprehension, fright and panic."[15] Again she stereotypes African Americans without offering any data, this time in psychological terms— and without reference to how racism, including antiblack lynchings and other antiblack violence in her region, might have contributed to some of these psychological reactions. In this article, Poe offers her reasons for the greater death rate of African Americans under anesthesia in surgery. There is not even a hint that racial discrimination inside and outside the medical profession might play a significant role in this higher death rate. Even today, some contemporary medical and health research carried out by white institutions focuses on the supposedly deviant lifestyles of African Americans as the cause of their major health problems.

The racist attitudes held by white health practitioners and researchers have sometimes had extreme discriminatory consequences. Take, for example, the Tuskegee, Alabama, experiments by the U.S. Public Health Service. Beginning in the 1930s, over several decades, white doctors experimented on 399 black men with late-stage syphilis. The men were regularly examined in a research study of the effects of this disease. However, even after penicillin was developed as a cure, the black men got *no* medical treatment for syphilis from the white physician-researchers and, as a result, some died horrible deaths.[16] In addition, there was a severe impact on the families of these men, yet no one has bothered to study that impact, nor has the government yet offered serious compensation for the men or their families.[17] An attorney for the men called this a "program of controlled genocide."[18] Today, this medical history is well known among African Americans, and doubtless shapes their views of, and even willingness to use, white-dominated health care professions.

RACIAL BIAS IN HEALTH CARE SERVICES:
THE CURRENT SCENE

Care for Physical Illness

In addition to stressful discrimination in the workplace, African Americans face discrimination in the health care system itself that increases their likelihood of illness. They often receive less adequate care than otherwise comparable whites. Indeed, the National Medical Association (NMA), which represents more than 25,000 African American physicians, has periodically called for less racial discrimination and more equality in the provision of health care in the United States.[19] This problem of racism in medical care does not stand alone, but is woven together with the other problems we have examined throughout this book. Reviewing the literature on cancer, medical researchers Clayton and Byrd underscore the need to study the impact of racism: "The circumstances that govern the incidence and course of the disease in a given person or population depend on a multitude of factors, some social, some political, and some medical; many of them unacknowledged, all of them historical. Interwoven with these historical determinants of cancer, especially in western culture, is the influence of race."[20]

The current data on illness outcomes point to a range of medical and other health care problems for African Americans. Not only do they have higher rates of contracting certain major illnesses, but they often have poorer outcomes and survival rates for many of these illnesses. This suggests that the health care they receive is far from adequate. For example, the cancer survival rate for African Americans is 12 percent lower than that of whites.[21] According to the American Cancer Society, although the breast cancer incidence rate is lower for black women, the death rate for them from breast cancer is 22 percent *higher* than it is for white women. Other research shows that black women are more likely to receive a total mastectomy rather than a lumpectomy when either procedure would have been appropriate. Recent American Cancer Society data also indicate that African American women have a significantly higher overall mortality rate than white women.[22] In addition, black men have higher rates of death from cardiovascular disease than any other major group, yet recent research shows that physicians are *less likely* to refer their black patients for further medical diagnoses or therapy for cardiovascular problems than their white patients.[23] The consequences of such differential treatment can be seen readily. Other research studies show that, when black patients are diagnosed at a similar stage of a major disease and are given the same treatment opportunities as whites, racial differences in recurrence of disease and death rates virtually disappear.[24] For example, when black women's breast cancer is diagnosed and treated as early as white women's, their medical outcomes are on the whole similar.

In general, black Americans do not receive the same levels of preventive health care as white Americans. More, and better quality, prenatal care would likely reduce low birth weight problems and lower infant mortality rates. When detected early, several diseases, like diabetes and cancer, are less likely to recur or cause death. Adequate preventive care also can reduce the complications that result from diabetes.[25] Yet access to good, and affordable, medical care is difficult in many working-class areas. Young black men, who are more likely than comparable whites to be unemployed or underemployed, have the lowest physician visit rates of any other subgroup, and are more likely to seek treatment in an emergency room when they do need help. In part, this results from little or no health care insurance coverage; they often do not have the type of coverage that would come with a full-time, well-paying job. They must wait until a problem is an emergency before seeking care. In a survey of two thousand African Americans, 20 percent reported never having seen a doctor in an independent office setting; 21 percent reported no health insurance, as well.[26] Here we see a likely connection between restricted economic circumstances—which result in part from the long-term impact of systemic racism—and access to important health benefits and services. The impact of restricted income can also be seen in the fact that numerous hospitals in moderate-income and working-class areas have been closed in recent decades. Many of these areas have populations that are predominantly composed of African Americans and other Americans of color. In addition, some managed health care plans have excluded physicians of color because these physicians are more likely to have patients with serious and chronic health problems. A number of observers have called for stricter regulation of these managed care plans to prevent this kind of rationing by income, which has the side effect of seriously disadvantaging many patients of color.[27]

Discrimination in the Provision of Health Care

Some of the racial differentials in access to health care and treatment are not a matter of later diagnoses or a lack of good health insurance. Recent studies, such as the aforementioned Institute of Medicine review of research, still show major differences in the provision of health care along racial lines, even when controls are applied for access to health insurance and severity of illness.[28] Some studies suggest that many white doctors and other white health care providers are like other white Americans; they often harbor stereotypical ideas about African Americans, which prevents them from providing equitable care. This racial bias may be overt or subtle, and may thus shape doctors' judgements about the range of possible treatment procedures. For example, stereotyping can shape views of how suitable black patients are for various medical procedures or of how likely the patients are to follow a physician's directions.[29] One recent study found that doctors tend to view black patients and those with low incomes less favorably than white patients and those with higher incomes. White patients were viewed as more intelligent and more likely to follow medical advice.[30] In another recent study, researchers asked several hundred physicians to view videotapes of actors playing patients with heart disease. Although all of the "patients" reported similar symptoms, test results, socioeconomic status, and occupations, the physicians interviewed were more likely to recommend various high-tech cardiac procedures for white men than for black men and women.

Some studies have found differential treatment for cancer along racial lines. Researchers discovered that older black patients are less likely than comparable white patients to get certain often-successful surgical procedures for early-stage lung cancer and adequate pain medication for cancer disease.[31] Another major medical study found that African American patients with lung cancer were less likely to secure the best surgical treatment than were comparable white patients. Not surprisingly, the former patients also died sooner than the white patients.[32] One widely cited review of numerous studies on medical treatment for heart disease and stroke found that "researchers have repeatedly documented racial and ethnic differences in access to invasive diagnostic and therapeutic interventions for heart disease and stroke. Study findings have consistently indicated that African Americans are less likely to receive pharmacological therapy, diagnostic angiography and catheterization, and invasive surgical treatments for heart disease and stroke relative to white Americans with similar clinical disease characteristics."[33]

Two recent studies examined what happens in the case of kidney transplants. One study looked at the major steps in the process of getting kidney transplants and found major barriers for blacks and the poor, including problems at the stage of the pretransplant workup, and the fact that blacks are less likely to receive transplants than whites. The researchers suggested several possible reasons for this major difference in access to kidney transplants, including "subconscious bias and financial disincentives" in regard to medical providers.[34]

Another recent study found data further supporting this explanation. In this study, a large number of eligible black and white patients (those with end-stage renal disease) were interviewed. The researchers found that most black patients desired such renal transplants. There was only a slight difference in the black and white percentages expressing this desire (76 percent versus 79 percent). However, there were *large* racial differences in the proportions of the black and white patients who were actually referred for evaluation at a transplantation center and in the proportions who were placed on a waiting list for transplantation. In the case of waiting lists, only 31 percent of black women and 35 percent of black men were put on the list for transplantation, compared to 57 percent of white women and 61 percent of white men. These racial differentials in treatment remained significant after a number of control variables were examined. The researchers suggest that one possible reason for the differentials is that "blacks may be more likely than whites to encounter problems in communicating with their physicians and may have less trust in the health care system."[35] Since today many health care providers are white, medical decisions and actions that incorporate stereotypes, even subtle stereotypes, about African Americans can have a negative, even severe, effect on their physical health. Serious problems in communication can affect the quality of care.

Yet another recent study showed that, after controlling for severity of illness, patient preference, and socioeconomic factors, African Americans hospitalized with a serious illness are *less likely* to receive one of five intensive care procedures than are whites.[36] This is due, in part, to the fact that African American patients are less likely to be under the care of a medical specialist. Ironically, in this study, the black patients had better health outcomes than did the whites, a finding that seems to raise the broader medical care question of whether patients' needs are better met by medical generalists or medical specialists. Still, the study shows that blacks and whites are treated differently in this aspect of health care.[37]

Some studies, including the aforementioned Institute of Medicine review, have found significant racial or ethnic differences in access to the best medical therapies for diseases like HIV/AIDS, as well as in regard to prenatal and other child health services.[38] One of the most dramatic of the studies showing racial differentials in medical treatment was reported in the prestigious *New England Journal of Medicine*. This study showed that blacks and whites who receive Medicare are treated quite differently in the health care system, regardless of their income.[39] For example, black patients who had circulatory problems were far more likely (264 percent) to have a leg amputated than comparable whites. Black men with prostate cancer were far more likely (145 percent) than other men to have their testicles removed. During routine visits to doctors, moreover, black patients received less attention from nurses, and fewer lab tests were ordered for them than for others. Finally, this study found that black patients with heart disease were 55 percent *less* likely to receive bypass surgery, balloon angioplasty, or other more sophisticated heart treatments. The study offered conclusive evidence that the "health care system is less responsive to black patients than to white patients, and that systemic change will therefore be required."[40] Phrasing the problem this way is clearly a substantial understatement of what is actually going on, given the centuries of racial stereotyping, scientific racism, and overt and subtle discrimination in U.S. medical institutions.

Bias in Mental Health Services and Diagnoses

Racially linked mistreatment is also to be found in mental health services. Contemporary research evidence suggests that stereotypes, especially those regarding black Americans, have sometimes led to significant bias in mental health diagnoses. Mental health professionals often misdiagnose African Americans. Researchers have found that black and white people presenting similar symptoms to doctors are sometimes, or often, diagnosed with very different illnesses.[41] For example, whites are often diagnosed with depression, a condition that has fewer stigmas attached to it, and that may or may not be treated with medication. Depression is often treated with counseling or psychotherapy and has a good prognosis. In contrast, *with the same symptoms*, African Americans are more likely to be diagnosed with schizophrenia, a condition that is generally viewed as much more permanent and serious—and that is usually treated with significant medication, as well as with voluntary or involuntary commitment.[42]

Since they usually come from the same type of background as most white Americans, many white therapists likely harbor negative and stereotypical views of African Americans, and thus of their African American patients. These negative stereotypes can affect the health care black Americans receive. In a survey of practicing psychiatrists, Doris Wilkinson found that "cultural conditioning to racial beliefs and attitudes . . . pervades therapeutic contexts in which minority women are clients."[43] Racial stereotypes among medical practitioners often stem from hoary societal stereotypes and centuries-old myths, some of which may be linked to scientific racism and its notions of biological "races."[44] Physicians who accept any of these old stereotypes, even unconsciously, are likely to communicate some negative feelings in their verbal or nonverbal behavior, thereby causing many black patients to withhold the kind of self-disclosure that is necessary for effective psychotherapy.[45] Doing so may cause them to be labeled as "noncompliant," which is a further stigma provided by the mental health care profession. Some researchers have found that, for African Americans, psychotherapy with a white caregiver often leads to "unhealthful consequences."[46] In addition, diagnostic tests themselves are sometimes racially biased and thereby elevate the observed rates of certain types of mental illness for black Americans.[47] Indeed, most diagnostic measures for mental illness, which are routinely used to assess the mental health of African Americans, have been validated only for whites. A white standard of "normal" is usually taught to, and used by, therapists. Yet, the subcultural norms for what is "normal" and "abnormal" behavior are sometimes different for blacks and whites.[48]

Black Americans sometimes have different ways of expressing symptoms and complaints, different culturally normative behaviors, and different coping mechanisms than whites. Thus, numerous observers have called for better crosscultural training for white psychiatrists and psychotherapists. It has been suggested that, as psychological therapists become more aware of mental health issues unique to black and other Americans of color, they will need to retrospectively diagnose some patients in order to correct earlier misdiagnoses made because of racial stereotyping.[49]

A Note on Mental Illness among African Americans

The findings of current research on serious mental illness among African Americans are contradictory. Some research studies have found that the rates of mental illness for African Americans are higher than those of white Americans.[50] Yet other studies conclude that blacks have lower rates of mental illness than do whites, and point to the resilience and coping skills of African Americans in this regard. One study of one hundred white and one hundred black women (matched by age) who had visited an outpatient family practice center explored the rate of primary or secondary diagnoses of emotional disorder by physicians.[51] The researchers found that 44 percent of the white women, but only 24 percent of the black women, had either a primary or secondary diagnosis of psychiatric disorder. The reason for this difference is unclear. In this case, the researchers suggested three possibilities for this discrepancy: (1) Black women actually have fewer psychiatric disorders (perhaps because of better family and community support networks, which we discussed in an earlier chapter); (2) black women are more reluctant to discuss personal problems with (mostly white) physicians; or (3) black women are receiving poorer care from physicians than white women—in other words, physicians are overlooking or misdiagnosing serious psychological disorders in black women.

It seems likely that at least some of the discrepant findings on the mental health of African Americans may result from white physicians' or other health practitioners' attitudes toward and perceptions of their African American patients. For this reason, one should examine findings on the mental health of African Americans very critically. These contradictory findings have led some to suggest that public health researchers abandon research on the mental health of racial groups altogether. Others have called for much more in-depth qualitative research, case studies, and studies that cover longer periods of time to help adjudicate these contradictory research findings.[52]

PROPOSALS FOR CHANGE

Racial disparities in health care have received some increasing attention by the federal government. For example, addressing these differentials was part of President Bill Clinton's Initiative on Race in the mid-1990s.[53] A more recent report in the *New England Journal of Medicine* not only shows that blacks and whites are treated differently in the health care system, but also calls for significant changes in the health care system. First, these researchers call on medical researchers to increase the study of racial inequality and bias in the provision of health care. The role of racial differentials must be examined in such research. Second, the authors point out that the specific clinical consequences and importance of the racial disparities must be made very clear, for, if not, "the existence of racial disparities will remain of far greater interest to social scientists than to policy makers and physicians."[54] The final recommendation is that the focus should be on *systemic* change in the health care profession, rather than on trying to change the behavior of individual physicians. After acknowledging that the elimination of racial disparities in U.S. health care will be a difficult undertaking, the authors end by stating: "We should get on with it."[55] In addition, another aforementioned report, "Unequal Treatment:

Confronting Racial and Ethnic Disparities in Health Care" of the prestigious Institute of Medicine, suggested the need for such reforms as increasing the ability of Americans of color to get into high-quality health care plans and increasing civil rights enforcement by government health agencies.[56]

A Broad Range of Reforms

A review of the data presented in this and previous chapters indicates that there are many reforms that need to be implemented if we are to decrease racial bias and discrimination in the medical and other health care systems in the United States. One necessary reform is to increase the number of African Americans who are admitted to medical schools. The proportion of African American physicians has increased very slowly over the last few decades, and is currently low—less than 3 percent of all physicians. The same is generally true for most other communities of color. Practitioners from communities of color are often more sensitive to the views and experiences of their residents, as well as to any distinctive cultural expressions of illness and health and orientations to health care. Research has shown that African American physicians and other physicians of color are also much more likely to serve poor and black patients. As a study published by the NMA recently noted, when compared to white physicians, black physicians "are five times more likely to treat African American patients and four times more likely to treat poor and underserved patients."[57] Given their usually negative experiences with whites generally, as well as with many white health care practitioners, African American patients may be more likely to disclose their problems to, and to trust, African Americans doctors and other health practitioners. Another partial solution is to greatly expand the availability of quality health insurance, especially for those who are unemployed or part-time workers.

In addition, many elements of the medical training system need to be substantially reformed or revamped. The curriculum in most medical schools does not deal adequately (or at all) with the history of "scientific" racism that lies behind the idea of biological "races." The latter notion was created originally, and later circulated widely, by medical anatomists and other medical researchers like Germany's Johann Blumenbach beginning in the eighteenth century. Blumenbach was a prominent researcher who first came up with a ranked hierarchy of biological "races," and who first named those Europeans at the top of that hierarchy as "Caucasians."[58] Given these scientific origins of racist thinking and analysis, it is well past the time for all medical schools and other medical training facilities to offer a serious and required course that deals with the intrusion of racism into medical thought. It is also necessary for required medical school courses to deal with the many overt and subtle ways that a racist legacy can still be found in the operational procedures of medicine today. Medical schools should offer courses that spend some time critically assessing biological notions of "race," and that examine how such notions came to be developed by scientists. These courses should also deal at length with the racist images and stereotypes held by many white medical students and physicians, as well as examine the medical practices that are still based on racial stereotyping. Such changes in the medical school curriculum will not likely come easily, for there is much resistance to dealing with institutional racism in U.S. medical schools.[59]

The widely used diagnostic manuals for assessing mental illness must also be accurately and regularly updated to remove the white (and white-male) biases that are often still imbedded there. Major efforts need to be made in medical schools to deal with the racial and other stereotypes often harbored in the minds and inclinations of mental health practitioners. The finding that much psychotherapy with a white caregiver leads to unhealthful consequences for black Americans is disturbing. Harold Cheatham suggests, "Empowering the client through therapeutic intervention means transcending subtle and unintended adjustment to the disabling, dysfunctional conventions of the 'dominant culture.' It means assisting the client to validate his or her sense of self-efficacy and ability to productively confront and dismantle disabling events."[60] He then discusses the important idea that therapists should normally make use of a black client's support networks, such as by including family members and friends in the therapy process. The idea is to use the assets of black families and communities in mental health services, and thereby rely less on the culture of (white) organized medicine.

Due to racial bias in health care, many African Americans have traditionally relied on other forms of help for psychological difficulties. Some research shows differences in help-seeking behaviors of white and black Americans, with blacks being more likely to rely on their families.[61] The data in previous chapters also support this finding. Racial biases in mental health care, as well as low incomes, often lead African Americans to care for mentally ill family members at home.[62] Today, African Americans in need of psychological support are still more likely to seek help from family members than from health professionals.[63]

Research indicates that black Americans are likely to see both physical and mental health as dependent on a healthy spiritual life. Black Americans often rely on prayer, ministers, and church services for psychological help. Some analysts have noted that many African American church services are similar to group therapy in offering psychological relief. This might explain why group therapy seems more useful than individual psychotherapy for black women.[64] Indeed, studies of black communities show that people who have supportive extended-kinship networks report fewer symptoms of personal depression.[65] Thus, given these data, much more support and provision need to be made for holistic medical treatment within the contours of mainstream medicine, including viable alternative medical care practices long seen as unpalatable to many in mainstream medicine. The aforementioned NMA report made the reasonable suggestion that mainstream medicine "should recognize the benefits of prayer, meditation, relaxation responses, and other alternative holistic approaches to improving health and should include them as appropriate."[66]

This same insightful NMA report listed a number of strategies to deal with what they termed the long-term "slave health deficit" of African Americans. These strategies include better data collection, reporting, and analysis. One idea is the Health Policy and Research Institute, established by the NMA, which is an organization of 25,000 African American physicians. The NMA report also calls for much better data collection by government agencies on disease prevalence along racial and ethnic lines, as well as on the "best practices" programs that improve health care for populations of color. It further recommends congressional hearings on the impact of racism on health care in the United States, as well as the creation of a national advisory committee on racial and ethnic bias in health care that reports annually to the president or Congress. In addition, the report recommends increased efforts by health care providers to develop some cultural competence to reflect the racial and ethnic diversity of their patients.[67]

Ultimately, many reforms aimed at reducing bias in the health care system will run up against the national crisis in health care in the United States. In fact, this so-called system is, as physicians Clayton and Byrd note eloquently, really "a poorly stitched together nonsystem of autonomous institutions, profit-taking and non-profit . . . health provider microsystems and networks, Wall Street profit-taking corporations, government and private agencies all driven by quasi-market rather than public service or public health forces."[68] They go on to show that this so-called health system has multiple tiers, with a tier of first-rate care for the well-to-do, executive, and professional class, a tier with increasingly limited and problematical HMO care for the middle class, and a lower tier of crumbling public institutions trying, increasingly inadequately, to serve the poor. When it is mainly those Americans with substantial wealth who get really good care, it is not hard to see why African Americans—who are much less likely to be in that upper income group—are likely to suffer from poor to mediocre health care for both physical and mental illness problems. Moreover, when government budget cuts hit this health care system, African Americans tend to suffer even more from the effects than whites. One consequence of budget reductions is an increase in the inadequacy of access to good health care for African Americans and other Americans of color. As Clayton and Byrd note, the United States has actually set up a more or less permanent "health and health care underclass." As they note, "What is really at stake is whether African Americans and other disadvantaged sectors of the U.S. population will be afforded the opportunities for equitable health, absence from deformity, and disability status necessary to compete with mainstream White Americans."[69]

White Resistance to Change

What is the probability of real change in the health care system? Today, the probability seems quite low. One Kaiser Family Foundation survey of U.S. (mostly white) physicians found that 69 percent thought the health care system "rarely or never treats people unfairly because of their race or ethnicity." In contrast, only 23 percent of black physicians agreed.[70] Thus, it is likely that most white physicians see no need for major reforms to alleviate racism in the U.S. health care system. Certainly, the views of the white public on such matters as government intervention against discrimination are not encouraging. In another recent poll, a majority of white respondents thought too much attention is paid these days to racial issues in the United States. Only a fifth thought that too little attention is paid to such matters. Recall from chapter 1 the erroneous beliefs the majority of whites expressed in this same opinion survey about racial differentials in health, jobs, income, and education.[71] In that survey, 61 percent of the white respondents had the erroneous impression that the average black person had health care access that is equal to or better than that of the average white person. Yet the actual data show that whites are far more likely to have good health insurance and get adequate or better medical care than black Americans. Recall too that half of the white respondents also believed that blacks had a level of education similar to or better than that of whites and were, on the average, as well off as whites in the jobs they hold. Over half believed that black Americans had achieved equality or would soon achieve it.[72] It is very clear that the majority of whites are ignorant or misinformed when it comes to understanding the difficult and discriminatory conditions that African Americans—as individuals and as families and communities—face most days of their lives.

Sadly enough, in one recent survey, white respondents were asked if they "often have sympathy for blacks," and again if they "often feel admiration for blacks." Only five percent said yes to both questions.[73] Given their ignorance and lack of understanding, most whites are not supportive of government programs for *substantial* change in the discriminatory conditions still faced by African Americans. African Americans, in contrast, seek changes in the recurring patterns of discrimination they face in all major institutions of U.S. society, including the health care system.

The only somewhat encouraging sign in this picture of contemporary health care is that there is substantial support among all Americans for general reforms in the U.S. health care system. In recent decades, the several attempts at major reforms have not been frustrated by the general public, but rather by such health care organizations as Health Maintenance Organizations (HMOs) and pharmaceutical companies. Recent surveys indicate that a substantial majority of Americans would prefer *more* government involvement in the health care system. One recent national poll found that seven in ten Americans desire that the government work to increase health insurance coverage for all Americans. Eighty percent also believed there should a "patient's bill of rights," including the right to file lawsuits against medical care providers and insurance companies. There was also support for special action for lower-income Americans. As one summary of the poll's results noted, "Three-fourths favor expanding state government programs for low-income people . . . and about two-thirds favor offering uninsured Americans income tax deductions, tax credits, or other financial assistance to help them purchase private health insurance on their own."[74] It is possible that general reforms in the health care system, especially if they include improving care for those families with less income and wealth than the average family, might improve the health care services available to many African Americans and other Americans of color. Still, this would be only a partial reform. Thoroughgoing reform requires that the government target the widespread racial stereotyping and subtle and blatant discrimination in the health care system for reduction and elimination.

CHANGING THE RACIST WORKPLACE

Since the U.S. workplace is a major source of the stress generating serious health problems for African Americans, it is an arena in which major changes are long overdue. We have seen a great range of workplace racism in our respondents' accounts. Sentient human beings react seriously, in their minds and bodies, to recurring mistreatment and everyday discrimination in their workplaces and other social settings. The recurring and dehumanizing discrimination of the workplace, as we have seen, creates, among other things, anguish, pain, despair, and rage over persisting injustice. This situation is in great and immediate need of redress.

As can be seen clearly in their education, occupations, and other achievements, our respondents work hard to try to create good lives for themselves and their families. They are usually involved in their communities, as well. Interestingly, middle-class African Americans are viewed by many white people, including a variety of national commentators, as having generally achieved the American dream, just like the white middle classes.[75] Since the late 1960s, the typical workplace, particularly the white-collar workplace, has become less segregated along racial lines. However, while an important step forward, this desegregation has in many cases created yet other racially stressful workplace situations for black employees. Since the 1970s, the placement of well-educated African Americans in historically white workplaces has frequently meant a new kind of informal segregation or subtle restriction. For example, many of the first well-educated African Americans to integrate historically white workplaces were placed into more or less racialized jobs—"community liaison" or affirmative action positions, or other staff (rather than line) positions for professionals and managers. White executives and government officials who made such "ghettoized" placements usually had their own interests in mind. Placing black Americans in some of these positions helped protect white corporations and agencies from increased pressure for yet more radical change in their hiring and other policies. Once they occupied these and other staff-type positions, many black middle-class workers later were unable to move into higher-level positions—up the usual mobility ladders of corporation or government agencies.[76]

A number of the accounts in previous chapters illustrate other serious problems in the contemporary workplace. For workers of color, workplace integration has often brought forced assimilation, recurring discrimination, and the sense of being constantly watched or outvoted, if not regularly harassed.[77] To this point in time, integration in most employment settings has been primarily one-way. African American employees and other employees of color usually have been required to accept white-generated work norms, rules, and practices, yet they have not been given the power to significantly reshape this traditional workplace culture. This is true for other institutional settings besides the workplace. In practice, a major problem with racial integration lies in the fact that it mixes varying numbers of people of color into predominantly white institutional settings without giving them enough resources to restructure those settings. Not surprisingly, racial integration of the workplace has caused many people of color anguish, anger, and pain.[78]

If the United States is ever to become a *true* democracy—one in which all groups have proportionate resources and a significant say in how all major institutions are run—we must move to a system of meaningful, full-fledged racial and ethnic integration in our workplaces and other major institutions, especially those that historically have been all white. We must move well beyond the placement of African American employees in restricted or informally segregated positions that do not take into account their full capabilities. We must move beyond the usual one-way assimilation of the current era of desegregation and moderate integration. New employees from previously excluded groups should not be required to become "whitewashed" and give up their identities just to be accepted as coworkers, employees, and supervisors. As we see it, the goal should be a situation of mutual accommodation for all employees. Black Americans and other people of color must be given the same opportunity as whites to change the contours of the workplace by their presence in it. Those who have held the dominant positions, white employers and employees, must make major adaptations to those who were excluded or restricted in the past. Whites employers and employees must allow the *full* incorporation of those who are not white into workplaces, which includes full access to equitable resources and positions commensurate with abilities. If necessary, whites must also be forced to abandon their racially discriminatory practices, or suffer serious punishment for violating more aggressively enforced civil rights laws.

One major step must be to change the number of employees so as to create a critical mass of African Americans and other workers of color in many workplaces where there are now only token numbers of employees who are not white.[79] Not surprisingly, researchers have found that the fewer the members of one's racial group available in the workplace for support, the more health problems are experienced by persons of under-represented groups.[80] As our respondents have suggested, the cultures at most historically white workplaces also need significant change. Many African Americans feel they have to tone down their own styles and preferences at work more so than whites. For example, African American employees are often criticized for wearing their hair in dreadlocks or braids or for wearing African-style clothing. It is time for the U.S. workplace to implement the old, much-heralded ideal of "liberty and justice for all."

Finally, it is time for U.S. employers to make sure that all their employees have access to adequate health care services. In the aforementioned opinion survey, the overwhelming majority of Americans agreed that all Americans should have better health care insurance. They also supported government action to improve health care services. Developing a national health care system like those in many European countries, systems that even some major corporate executives have supported for the United States from time to time, might do this. Yet, while we await such a national government-funded system, employers should be pressed, by government and activist organizations, to take action *now* to improve the character of the health care provided to workers by private for-profit and nonprofit agencies. Many of these health plans and programs are inadequate in their coverage. Moreover, lower-paid workers are less likely to have adequate health care insurance than better-paid workers. And the former are more likely to be workers of color than are the latter, an example of institutional racism in U.S. society. Not only is the health care coverage generally poorer for these workers, but they also are generally not given certain other types of support for dealing with illness. They may have few or no sick leave or vacation days. One recent study of African American women receiving mammograms found that these women often would not be given time off to go get screening services like a mammogram. If they take time off on their own, they run the risk of being fired or otherwise punished by their employers.[81] It is time for employers to take action to eliminate all forms of blatant, subtle, and covert racial discrimination in their workplaces.

REDRESS THROUGH THE "JUSTICE" SYSTEM?

It is not only the health care system and the workplace that need to be dramatically reformed if the health and welfare of African Americans and other Americans of color are to be significantly improved. The U.S. court system must also be reformed so that Americans who face racial and other forms of discrimination in many sectors of society can get significant redress for the damage done to them, their families, and their communities. African American workers, who face recurring, high levels of stress in racially hostile workplaces, have frequently tried to turn to the U.S. justice system for redress and compensation. Yet this system has often not given much redress; indeed, it too often provides more injustice.

There are clear reasons for this. This U.S. legal system is very white-dominated. Most of its key figures and practitioners are white. Thus, one report on the U.S. justice system found that almost all (1,816 out of 1,838) of the district attorneys and similar officials across the nation with the power to make decisions about the death penalty and other major justice-system decisions are white. This study also cited evidence of the use of peremptory challenges by prosecutors to keep juries as white as possible.[82]

This dominance of white officials means that the culture of the U.S. justice system is substantially whitewashed in its norms and conditions. As a rule, the understandings and comprehension of those whites who dominate the system are limited by their own racial and class backgrounds. Most do not have the kind of experience or knowledge necessary to fully understand the African

American experience with everyday racism. Recall from chapter 1 that it seems that some important appellate courts are backpedaling on issues regarding racial discrimination.[83] In the *Etter v. Veriflo Corporation* case we discussed there, recurring racist epithets directed at a black man were not "severe or pervasive" enough to warrant a remedy to be imposed by the courts.[84] The California court seemed to be saying that the hostile racial climate that Etter, like many other similarly situated black employees experience, is painful only because they construct their experiences that way. In thinking about the arguments in this case, we are reminded of Justice Henry Brown's reasoning in the 1896 *Plessy v. Ferguson* case: "We consider the underlying fallacy of the plaintiff's argument to consist in the assumption that the enforced separation of the two races stamps the colored race with a badge of inferiority. If this be so, it is not by reason of anything found in the act, but solely because the colored race chooses to put that construction upon it."[85] In this all-white court's opinion, as expressed here by the chief justice, it was only the black man's (Plessy's) *perception* that he faced humiliating racism when he was put into a racially segregated railroad car. Any feeling by blacks that whites saw them as inferior was just in their heads. Today, this "blaming the victim" view still is echoed in many contemporary white analyses of the problems faced by black workers, families, and communities, inside and outside the legal system.

Let us consider a few trends in recent court debates over discrimination. Examining several important court cases, we have found that, although the idea of a "hostile work environment" was originally extended from racial discrimination cases to sex discrimination cases,[86] the courts have only occasionally accepted the kind of evidence to demonstrate a hostile racial climate that they accept to demonstrate a hostile sexual climate. As yet, although legal standards are about the same for proving hostile racial and sexual climates, judges are more lenient in the evidence they allow to demonstrate that there are hostile sexual climates than in the evidence they allow for proof of hostile racial climates. In our view, there is no reason that this standard should not be the same, for both environments can be dangerous to a person's psychological and physical health.

Interestingly, in a 1993 case, *Harris v. Forklift Systems, Inc.*, the U.S. Supreme Court ruled that a victim of sexual harassment did *not* have to prove "severe psychological injury" in order to be compensated for sexist discrimination in the workplace. In this case, a white female employee reported suffering a number of sexist comments and humiliating actions from her white male employer. In her majority opinion on this case, Supreme Court Justice Sandra Day O'Connor made it clear that a hostile sexual climate could be demonstrated by evidence of a string of humiliating actions or offensive comments by a male employer: "Whether an environment is hostile or abusive can be determined only by looking at all the circumstances. These may include the frequency of the discriminatory conduct; its severity; whether it is physically threatening or humiliating, or a mere offensive utterance; and whether it reasonably interferes with an employee's work performance."[87] In this case, the judges determined that a single major act of discrimination is not necessary to prove illegal sexual harassment in employment settings. A continuing pattern of minor acts is sufficient for the workplace climate to be considered hostile.

However, in cases alleging a hostile racial climate, African Americans and other people of color who go to the higher courts to remedy workplace discrimination are usually subject to a much more stringent burden of proof. As we saw in *Etter*, demonstrating that one faces moderately derogatory racist comments over some period of time generally is not enough. The judges seem to insist on proof of serious psychological stress and physical impact. Yet the standard in *Harris* is that the harassing conduct need *not* cause serious psychological distress, but only has to be "severe or pervasive enough to alter the conditions of the victim's employment." In *Faragher v. City of Boca Raton*, the Eleventh Circuit Court of Appeals further clarified this standard, explaining that the *Harris* factors should serve as a filter to eliminate complaints regarding "ordinary tribulations of the workplace" such as "occasional teasing."[88] In this case, Beth Ann Faragher was a lifeguard for the city of Boca Raton, to whom sexually harassing comments were made by male city employees. The Supreme Court ruled in her favor, overturning a lower court ruling.

Statutory relief should only be given, according to another decision cited favorably in the *Faragher* decision, for "incidents of harassment . . . occur[ing] with a regularity that can reasonably be termed pervasive." No remedy is necessary, this other court ruled, for "episodic patterns of racial antipathy."[89] According to this latter judicial view, judges (often white judges with little contact with African Americans) decide whether a black person faces a painful racial climate—and when a company or defendant should be held legally liable for allowing a hostile racial environment to exist. These white judges determine when that hostile environment is "pervasive enough to alter the conditions of the victim's employment." However, what may be a hostile racial environment for most African Americans may not be seen that way by these white judges with no experience with such difficult environments. The type of reasoning in these cases shows the institutional racism in the justice system—the reality that constitutional scholar Roy Brooks has called "juridical subordination."[90]

The rulings we have just cited seem to ignore a much better approach, which was delineated in one 1996 appellate court case, *Aman v. Cort Furniture Rental Corporation*. In that decision, an exception to those noted above, the Third Circuit Court of Appeals decided that when white supervisors and coworkers made repeated use of terms—such as "another one," "one of them," and "poor people"—to refer to two black employees, they were indeed using racial "code words" that created a "complex tapestry of discrimination" for which the company was legally accountable.[91] This circuit court recognized these comments as verbal acts of discrimination, and concluded that they constituted a racially hostile workplace. The standards the court asserted for proving a racially hostile workplace were that (1) the employee suffered intentional discrimination, (2) the treatment was pervasive and regular, (3) the discrimination detrimentally affected a particular employee and (4) the discrimination would also detrimentally affect "a reasonable employee in a similar situation." These four standards are similar to those set forth in the hostile sexual climate cases.

Here the judges were able to see conduct as generating a racially hostile workplace, but more recent court decisions, such as those in *Etter*, seem to have lost this understanding. To this point in time, the majority of U.S. courts have been more sympathetic to the arguments of women, mainly white women, that they face hostile, sexually harassing male workers in their workplaces—and thus hostile workplace climates—than they have been to the arguments of black workers that they face racially hostile white workers and, thus, racially hostile workplace climates. Perhaps the reason for this is that in their own lives every white male judge and jury member has had close contacts with a woman, whether she be his grandmother, mother, daughter, wife, or friend. Thus, most will have some idea of what a "reasonable woman" might find offensive, as well as have some sympathy toward a white woman. However, white juries and judges often assess the evidence of racial hostility in white workplaces, and that evidence may be considered to be the "perceptions" of some "oversensitive" African Americans. Thus, the test presented by the courts, in which the standard of "a reasonable person of the plaintiff's race" is invoked, is empty of meaning. Few white people have a real understanding of what African Americans' experience in white workplaces is like.

The Law and a Better Workplace

Some legal scholars have suggested the need for a much better standard to use in judging racially hostile workplaces. For example, Barbara Flagg has discussed a situation that exists in predominantly white workplaces that she calls the "transparency phenomenon."[92] Because whites are generally unaware of racial discrimination in the workplace, they are not conscious that decision-making that appears neutral often benefits whites and disadvantages African Americans and other employees of color. We agree with this analysis, but we suggest that discrimination that automatically advantages whites and disadvantages people of color, but is thought of as applying "neutral standards," is best referred to as yet another type of the "woodwork racism" we have discussed previously. Such discrimination is usually *not* transparent to its targets. It is clearly seen and very real.

Flagg suggests that instead of a disparate treatment test for racial discrimination, which relies on proof of intentional discrimination, the courts should consider finding employers liable for failure to create a culturally diverse workplace environment that imbeds the perspectives and norms of newly integrated groups. Flagg suggests two possible new standards, a "foreseeable impact" approach and an "alternatives" approach. Both would make it necessary for courts to consider the transparent-to-whites phenomenon in deciding what constitutes a racially hostile workplace. Flagg advocates the alternatives approach, in which a historically and predominantly white workplace likely indicates that there are distinctively white norms of decision-making in routine operation—and this, in turn, requires and activates strict judicial scrutiny. The employer is then responsible for explaining the specific criteria used in the particular workplace that led to the suit; after that, a plaintiff could propose alternative criteria that would not have a disparate impact on employees of color.[93]

Charles Lawrence has suggested another solution to the difficulty of proving a racially hostile workplace. From his perspective, the courts' reliance on proof of intent and a show of individualized fault should be replaced with a "cultural meanings" standard.[94] Such a standard would take into account the often unconscious and half-conscious discrimination practiced every day by whites who have grown up in a racist society. Legal scholars and judges can look to social science research to offer some evidence on the racially derogatory cultural meanings of seemingly "neutral" acts by white employees and supervisors. Such insights are useful for crafting a new standard for judging the "reasonableness" of African Americans' complaints of discrimination in their workplaces. Somehow, their long-term experience must be factored into any meaningful approach that tries to judge the character and impact of hostile racial climates.

CONCLUSION

A racist society is not a healthy society, for the perpetrators of racial discrimination as well as for the targets of that discrimination. In an earlier book, Joe Feagin and his colleagues argued that all Americans have paid a heavy price for continuing racism:

> Racist notions have brought ill-gotten resources and benefits to many white Americans. Yet few whites realize the heavy price that they, their families, and their communities have paid and will pay for this institutionalized racism. White Americans have paid greatly in the form of their ignorance and fears, in human contributions and achievements sacrificed, in the failure to create a just and egalitarian society, in the resistance and lashing out of the oppressed, and in the fundamental ideals and egalitarian morality thus betrayed. In our view, U.S. society certainly cannot afford white racism in the long run, for it may well destroy this society as we know it sometime in this century.[95]

Clearly, it is African Americans and other Americans of color who pay the heaviest cost for continuing racism, for the price they pay is direct and immediately painful. Notwithstanding, the society as a whole does indeed pay a heavy price for continuing racism.

In 1991, Billy Tidwell crafted this eloquent assessment of U.S. society: "Arguments against American racism have moved beyond the historical issues of morality. The more pressing issue to be addressed is the serious threat that racism poses to our national security. Perhaps, most importantly, the costs of racism severely constrain this society's ability to produce and progress."[96] This is even truer today.

For nearly four hundred years, African Americans have been central to the costly system of racial oppression. Not surprisingly given so many generations of oppression, African Americans have always been among the strongest carriers of the ideals of liberty and social justice in this country. In spite of the weight of racial oppression, most African Americans have been creative and more or less successful in building their lives and communities, and many have regularly pressed the society in the direction of greater liberty, equality, and justice. African Americans' sense of social justice continues to have great potential in regard to stimulating further movement by this society in the direction of its formal egalitarian and democratic ideals. African Americans have periodically developed large-scale social movements in U.S. history. Significantly, most African Americans have not retreated to debilitating pessimism, but have slowly pressed onward as individuals, families, and communities. Today, significant numbers of African Americans create and join many religious, civic, and civil rights organizations that are working to eradicate systemic racism, get civil rights laws enforced, and secure better living conditions for Americans of all social backgrounds. There are lessons here for all Americans concerned with building a truly democratic United States.

Today, the United States faces many challenges, not the least of which is the fact that the U.S. population is rapidly becoming much less white and European, and much more Asian, Latino, African, Middle Eastern, and Native American in its composition. In spite of these changes over the last few decades, however, at least 95 percent of the country's top leaders—in most of its major institutions—are still white men. And most of the rest are white women. This exclusiveness in leadership now means major and increasing problems for the country. As the members of the white elite look out over the country, most seem ignorant about its racial and ethnic past and fearful about its racial and ethnic future. So, it seems, are many ordinary whites who are reacting to significant increases in the number of Americans of color by seeking greater separatism like that of the old

South Africa. Some whites are choosing guarded communities, private schools, and armed militias; others are moving to whiter counties and states, away from the increasingly diverse metropolitan areas on the West Coast, the Gulf Coast, and the East Coast. A key problem for most whites is that they have been raised in, and mostly lived in, predominantly white or all-white communities. Most do not understand the painful experiences of racial antipathy and discrimination. Most whites have not seriously listened to the views of those who are not white. As philosopher Laurence Thomas put it, "as far as I can see, many white folks do not think they have to listen to Black people. They seem to think that they understand who we are, what we're about, what our needs are, and where they come from without listening to us."[97] He adds that whites must not only listen to African Americans, but also respect them and be interested in earning their trust.

There is a positive possibility for the future of the United States. Working with respectful and antiracist whites, African Americans and other Americans of color can build effective multiracial coalitions that will break down the racist barriers and institutions of U.S. society once and for all. They can move the United States toward the goal of a true and viable democracy. Many Americans, fortunately, are committed to this view of the future and are working in a large number of multiracial organizations to end all forms of dehumanizing discrimination, and finally achieve the heralded "ideals of liberty and justice for all."

James Baldwin once described how U.S. racism created black *Americans*, men and women who are fully American and whose oppressive and turbulent history is central to that of the nation. This extraordinarily damaging and painful white-on-black experience, he predicted, "may prove of indispensable value to us in the world we face today. This world is white no longer, and it will never be white again."[98] Reflecting on the contemporary state of Americans, he concluded that the dehumanization of African Americans is "indivisible" from the dehumanization of all Americans.[99]

Notes

Introduction

1. L. M. Sixel, "Prince Will Settle EEOC Bias Case; Cafeteria Company to Pay $175,000 Fine," *Houston Chronicle*, April 2, 2002, p. 2.

2. Elliot Grossman, "Jury to Hear Officer's Evidence of Hostility," *Morning Call* (Allentown), April 25, 2002, p. A1.

3. For specific examples see Andrew R. McIlvaine, "Hostile Environments," *Human Resource Executive Magazine*, at www.workindex.com/editorial/hre/hre0101-2.asp (retrieved May 31, 2001); and Gregory Weaver, *Indianapolis Star*, January 14, 2001, at www.iww.org/pipermail/iww-news/2001-January/002136.html.

4. Jim Skeen, "Racial Bias Suit Files; Lockheed Racist, 3 Workers Say," *Los Angeles Daily News*, March 13, 2002, p. AV1.

5. Lance Williams, "Lawsuit Describes Jim Crow Workplace," *San Francisco Chronicle*, March 23, 2002, p. A25.

6. Bari-Ellen Roberts, *Roberts v. Texaco: A True Story of Race and Corporate America* (New York: Avon Books, 1998); Kurt Eichenwald, "The Two Faces of Texaco," New York Times (November 10, 1996): Section 3, p. 1.

1 The Many Costs of White Racism

1. See Joe R. Feagin and Melvin P. Sikes, *Living with Racism: The Black Middle Class Experience* (Boston: Beacon Press, 1994), p. vii.

2. Feagin and Sikes, *Living with Racism*, p. ix.

3. See S. S. Fluss, "International Public Health Law: An Overview," in *The Scope of Public Health*, vol. 1 of *Oxford Textbook of Public Health*, ed. R. Detels et al. (New York: Oxford University Press, 1997), pp. 371–390.

4. National Medical Association, "Racism in Medicine and Health Parity for African Americans: 'The Slave Health Deficit,'" Second Annual National Colloquium on African American Health, March 12, 2001, p. 1.

5. For example, see Rodney Clark, Norman B. Anderson, Vanessa R. Clark, and David R. Williams, "Racism as a Stressor for African Americans," *American Psychologist* 54 (October 1999): 811.

6. George Lipsitz, "The Possessive Investment in Whiteness: How White People Profit From Identity Politics," in *The Meaning of Difference: American Constructions of Race, Sex, and Gender, Social Class and Sexual Orientation*, eds. Karen E. Rosenblum and Toni-Michelle C. Travis, 2d ed. (Boston: McGraw Hill, 2000), p. 355; see also George Lipsitz, *The Possessive Investment in Whiteness: How White People Profit From Identity Politics* (Philadelphia: Temple Press, 1998).

7. Richard Morin, "Misperceptions Cloud Whites' View of Blacks," *Washington Post*, July 11, 2001, p. A01.

8. For data on these economic matters, see Joe R. Feagin and Clairece B. Feagin, *Racial And Ethnic Relations* (Upper Saddle River, N.J.: Prentice-Hall, 2003), chapter 7.

9. "Washington Post/Kaiser/Harvard Racial Attitudes Survey," *Washington Post*, July 11, 2001, p. A01.

10. See, for example, Yanick St. Jean and Joe R. Feagin, *Double Burden: Black Women and Everyday Racism* (New York: M. E. Sharpe, 1998); and Joe R. Feagin, *Racist America: Roots, Current Realities, and Future Reparations* (New York: Routledge, 2000).

11. See Thomas Pettigrew, "The Mental Health Impact," in *Impacts of Racism on White Americans*, Benjamin Bowser and Raymond G. Hunt, eds. (Beverly Hills, Calif.: Sage, 1981), pp. 116–118.

12. Lawrence Bobo, "Inequalities that Endure?: Racial Ideology, American Politics, and the Peculiar Role of the Social Sciences," paper presented at conference "The Changing Terrain of Race and Ethnicity," University of Illinois, Chicago, Illinois, October 26, 2001.

13. A 1992 national survey by the Anti-Defamation League asked whites whether they agreed with one or more of eight antiblack stereotypes. The majority (55 percent) agreed with two or more, and 30 percent agreed with four or more. Anti-Defamation League, *Highlights from an Anti-Defamation League Survey on Racial Attitudes in America* (New York: ADL, 1993), pp. 8–25.

14. See Norman R. Yetman, "Introduction," in *Majority and Minority: The Dynamics of Race and Ethnicity in American Life*, ed. Norman R. Yetman, 4th ed. (Boston: Allyn and Bacon, 1985), p. 15. On white views of poverty and individualism, and on links between these views and racial views, see generally Joe R. Feagin, *Subordinating the Poor* (Englewood Cliffs, N.J.: Prentice-Hall, 1975).

15. Sally Satel, *PC, M.D.: How Political Correctness Is Corrupting Medicine* (New York: Basic Books, 2000), p. 192.

16. Ibid., p. 27.

17. Ibid., p. 25.

18. See J. C. Quick, L. R. Murphy, and J. J. Hurrell, eds., *Stress and Well-Being at Work: Assessments and Interventions for Occupational Mental Health* (Washington, D.C.: American Psychological Association, 1992); and Clark, Anderson, Clark, and Williams, "Racism as a Stressor for African Americans," p. 809.

19. Satel, *PC, M.D.*, p. 14.

20. Dinesh D'Souza, *The End of Racism: Principles for a Multiracial Society* (New York: Free Press, 1995), p. 538.

21. See Jean Stefancic and Richard Delgado, *No Mercy: How Conservative Think Tanks and Foundations Changed America's Social Agenda* (Philadelphia: Temple University Press, 1996), pp. 3–4.

22. See Steven Keeva, "A Bumpy Road to Equality: Panelists Say Courts are Backpedaling on Minority Issues," 82 *ABA Journal* 32 (1996).

23. *Etter v. Veriflo Corporation*, 67 Cal.App.4th 457, 79 Cal.Rptr.2d 33 (1st Dist. Ct. App. 1998).

24. See St. Jean and Feagin, *Double Burden*.

25. See Feagin and Sikes, *Living with Racism*, pp. 135–222.

26. *Etter v. Veriflo Corporation*, 67 Cal.App.4th 457, 79 Cal.Rptr.2d 33 (1st Dist. Ct. App. 1998).

27. Roy L. Brooks, *The Structure of Judicial Decision-Making From Legal Formalism to Critical Theory* (Durham, N.C.: Carolina Academic Press, forthcoming 2002). We are indebted here to the suggestions of Roy Brooks.

28. See Joe R. Feagin and Hernan Vera, *White Racism: The Basics* (New York: Routledge, 1995), pp. 135–194.

29. See ibid.

30. See Ruth A. Wallace and Alison Worl, *Contemporary Sociological Theory*, 4th ed. (Englewood Cliffs, N.J.: Prentice-Hall, 1995), pp. 290–292.

31. Magnus Hirschfeld, *Racism* (London: Gollancz, 1938).

32. Stokely Carmichael (Kwame Ture) and Charles V. Hamilton, *Black Power: The Politics of Liberation in America* (New York: Vintage, 1967).

33. Randall Collins, *Theoretical Sociology* (New York: Harcourt, Brace, Jovanovich, 1988), p. 406.

34. We are indebted to Bette Woody for reminding us of this key point.

35. James Jones, *Prejudice and Racism*, 2d ed. (New York: McGraw-Hill, 1997), p. 472.

36. Philomena Essed, *Understanding Everyday Racism* (Newbury Park, Calif.: Sage, 1991).

37. See Patricia Hill Collins, *Black Feminist Thought: Knowledge, Consciousness, and the Politics of Empowerment* (Boston, Mass.: Unwin Hyman, 1990); and St. Jean and Feagin, *Double Burden.*

38. Denise A. Segura, "Chicanas and Triple Oppression in the Labor Force," in *Chicana Voices: Intersections of Class, Race, and Gender,* ed. Teresa Cordova et al. (Austin, Tex.: Center for Mexican American Studies, 1986), p. 48.

39. Herbert Blumer, "Race Prejudice as a Sense of Group Position," *The Pacific Sociological Review* 1 (Spring 1959): 3–7; see also Robert Blauner, *Black Lives, White Lives* (Berkeley: University of California Press, 1989); and Feagin and P. Sikes, *Living with Racism.*

40. Feagin and Sikes, *Living with Racism,* p. 54.

41. Our analysis here is inspired by a similar discussion in W. Michael Byrd and Linda A. Clayton, "Race, Medicine, and Health Care in the United States: A Historical Survey," *Journal of the National Medical Association* 93 (March 2001): 254–255.

42. Frederick Douglass, *Narrative of the Life of Frederick Douglass, an American Slave Written by Himself Entered, According to Act of Congress, in the Year 1845* (Clerk's Office of the District Court of Massachusetts, 1845), www.pinkmonkey.com/dl/library1/digi009.pdf (retrieved March 10, 2002), pp. 60–61.

43. Angela Davis, *Women, Race, and Class* (New York: Vintage Books, 1981), p. 29.

44. Douglass, *Narrative of the Life of Frederick Douglass,* p. 68.

45. W. E. B. DuBois, *Darkwater,* as published in Eric Sundquist, ed., *The Oxford W. E. B. Du Bois Reader* (New York: Oxford University Press, 1996), p. 551.

46. Depending on assumptions made about multiple ownership, mortality, marriage, and childbearing patterns, she estimates that somewhere between 20 and 93 million Americans are current beneficiaries of this wealth-generating program. The 46 million figure is in the middle range. Trina Williams, "The Homestead Act—Our Earliest National Asset Policy," paper presented at the Center for Social Development's symposium, "Inclusion in Asset Building," St. Louis, Missouri, September 21–23, 2000.

47. For extensive evidence, see Feagin, *Racist America.*

48. Ibid.

49. James Marketti estimates slave prices and the number of those enslaved for the decades between 1790 and 1860, with allowance for price variations

by age and other status, and uses these figures to estimate the value of slave-holders' income from slaves. He also calculates roughly the value of the diverted labor income (compounded via interest) for later points in time. James Marketti, "Estimated Present Value of Income Diverted during Slavery," in *The Wealth of Races: The Present Value of Benefits from Past Injustices,* ed. Richard F. America (New York: Greenwood Press, 1990), p. 118.

50. See Feagin, *Racist America.*

51. Lawrence D. Bobo and Susan A. Suh, "Surveying Racial Discrimination: Analyses from a Multiethnic Labor Market," in *Prismatic Metropolis: Inequality in Los Angeles*, eds. Lawrence D. Bobo, Melvin L. Oliver, James H. Johnson, Jr., and Abel Valenzuela, Jr. (New York: Russell Sage, 2000), pp. 527–529.

52. Richard Morin and Michael H. Cottman, "Discrimination's Lingering Sting," *Washington Post*, June 22, 2001, p. A1.

53. Jacquelyn Scarville et al., *Armed Forces Equal Opportunity Survey* (Arlington, Va.: Defense Manpower Data Center, 1999), pp. 46–78; Office of the Under Secretary of Defense Personnel and Readiness, *Career Progression of Minority and Women Officers* (Washington, D.C.: Department of Defense, 1999), pp. 46–85.

54. T. A. Forman, D. R. Williams, and J. S. Jackson, "Race, Place, and Discrimination," in *Perspectives on Social Problems*, ed. C. Gardner (New York: JAI Press, 1997), pp. 231–261.

55. American Civil Liberties Union, "ACLU Moves to Have Maryland State Police held in Contempt," Press Release, November 14, 1996, at www.aclu.org/news/n111496a.html (retrieved December 10, 2001).

56. Morin and Cottman, "Discrimination's Lingering Sting."

57. Kathy Ciotola, "Black Tourists Report Discrimination in Study," *Gainesville Sun*, October 2, 2001, pp. B1, B3.

58. Ian Ayres and Joel Waldfogel, "A Market Test for Race Discrimination in Bail Setting," *Stanford Law Review* 46 (May 1994): 993; Ian Ayres, "Fair Driving: Gender and Race Discrimination in Retail Car Negotiations," *Harvard Law Review* 104 (February 1991): 820–830; Kevin A. Schulman et al., "The Effect of Race and Sex on Physicians' Recommendations for Cardiac Catherization," *New England Journal of Medicine* (February 25, 1999): 618–626.

59. See Fair Housing Council of Fresno County, "Audit Uncovers Blatant Discrimination against Hispanics, African Americans, and Families with Children in Fresno County," press release, Fresno, California, October 6, 1997; Central Alabama Fair Housing Center, "Discrimination in the Rental Housing Market: A Study of Montgomery, Alabama, 1995–1996," Montgomery, Alabama, January 13, 1996; Fair Housing Action Center, Inc., "Greater New Orleans Rental Audit," New Orleans, Louisiana, 1996; San Antonio Fair

Housing Council, "San Antonio Metropolitan Area Rental Audit 1997," San Antonio, Texas, 1997; Greater Houston Fair Housing Center, "Houston Rental Audit," Houston Texas, 2001; and Fair Housing Center of Greater Boston, "We Don't Want Your Kind Living Here: A Report on Discrimination in the Greater Boston Rental Market," Boston, April 2001.

60. Michael O. Emerson, George Yancey, and Karen Chai, "Race versus Race-as-Proxy in Residential Segregation: Exploring the Mind's Eye of White Americans," unpublished research paper, Rice University, January 2001, p. 11. The researchers note, too, that finding a pure "race effect" is impossible, because for many whites violent crime and poor schools (two of the control variables) are part of their very mental images of African Americans and African American communities. This negative effect was greatest for whites with young children.

61. Diane R. Brown, Verna M. Keith, and James S. Jackson, "(Dis)respected and (Dis)regarded: Race Discrimination and Mental Health," in D. R. Brown and V. M. Keith, eds., *In and Out of Our Right Minds: African American Women and Mental Health*) (New York: Columbia University Press, forthcoming); see also Melvin L. Oliver and Thomas M. Shapiro, *Black Wealth/White Wealth: A New Perspective on Racial Equality* (New York: Routledge, 1995).

62. See Carole Collins, "U.N. Report on Minorities: U.S. Not Measuring Up," *National Catholic Reporter* (June 18, 1993): 9.

63. *Jones et ux. v. Alfred H. Mayer Co.*, et al., 392 U.S. 409, 445 (1968). Our italics.

64. Joe R. Feagin and Clairece B. Feagin, *Racial and Ethnic Relations*, 7th ed. (Upper Saddle River: Prentice-Hall, 2003), pp. 170–177; William A. Darity, Jr. and Samuel L. Myers, *Persistent Disparity: Race and Economic Inequality in the United States since 1945* (Northampton, Mass.: Edward Elgar, 1998), pp. 7–10; U.S. Bureau of the Census, *Household Wealth and Asset Ownership: 1991*, Current Population Reports P70–34 (Washington, D.C., 1994), pp. xiii–xiv.

65. Studs Terkel, *Race: How Blacks and Whites Think and Feel About the American Obsession* (New York: The New York Press, 1992), p. 97.

66. Ellis Cose, *The Rage of a Privileged Class* (New York: HarperCollins, 1993), p. 1.

67. A. Schultz, B. Israel, D. Williams, E. Parker, A. Becker, and S. James, "Social Inequalities, Stressors, and Self-Reported Health Status among African American and White Women in the Detroit Metropolitan Area," *Social Science and Medicine* 51 (2000): 1639–1653.

68. David R. Williams, Yan Yu, and James Jackson, "The Costs of Racism: Discrimination, Race, and Health," paper presented at joint meeting of Public Health Conference on Records and Statistics and the Data User's Conference, Washington, D.C., July 1997.

69. Tony Brown, David Williams, James Jackson, Harold Neighbors, Myriam Torres, Sherrill L. Sellers, and Kendrick Brown, "Being Black and Feeling Blue: The Mental Health Consequences of Racial Discrimination," *Race and Society* 2 (2000): 117–131.

70. See H. Landrine and E. A. Klonoff, "The Schedule of Racist Events: A Measure of Racial Discrimination and a Study of Its Negative Physical and Mental Health Consequences," *Journal of Black Psychology* 22 (1996): 144–168; and X. S. Ren, B. Amick, and D. R. Williams, "Racial/Ethnic Disparities in Health: The Interplay Between Discrimination and Socioeconomic Status," *Ethnicity and Health* 9 (1999): 151–165.

71. Clark, Anderson, Clark, and Williams, "Racism as a Stressor for African Americans," pp. 805–816.

72. Keith James, "Social Identity, Work Stress, and Minority Workers' Health," in *Job Stress in a Changing Workforce*, eds. Gwendolyn P. Keita and Joseph Hurrell (Washington, D.C.: American Psychological Association, 1994), pp. 127–145.

73. Clark, Anderson, Clark, and Williams, "Racism as a Stressor for African Americans," pp. 811–812.

74. See the summary in Amy Schultz, David Williams, Barbara Israel, Adam Becker, Edith Parker, Sherman A. James, and James Jackson, "Unfair Treatment, Neighborhood Effects, and Mental Health in the Detroit Metropolitan Area," *Journal of Health and Social Behavior* 41 (September 2000): 314–332.

75. Feagin and Sikes, *Living with Racism*, p. 16.

76. Ibid.

77. Ibid., pp. 295–296.

78. William James, *The Principles of Psychology*, vol. 2 (New York: Henry Holt, 1890), p. 430.

79. Gunnar Myrdal, *An American Dilemma*, vol. 2 (New York: McGraw-Hill, 1964 [1944]), pp. 57–59 and passim; also see Robert H. Lauer and Warren H. Handel, *Social Psychology: The Theory and Application of Symbolic Interactionism* (Boston: Houghton Mifflin, 1977), p. 330.

80. Howard P. Ramseur, "Psychologically Healthy Black Adults," in *Black Psychology*, ed. Reginald Jones, 3d ed. (Berkeley, Calif.: Cobb & Henry, 1991), p. 355.

81. The participants included a dental assistant, several nurses, a community health specialist, a psychologist, a counselor, several government administrators, a planner, a social services coordinator, a sheriff, postal service managers, teachers, a college admissions advisor, a college residential coordinator, two

college students, several secretaries, a purchasing agent, and several corporate managers and engineers. Three held skilled blue-collar jobs. We used black moderators to conduct the focus groups. We are indebted to John McKnight and Kevin Early for moderating the groups.

82. For more details on the interview study, see Feagin and Sikes, *Living with Racism,* chapter 1. We use portions of the individual interviews in this book that are not generally quoted or analyzed in the earlier book.

83. Some quotes have been lightly edited for stutter words, spoken grammar, and anonymity. We have deleted some filler words like "you know" and "uh" and changed a few spoken words to their standard written forms. We have kept respondents anonymous by deleting or disguising names and places.

84. *See* Anthony J. Marsellas, "Work and Well-Being in an Ethnoculturally Pluralistic Society: Conceptual and Methodological Issues," in *Job Stress in a Changing Workplace,* eds. Gwendolyn P. Keita and Joseph J. Hurrell (Washington, D.C.: American Psychological Association, 1994), pp. 147–160; Sharon Collins, "Blacks on the Bubble: The Vulnerability of Black Executives in White Corporations," *Sociological Quarterly* 34 (August 1993): 429–447.

85. Susan D. Toliver, *Black Families in Corporate America* (Thousand Oaks, Calif.: Sage, 1998), p. 8.

86. James C. Quick, Lawrence R. Murphy, Joseph J. Hurrell, Jr., and Dusty Orman, "The Value of Work, the Risk of Distress, and the Power of Prevention," in *Stress and Well-Being at Work: Assessments and Interventions for Occupational Mental Health,* eds. J. C. Quick, L. R. Murphy, and J. J. Hurrell (Washington, D.C.: American Psychological Association, 1992), p. 4.

87. Mitchell Duneier, *Slim's Table: Race, Respectability, and Masculinity* (Chicago: University of Chicago Press, 1992).

2 Workplace Discrimination: The Social Generation of Anger and Rage

1. See Jock McCulloch, *Black Soul, White Artifact: Fanon's Clinical Psychology and Social Theory* (New York: Cambridge University Press, 1983), pp. 126–127.

2. William E. B. DuBois, *The Souls of Black Folk* (New York: Bantam Books, 1989 [1903]), pp. 7–9.

3. Dinesh D'Souza, *The End of Racism: Principles for a Multiracial Society* (New York: Free Press, 1995), p. 491.

4. bell hooks, *Killing Rage: Ending Racism* (New York: H. Holt and Company, 1995), p. 12.

5. Ibid., p. 14.

6. Ibid., p. 20.

7. Frances Terrell and Sandra Terrell, "An Inventory to Measure Cultural Mistrust Among Blacks," *The Western Journal of Black Studies* 5 (1981): 180–185.

8. Chalmer E. Thompson, Helen Neville, Pamela L. Weathers, W. Carlos Poston, and Donald R. Atkinson, "Cultural Mistrust and Racism Reaction Among African-American Students," *Journal of College Student Development* 31 (1990): 162–168.

9. Charles R. Ridley, "Clinical Treatment of the Nondisclosing Black Client," *American Psychologist* 39 (1984): 1234–1244.

10. See Ezra E. H. Griffith and F. M. Baker, "Psychiatric Care of African Americans," in *Culture, Ethnicity, and Mental Illness*, ed. Albert C. Gaw (Washington, D.C.: American Psychiatric Press, 1993), pp.147–173; Billy E. Jones and Beverly A. Gray, "Problems in Diagnosing Schizophrenia and Affective Disorders Among Blacks," *Hospital and Community Psychiatry* 37 (1986): 61–65; S. I. Abramowitz and Joan Murray, "Race Effects in Psychotherapy," in *Bias in Psychotherapy*, eds. Joan Murray and Paul R. Abramson (New York: Praeger, 1983), pp. 215–255; Raymond M. Costello, "Construction and Cross-Validation of an MMPI Black-White Scale," *Journal of Personality Assessment* 41 (1977): 514–519; Jerome M. Sattler, "The Effects of Therapist-Client Racial Similarity," in *Effective Psychotherapy: A Handbook of Research,* eds. Alan S. Gurman and Andrew M. Razin (New York: Pergamon Press, 1977), pp. 151–190.

11. "[Interview with] Laurence Thomas," in *African-American Philosophers: Seventeen Conversations*, ed. George Yancey (New York: Routledge, 1998), p. 298.

12. See, e.g., Sara E. Gutierres, Delia S. Saenz, and Beth L. Green, "Job Stress and Health Outcomes among White and Hispanic Employees," in *Job Stress in a Changing Workforce*, eds. Gwendolyn P. Keita and Joseph J. Hurrell (Washington, D.C.: American Psychological Association, 1994), pp. 107–125.

13. See ibid., pp. 107–125; Anthony J. Marsella, "Work and Well-Being in an Ethnoculturally Pluralistic Society: Conceptual and Methodological Issues," in *Job Stress in a Changing Workforce*, eds. Gwendolyn P. Keita and Joseph J. Hurrell (Washington, D.C.: American Psychological Association, 1994), pp. 147–160.

14. See Vickie M. Mays, Lerida M. Coleman, and James S. Jackson, "Perceived Race-Based Discrimination, Employment Status, and Job Stress in a National Sample of Black Women: Implications for Health Outcomes," *Journal of Occupational Health Psychology* 1 (3) (1996): 319–329; Charles B.

Wilkinson and Jeanne Spurlock, "Mental Health of Black Americans: Psychiatric Diagnosis and Treatment," in *Ethnic Psychiatry*, ed. Charles B. Wilkinson (New York: Plenum Medical Book Company, 1986) pp. 13–50; Jewelle Taylor Gibbs and Diana Fuery, "Mental Health and Well-Being of Black Women: Toward Strategies of Empowerment," *American Journal of Community Psychology* 22 (1994): 559–582; Ezra E. H. Griffith and F. M. Baker, "Psychiatric Care of African Americans," in *Culture, Ethnicity, and Mental Illness*, ed. Albert C. Gaw (Washington, D.C.: American Psychiatric Press, 1993), pp. 147–173; and Tony R. Brown et al., "'Being Black and Feeling Blue': The Mental Health Consequences of Racial Discrimination," *Race & Society* 2 (2000): 117–119.

15. See James S. Jackson and Sherrill L. Sellers, "African-American Health over the Life Course: A Multidimensional Framework," in *Handbook of Diversity Issues in Health Psychology*, eds. Pamela M Kato and Traci Mann (New York: Plenum Press, 1996), pp. 301–317; James S. Jackson and Monica L. Wolford, "Changes from 1980 to 1987 in Mental Health Status and Help-Seeking among African Americans," *Journal of Geriatric Psychiatry* 25 (1992): 15–67.

16. James Baldwin, *Notes of a Native Son* (Boston: Beacon Press, 1955), p. 95.

17. William H. Grier and Price M. Cobbs, *Black Rage* (New York: Basic Books, 1968).

18. Ibid., p. 4.

19. See Price M. Cobbs, "Critical Perspectives on the Psychology of Race," in *The State of Black America: 1988*, ed. J. Dewart (New York: National Urban League, 1988), pp. 61–70.

20. See John Mirowsky and Catherine Ross, *Social Causes of Psychological Distress* (New York: Aldine de Gruyter, 1989); James C. Quick, Lawrence R. Murphy, Joseph J. Hurrell, Jr., and Dusty Orman, "The Value of Work, the Risk of Distress, and the Power of Prevention," in *Stress and Well-Being at Work: Assessments and Interventions for Occupational Mental Health*, eds. J. C. Quick, L. R. Murphy, and J. J. Hurrell (Washington, D.C.: American Psychological Association, 1992) pp. 4ff.

21. M. M. Manring, *Slave in a Box: The Strange Career of Aunt Jemima* (Charlottesville, Va.: University Press of Virginia, 1998), pp. 6–8.

22. Irving Lewis Allen, *Unkind Words: Ethnic Labeling from Redskin to WASP* (New York: Bergin and Garvey, 1990), pp. 29, 49.

23. Thomas Fields-Meyer, Bob Stewart, Michelle McCalope and Michael Haederle, "One Deadly Night; Deep in the Woods of East Texas, James Byrd Died a Terrible Death, Leaving a Town and a Nation in Shock," *People*, June 29, 1998, p. 46.

24. Howard Chua-Eoan and Hilary Hylton/Austin "Beneath The Surface; A 'New South' Town is Haunted by 'Deep South' Ghosts—And a Fresh, Ugly Murder," *Time*, June 22, 1998, p. 34.

25. James Byrd, Jr.'s sister and others have created a foundation to work actively against such hate crimes. The foundation's Web address is www.byrdfoundation.org.

26. Sharon Waxman, "White and Black and Blue; Documentary about Texas Lynching Proves 'Bruising' to Creators' Friendship," *Washington Post*, January 22, 2002, p. C1.

27. See Frantz Fanon, *Black Skin, White Masks* (New York: Grove Press, 1967). Some whites who are parents of African American children face similar circumstances and often develop important insights into dealing with the discrimination their children face. See, for example, Sharon Rush, *Loving Across the Color Line* (Lanham, Md.: Rowman & Littlefield, 2000); and Jane Lazarre, *Beyond the Whiteness of Whiteness* (Durham, N.C.: Duke University Press, 1996).

28. See, e.g., F. M. Baker, "The Afro-American Life Cycle: Success, Failure, and Mental Health," *Journal of the National Medical Association* 79 (1987): 625–633.

29. Robert Karasek and Tores Theorell, *Healthy Work* (New York: Basic Books, 1990), pp. 69–72; John Mirowsky and Catherine E. Ross, "The Consolation-Prize Theory of Alienation," *American Journal of Sociology* 95 (1990): 1505–1535; Catherine E. Ross and John Mirowsky, "Households, Employment, and the Sense of Control," *Social Psychology Quarterly* 55 (1992): 217–235.

30. William A. Darity, Jr. and Samuel L. Myers, *Persistent Disparity: Race and Economic Inequality in the United States Since 1945* (Northampton, Mass.: Edward Elgar, 1998) pp. 7–10; see also Melvin L. Oliver and Thomas M. Shapiro, *Black Wealth/White Wealth: A New Perspective on Racial Equality* (New York: Routledge, 1995).

31. Philomena Essed, *Everyday Racism: Reports from Women of Two Cultures* (Claremont: Hunter House, 1990); Joe R. Feagin and Melvin P. Sikes, *Living with Racism: The Black Middle Class Experience* (Boston: Beacon Press, 1994); James S. Jackson and Marita R. Inglehart, "Reverberation Theory: Stress and Racism in Hierarchically Structured Communities," in *Extreme Stress and Communities: Impact and Intervention*, eds. Stevan E. Hobfoll and Marten W. deVries (Boston, Mass.: Kluwer Academic Publishers, 1995) pp. 353–373.

32. Robert N. Bellah, Richard Madsen, William M. Sullivan, Ann Swidler, and Steven M. Tipton, *Habits of the Heart: Individualism and Commitment in*

American Life (Berkeley: University of California Press, 1985), p. 153.

33. Ibid., p. 157.

34. Feagin and Sikes, *Living with Racism*, p. 294.

35. Lydia Rappoport, "The State of Crisis: Some Theoretical Considerations," in *Crisis Intervention: Selected Readings*, ed. Howard J. Parad (New York: Family Service Association, 1965), pp. 22–31; Karasek and Theorell, *Healthy Work*, p. 71.

36. Mirowsky and Ross, *Social Causes of Psychological Distress*.

37. Hortensia Amaro, Nancy F. Russo, and Julie Johnson, "Family and Work Predictors of Psychological Well-Being among Hispanic Women Professionals," *Psychology of Women Quarterly* 11 (1987): 505–521; V. Nelly Salgado de Snyder, "Factors Associated with Acculturative Stress and Depressive Symptomology among Married Mexican Immigrant Women," *Psychology of Women Quarterly* 11 (1987): 475–488; see, e.g., Gutierres, Saenz, and Green, "Job Stress and Health Outcomes among White and Hispanic Employees," pp. 107–125.

38. David R. Williams and An-Me Chung, "Racism and Health," in *Health in Black America*, eds. Rose C. Gibson and James S. Jackson (Newbury Park, Calif.: Sage, 1995).

39. See Linda M. Chatters and James S. Jackson, "Quality of Life and Subjective Well-Being among Black Americans," in *Black Adult Development and Aging*, ed. Reginald L. Jones (Berkeley, Calif.: Cobb and Henry, 1989), pp. 191–213; James S. Jackson and Sherrill L. Sellers, "Psychological, Social, and Cultural Perspectives on Minority Health in Adolescence: A Life-Course Framework," in *Health-Promoting and Health Compromising Behaviors among Minority Adolescents*, eds. Dawn K. Wilson, James R. Rodrigue, and Wendell C. Taylor (Washington, D.C.: American Psychological Association, 1997), pp. 29–49.

40. Karasek and Theorell, *Healthy Work;* Sherman A. James, Andrea Z. Lacroix, David G. Kleinbaum, and David S. Strogatz, "John Henryism and Blood Pressure Differences among Black Men: The Role of Occupational Stressors," *Journal of Behavioral Medicine* 7 (3) (1984): 259–275. On white attitudes about black employees and students, see Joe R. Feagin, Hérnan Vera, and Pinar Batur, *White Racism: The Basics*, 2d. ed. (New York: Routledge, 2001) and Joe R. Feagin, Hernán Vera, and Nikitah Imani, *The Agony of Education* (New York: Routledge, 1996).

41. See Robert Joseph Taylor et al., "Changes Over Time in Support Network Involvement among Black Americans," in *Family Life in Black America*, eds. Robert Joseph Taylor, James S. Jackson, and Linda M. Chatters (Thousand Oaks, Calif.: Sage, 1997), pp. 293–316; William W. Dressler,

"Extended Family Relationships, Social Support, and Mental Health in a Southern Black Community," *Journal of Health and Social Behavior* 26 (1985): 39–48; Ezra E. H. Griffith and F. M. Baker, "Psychiatric Care of African Americans," in *Culture, Ethnicity, and Mental Illness*, ed. Albert C. Gaw (Washington, D.C.: American Psychiatric Press, 1993), pp. 147–173.

42. James S. Coleman, "Human Capital and Social Capital," in *Social Theory: Roots and Branches*, ed. Peter Kivisto (Los Angeles, Calif.: Roxbury, 2000), p. 297.

43. See, for example, Carmenza Gallo, "The Construction Industry in New York City: Immigrant and Black Entrepreneurs," unpublished working manuscript, Conservation of Human Resources Project (New York: Columbia University, 1983).

44. Feagin and Sikes, *Living with Racism*, pp. 295–296.

45. Diane R. Brown, Verna M. Keith, and James S. Jackson, "(Dis)respected and (Dis)regarded: Race Discrimination and Mental Health," in D. R. Brown and V. M. Keith, eds., *In and Out of Our Right Minds: African American Women and Mental Health* (New York: Columbia University Press, forthcoming.)

46. See Essed, *Everyday Racism*; Lois Benjamin, *The Black Elite* (Chicago: Nelson-Hall, 1991); Feagin and Sikes, *Living with Racism*.

47. DuBois, *The Souls of Black Folk*, p. 3.

48. Kelly M. Barlow, Donald M. Taylor, and Wallace E. Lambert, "Ethnicity in America and Feeling 'American'," *Journal of Psychology* 134 (November 2000): 581–600.

49. We draw here on Joe R. Feagin, *Racist America: Roots, Current Realities, and Future Reparations* (New York: Routledge, 2000), pp. 192–194.

3   The Physical Health Consequences of Racism

1. Megan Garvey, "Federal Health Survey Finds Racial Gaps; Study: Disparities between Whites and Minorities Narrow but Persist in Many Cases, Researchers Report," *Los Angeles Times*, January 25, 2002, p. A16.

2. "Racial Disparities in Medical Care," *The New England Journal of Medicine* 344 (19) (May 10, 2001): 1471–1473.

3. John A. Rich, "The Health of African American Men," *Annals of the American Academy of Political and Social Science* 569 (2000): 149–160.

4. See David R. Williams and Chiquita Collins, "U.S. Socioeconomic and Racial Differences in Health: Patterns and Explanations," *Annual Review of Sociology* 21 (1995): 349–387.

5. Williams and Collins, "U.S. Socioeconomic and Racial Differences in Health."

6. Linda A. Clayton and W. Michael Byrd, "Race: A Major Health Status and Outcome Variable 1980–1999," *Journal of the National Medical Association* 93 (March, 2001): 395.

7. See Linda Chatters, "Physical Health," in *Life in Black America*, ed. James S. Jackson, (Newbury Park, Calif.: Sage, 1991), pp. 199–220; Wornie L. Reed, William Darity, Sr., Stanford Roman, Claudia Baquet, and Noma L. Roberson, "Cross-Cutting Issues in the Health of African-Americans," in *The Health and Medical Care of African-Americans*, ed. Wornie L. Reed, (Boston: William Monroe Trotter Institute, University of Massachusetts at Boston, 1992), pp. 155–158.

8. Linda A. Clayton and W. Michael Byrd, "The African American Cancer Crisis, Part I: The Problem," *Journal of Health Care for the Poor and Underserved* 4 (1993): 85.

9. Reed, Darity, Roman, Baquet, and Roberson, "Cross-Cutting Issues."

10. See Williams and Collins, "U.S. Socioeconomic and Racial Differences in Health."

11. "Racist Slights That Blacks Face Every Day are Linked to Higher Illness Rates," *Jet*, October 20, 1997, p. 24.

12. Reed, Darity, Roman, Baquet, and Roberson, "Cross-Cutting Issues."

13. See Frank Michel, "Racism Can be Cancer on the Health System," *Houston Chronicle* September 21, 1998, p. 18.

14. Camara P. Jones, quoted on radio broadcast "NPR Weekend," October 31, 1998, Transcript # 98103106-214, Frank Browning, moderator; see also Camara P. Jones, T. A. LaVeist, and M. Lillie-Blanton, "'Race' in the Epidemiologic Literature: An Examination of the American Journal of Epidemiology, 1921–1990," *American Journal of Epidemiology* 134 (1991): 1079–1084.

15. Jones, quoted on "NPR Weekend," October 31, 1998.

16. "Racist Slights," p. 24. This reports a study by David R. Williams and associates.

17. Linda A. Clayton and W. Michael Byrd, personal communication, February 19, 2002; see also Chatters, "Physical Health."

18. Chatters, "Physical Health."

19. See also John Mirowsky and Catherine E. Ross, *Social Causes of Psychological Distress* (New York: Aldine de Gruyter, 1989), p. 21; Keith James, "Social Identity, Work Stress, and Minority Workers' Health," in *Job Stress in a Changing Workforce*, eds. Gwendolyn P. Keith and Joseph J. Hurrell (Washington, D.C.: American Psychological Association, 1994), pp. 127–145.

20. Jewelle Taylor Gibbs, "Anger in Young Black Males: Victims or Victimizers?" in *The American Black Male*, eds. Richard G. Majors and Jacob U.

Gordon (Chicago: Nelson-Hall, 1994), pp. 127–143.

21. Yanick St. Jean and Joe Feagin, *Double Burden: Black Women and Everyday Racism* (Armonk, N.Y.: M. E. Sharpe, 1998), p. 203.

22. Ann M. Gerber, Sherman A. James, Alice S. Ammerman, Nora L. Keenan, Joanne M. Garrett, David S. Strogatz, and Pamela Haines, "Socioeconomic Status and Electrolyte Intake in Black Adults: The Pitt County Study," *The American Journal of Public Health* 81 (1991): 1608–1613; see also Reed, Darity, Roman, Baquet, and Roberson, "Cross-Cutting Issues"; and Alphonso Pinkney, *Black Americans* (Englewood Cliffs, N.J.: Prentice Hall, 1993).

23. See George D. Smith, James D. Neaton, Deborah Wentworth, Rose Stamler, and Jeremiah Stamler, "Mortality Differences between Black and White Men in the USA: Contribution of Income and Other Risk Factors Among Men Screened for the MRFIT," *The Lancet* 351 (1998): 934–939.

24. James, "Social Identity, Work Stress, and Minority Workers' Health;" Sherman A. James, Andrea Z. Lacroix, David G. Kleinbaum, and David Strogatz, "John Henryism and Blood Pressure Differences among Black Men: The Role of Occupational Stressors," *Journal of Behavioral Medicine* 7 (3) (1984): 259–275; Norman B. Anderson, "Racial Differences in Stress-Induced Cardiovascular Reactivity and Hypertension," *Psychological Bulletin* 105 (1989): 89–105.

25. See James, "Social Identity."

26. Nancy Krieger and Stephen Sidney, "Racial Discrimination and Blood Pressure: The CARDIA Study of Young Black and White Adults," *American Journal of Public Health* 86 (1996): 1370–1378.

27. Nancy Krieger, "Racial and Gender Discrimination: Risk Factors for High Blood Pressure?" *Social Science and Medicine* 30 (1990): 1273–1281.

28. Barbee C. Myers, "Hypertension as a Manifestation of the Stress Experienced by Black Families," in *Black Families: Interdisciplinary Perspectives*, eds. Harold E. Cheatham and James B. Stewart (New Brunswick, N.J.: Transaction Publishers, 1990), p. 211.

29. James, Lacroix, Kleinbaum, and Strogatz, "John Henryism."

30. Michelle Marble, "Jobs May Raise Blood Pressure in Women and African-Americans, But Not Caucasian," *Women's Health Weekly,* April 3, 1995, pp. 12–14.

31. Amy B. Curtis, Sherman A. James, Trivellore E. Raghunathan, and Kirsten H. Alcser, "Job Strain and Blood Pressure in African Americans: The Pitt County Study," *American Journal of Public Health* 187 (1997): 1297–1303; see also James, Lacroix, Kleinbaum, and Strogatz, "John Henryism."

32. See Sharon M. Collins, "Blacks on the Bubble: The Vulnerability of Black Executives in White Corporations," *Sociological Quarterly* 34 (August

1993): 429–447; and Sharon M. Collins, *Black Corporate Executives: The Making and Breaking of a Black Middle Class* (Philadelphia, Pa.: Temple University Press, 1997).

33. Philomena Essed, *Everyday Racism: Reports from Women of Two Cultures* (Claremont, Calif.: Hunter House, 1990); Ellis Cose, *The Rage of a Privileged Class* (New York: Harper Collins, 1993).

34. Bari-Ellen Roberts, *Roberts v. Texaco: A True Story of Race and Corporate America* (New York: Avon Books, 1998), pp. 1, 283.

35. Kurt Eichenwald, "The Two Faces Of Texaco," *New York Times*, November 10, 1996, section 3, p. 1.

36. Joel Kovel, *White Racism: A Psychohistory*, rev. ed. (New York: Columbia University Press, 1984).

37. See Feagin and Sikes, *Living with Racism*, especially chapter 2; Joe R. Feagin, Hernan Vera, and Nikitah Imani, *The Agony of Education: Black Students in White Colleges and Universities* (New York: Routledge, 1996).

38. Kovel, *White Racism*, pp. xli–xlvii.

39. Reed, Darity, Roman, Baquet, and Roberson, "Cross-Cutting Issues."

40. Ibid.

41. Jacqueline A. Walcott-McQuigg and Judith Sullivan, "Psychosocial Factors Influencing Weight Control Behavior of African American Women," *Western Journal of Nursing Research* 17 (5) (1995): 502–521.

42. Ibid.

4 The Family and Community Costs of Racism

1. Bertell Ollman, *Alienation: Marx's Conception of Man in Capitalist Society*, 2d ed. (Cambridge: Cambridge University Press, 1976), p. 18.

2. Jerold Heiss, *The Case of the Black Family: A Sociological Inquiry* (New York: Columbia University Press, 1975).

3. E. Franklin Frazier, *The Negro in the United States* (New York: Macmillan, 1957), p. 636.

4. Daniel P. Moynihan, *The Negro Family: The Case for National Action* (Washington, D.C.: U.S. Department of Labor, 1965).

5. Ibid, p. 30.

6. See Robert B. Hill, *The Strengths of Black Families* (New York: Emerson, 1971); Heiss, *The Case of the Black Family*.

7. This term was first coined by Oscar Lewis to refer to Mexicans, in Oscar Lewis, *The Children of Sanchez* (New York: Random House, 1961). He later applied the term to Puerto Ricans. Lewis saw the "culture of poverty," at least

in part, as a response to oppressive circumstances. It was Moynihan and others who later applied the term to black Americans and used it in more of a victim-blaming manner.

8. See Joe R. Feagin, *Subordinating the Poor* (Englewood Cliffs, N.J.: Prentice Hall, 1975); and Lawrence Bobo, "Inequalities that Endure?: Racial Ideology, American Politics, and the Peculiar Role of the Social Sciences," paper presented at conference "The Changing Terrain of Race and Ethnicity," University of Illinois, Chicago, Illinois, October 26, 2001.

9. Robert Staples and Leanor Boulin Johnson, *Black Families at the Crossroads: Challenges and Prospects* (San Francisco: Jossey-Bass Publishers, 1993), p. 194.

10. Ibid.

11. Ibid.

12. Andrew Billingsley, *Black Families in White America* (Englewood Cliffs, N.J.: Prentice Hall, 1968); see Susan D. Toliver, *Black Families in Corporate America* (Thousand Oaks, Calif.: Sage Publications, 1998), pp. 23–25 for a review of this body of research.

13. Robert B. Hill, *The Strengths of African American Families: Twenty-Five Years Later* (Lanham, Md.: University Press of America, 1999).

14. Hill, *The Strengths of Black Families*, p. 10.

15. Ibid., p. 20.

16. Ibid., p. 7; Staples and Johnson, *Black Families at the Crossroads*, p. 202.

17. Hill, *The Strengths of Black Families*, p. 31.

18. Ibid., p. 33.

19. William W. Dressler, *Stress and Adaptation in the Context of Culture: Depression in a Southern Black Community* (Albany, N.Y.: State University of New York Press, 1991).

20. Staples and Johnson, *Black Families at the Crossroads*, pp. 211–217.

21. E. H. Hall and G. C. King, 1982, quoted in Toliver, *Black Families in Corporate America*, p. 27.

22. Bob Blauner, *Black Lives, White Lives: Three Decades of Race Relations in America* (Berkeley: University of California Press, 1989), p. 305.

23. Dressler, *Stress and Adaptation in the Context of Culture*, p. 126.

24. Howard P. Ramseur, "Psychologically Healthy Black Adults," in Black Psychology, ed. Reginald Jones, 3d. ed. (Berkeley, Calif.: Cobb & Henry, 1991), p. 355.

25. Joanne M. Martin and Elmer P. Martin, *The Helping Tradition in the Black Family and Community* (Washington, D.C.: National Association of Social Workers, 1985), pp. 91–96; Paul Martin DuBois, Jacquelyn Madry-Taylor,

Robert L. Green, George E. Ayers, Marilyn Melkonian, and Roscoe Ellis, *Repairing the Breach: Key Ways to Support Family Life, Reclaim Our Streets, and Rebuild Civil Society in America's Communities* (report of the National Task Force on African-American Men and Boys, Andrew J. Young, chairman, Bobby William Austin, editor) (Dillon, Colo.: Alpine Guild, Inc., 1996), p. 84.

26. DuBois, Madry-Taylor, Green, Ayers, Melkonian, and Ellis, *Repairing the Breach*, p. 84; Martin and Martin, *The Helping Tradition*, pp. 5, 36.

27. See Joe R. Feagin and Clairece B. Feagin, *Racial and Ethnic Relations* 7th ed. (Upper Saddle River, N.J.: Prentice-Hall, 2003), chapter 1.

28. Harrison Y. Smith, "Building on the Strengths of Black Families: Self-Help and Empowerment," in *The Black Family: Strengths, Self-Help, and Positive Change* , ed. Sadye L. M. Logan (Boulder, Colo.: Westview, 2001), p. 27.

29. Quoted in Sadye L. Logan, "Strengthening Family Ties: Working with Black Female Single-Parent Families," in *The Black Family*, p. 164.

30. Ibid., 170.

31. Sidney Willhelm, *Who Needs the Negro?* (Cambridge: Schenkman, 1970), p. 250.

32. Robert B. Hill, "Economic Forces, Structural Discrimination, and Black Family Instability," in *Black Families: Interdisciplinary Perspectives*, eds. Harold E. Cheatham and James B. Stewart (New Brunswick, N.J.: Transaction Publishers, 1990), pp. 87–105, specifically p. 92.

33. Ibid., p. 94.

34. Ibid., p. 97.

35. Robert B. Hill with Andrew Billingsley, Eleanor Engram, Michelene R. Malson, Roger H. Rubin, Carol B. Stack, James B. Stewart, and James E. Teele, *Research on the African American Family: A Holistic Perspective* (Westport, Conn.: Auburn House, 1993). This report was prepared under the auspices of the William Monroe Trotter Institute, University of Massachusetts at Boston, with Wornie L. Reed as general editor.

36. Ibid.

37. Martin and Martin, *The Helping Tradition*, p. 84; see Hill, "Economic Forces" for a general discussion of intended and unintended consequences of government policies.

38. Hill, "Economic Forces," pp. 97–98; Ruth G. McRoy, "Racial Identity Issues for Black Children in Foster Care," in *The Black Family: Strengths, Self-Help, and Positive Change*, ed. Sayde L. M. Logan (Boulder, Colo.: Westview Press, 2001), pp. 131–143.

39. Hill, "Economic Forces," pp. 97–98; Hill et al., *Research on the African American Family,* p. 58.

40. McRoy, "Racial Identity Issues," p. 139.

41. Staples and Johnson, *Black Families at the Crossroads,* p. 205.

42. Brenda H. Crawley, "Effective Programs and Services for African American Families and Children: An African-Centered Perspective," in *The Black Family: Strengths, Self-Help, and Positive Change,* ed. Sayde L. M. Logan (Boulder, Colo.: Westview Press, 2001), pp. 112–130.

43. David L. Dudley, *My Father's Shadow: Intergenerational Conflict in African American Men's Autobiography* (Philadelphia: University of Pennsylvania Press, 1991), pp. 110–111.

44. James Baldwin, from *Notes from a Native Son,* excerpted in *Modern American Memoirs,* eds. Annie Dillard and Cort Conley (New York: Harper Perennial, 1995), p. 250.

45. Baldwin, pp. 250–251. Italics added.

46. Toi Derricotte, *The Black Notebooks: An Interior Journey* (New York: Norton, 1997), p. 13.

47. Ibid., pp. 44–45.

48. Ibid., pp. 46–47.

49. Ibid., p. 50.

50. Ibid., pp. 33–55.

51. Toliver, *Black Families in Corporate America,* p. 56.

52. Ibid., pp. 61–62.

53. Ibid., p. 62.

54. Blauner, *Black Lives, White Lives,* p. 183.

55. Arthur J. Norton and Louisa F. Miller, *Marriage, Divorce, and Remarriage in the 1990s* (U.S. Department of Commerce, 1992) pp. 3–5.

56. See, e.g., Moynihan, *The Negro Family.*

57. Leanor Boulin Johnson, "The Employed Black: The Dynamics of Work-Family Tension," in *Black Families: Interdisciplinary Perspectives,* eds. Harold E. Cheatham and James B. Stewart (New Brunswick, N.J.: Transaction Publishers, 1990), pp. 217–233.

58. Blauner, *Black Lives, White Lives,* p. 280.

59. bell hooks and Cornel West, *Breaking Bread: Insurgent Black Intellectual Life* (Boston: South End Press, 1991), p. 18.

60. Ibid., p. 19.

61. See Susan L. Smith, *Sick and Tired of Being Sick and Tired: Black Women's Health Activism in America, 1890–1950* (Philadelphia: University of Pennsylvania Press, 1995).

5 Fighting and Managing Everyday Racism: An Array of Strategies

1. Adrian Piper, "Passing for White, Passing for Black," *Transition* 58 (1992); on developing a shield, See Joe R. Feagin and Melvin P. Sikes, *Living with Racism: The Black Middle Class Experience* (Boston: Beacon Press, 1994), pp. 272–294.

2. Robert Karasek and Tores Theorell, *Healthy Work* (New York: Basic Books, 1990); Shawn O. Utsey and Joseph Ponterotto, "Racial Discrimination, Coping, Life Satisfaction, and Self-Esteem among African Americans," *Journal of Counseling and Development* 78 (1) (2000): 72–81.

3. Alexander Thomas and Samuel Sillen, *Racism and Psychiatry* (Secaucus, N.J.: Citadel Press, 1974).

4. See Joe R. Feagin, "The Continuing Significance of Race: Anti-Black Discrimination in Public Places," *American Sociological Review* 56 (1991): 101–116.

5. See Feagin and Sikes, *Living with Racism*, p. 281 and passim.

6. See John Mirowsky and Catherine Ross, *Social Causes of Psychological Distress* (New York: Aldine de Gruyter, 1989), p. 144.

7. Feagin and Sikes, *Living with Racism*, p. 295.

8. Gallup, *Black/White Relations in the United States* (Princeton, N.J.: The Gallup Organization, 1997), pp. 29–30, 108–110.

9. Joe R. Feagin, *Racist America: Roots, Current Realities, and Future Reparations* (New York: Routledge: 2000), p. 143.

10. Feagin and Sikes, *Living with Racism*, pp. 276–277.

11. Sherman A. James, Andrea Z. Lacroix, David G. Kleinbaum, and David Strogatz, "John Henryism and Blood Pressure Differences among Black Men: The Role of Occupational Stressors," *Journal of Behavioral Medicine* 7 (3) (1984): 259–275.

12. Barbee C. Myers, "Hypertension as a Manifestation of the Stress Experienced by Black Families," in *Black Families: Interdisciplinary Perspectives*, eds. Harold E. Cheatham and James B. Stewart (New Brunswick, N.J.: Transaction Publishers, 1990), pp. 211–212.

13. Dinesh D'Souza, *The End of Racism: Principles for a Multiracial Society* (New York: Free Press, 1995), p. 487.

14. David R. Williams and Ruth Williams-Morris, "Racism and Mental Health: The African American Experience," *Ethnicity and Health* 5 (August 2000): 243–246; and Claude M. Steele and Joshua Aronson, "Stereotype Threat and the Intellectual Test Performance of African Americans," *Journal of Personality and Social Psychology* 69 (1995): 797–811.

15. See Robert Joseph Taylor et al., "Changes Over Time in Support Network Involvement among Black Americans," in *Family Life in Black America*, eds. Robert Joseph Taylor, James S. Jackson, and Linda M. Chatters, (Thousand Oaks, Calif: Sage, 1997), pp. 293–316; William W. Dressler, "Extended Family Relationships, Social Support, and Mental Health in a Southern Black Community," *Journal of Health and Social Behavior* 26 (1985): 39–48; Ezra E. H. Griffith and F. M. Baker, "Psychiatric Care of African Americans," in *Culture, Ethnicity, and Mental Illness*, ed. Albert C. Gaw (Washington, D.C.: American Psychiatric Press, 1993), pp. 147–173.

16. Anita Underwood, "Coping With On-The-Job Stress," *Black Enterprise* 23 (1) (1992): 86–89.

17. Yanick St. Jean and Joe R. Feagin, *Double Burden: Black Women and Everyday Racism* (Armonk, N.Y.: M. E. Sharpe, 1998).

18. See David R. Williams, David T. Takeuchi, and Russell K. Adair, "Marital Status and Psychiatric Disorder among Blacks and Whites," *Journal of Health and Social Behavior* 33 (1992): 140–157; Harold W. Neighbors, "Mental Health," in *Life in Black America*, ed. James S. Jackson (Newbury Park, Calif.: Sage, 1991), pp. 221–237.

19. See Linda K. Sussman, "Treatment-Seeking for Depression by Black and White Americans," *Social Science and Medicine* 24 (1987): 187–196.

20. See Griffith and Baker, "Psychiatric Care of African Americans;" Jewelle Taylor Gibbs and Diana Fuery, "Mental Health and Well-Being of Black Women: Toward Strategies of Empowerment," *American Journal of Community Psychology* 22 (1994): 559–582.

21. Harold W. Neighbors, "Mental Health," in *Life in Black America*, ed. James S. Jackson, (Newbury Park: Sage, 1991), pp. 221–237; Griffith and Baker, "Psychiatric Care of African Americans"; Danielle Watts-Jones, "Toward a Stress Scale for African American Women," *Psychology of Women Quarterly* 14 (1990): 271–275.

6 Combating Racism: Active Behavioral Strategies

1. See Joe R. Feagin, *Racist America: Roots, Current Realities, and Future Reparations* (New York: Routledge, 2000), pp. 112–113.

2. John Hope Franklin, C. Eric Lincoln, Alvin F. Poussaint, Gaynelle Griffin Jones, and Anita L. Allen, "Black Scholars Recall Racism from Their Undergraduate Years," *Journal of Blacks in Higher Education* 14 (1996): 101–103.

3. "[Interview with] Laurence Thomas," in *African-American Philosophers: Seventeen Conversations*, ed. George Yancey (New York: Routledge, 1998), p. 296.

4. Gallup, *Black/White Relations in the United States* (Princeton, N.J.: The Gallup Organization, 1997), pp. 29–30, 108–110.

5. Dexter B. Gordon, "Humor in African American Discourse: Speaking of Oppression," *Journal of Black Studies* 29 (2) (1998): 254–276.

6. See, for example, Joe R. Feagin and Melvin P. Sikes, *Living with Racism: The Black Middle Class Experience* (Boston: Beacon, 1994), chapter two.

7. See Jan Ziegler, "Immune System May Benefit from the Ability to Laugh," *Journal of the National Cancer Institute* 87 (1994): 342–343; Douglas S. Nelson, "Humor in the Pediatric Emergency Department: A Twenty-Year Retrospective," *Pediatrics* 89 (1992): 1089–1090.

8. See Feagin and Sikes and Yanick St. Jean and Joe R. Feagin, *Double Burden: Black Women and Everyday Racism* (Armonk, N.Y.: M. E. Sharpe, 1998).

9. See ibid.

10. Felicenne H. Ramey, "Obstacles Faced by African American Women Administrators in Higher Education: How They Cope," *The Western Journal of Black Studies* 19 (1995): 116.

11. See Randy Hodson and Teresa Sullivan, *The Social Organization of Work* (Belmont, Calif.: Wadsworth, 1990), passim; Robert H. Lauer and Warren H. Handel, *Social Psychology: The Theory and Application of Symbolic Interactionism* (Boston: Houghton-Mifflin, 1977).

12. See Robert Joseph Taylor et al., "Changes over Time in Support Network Involvement among Black Americans," in *Family Life in Black America*, eds. Robert Joseph Taylor, James S. Jackson and Linda M. Chatters (Thousand Oaks, Calif.: Sage, 1997), pp. 293–316; William W. Dressler, "Extended Family Relationships, Social Support, and Mental Health in a Southern Black Community," *Journal of Health and Social Behavior* 26 (1985): 39–48; Ezra E. H. Griffith and F. M. Baker, "Psychiatric Care of African Americans," in *Culture, Ethnicity, and Mental Illness*, ed. Albert C. Gaw (Washington, D.C.: American Psychiatric Press, 1993), pp. 147–173.

13. James S. Coleman, "Human Capital and Social Capital," in *Social Theory: Roots and Branches*, ed. Peter Kivisto (Los Angeles, Calif.: Roxbury, 2000), pp. 297–298.

14. See Shawn O. Utsey and Joseph Ponterotto, "Racial Discrimination, Coping, Life Satisfaction, and Self-Esteem among African Americans," *Journal of Counseling and Development*, 78 (1) (2000): 72–81; James S. Jackson, "Black American Life Course," in *Life in Black America*, ed. James S. Jackson (Newbury Park, Calif.: Sage, 1991); pp. 264–273; Carol B. Stack, *All our Kin: Strategies for Survival in a Black Community* (New York: Harper and Row, 1974); Sayde L. Logan, *The Black Family: Strengths, Self-Help, and Positive Change*, 2d. ed. (Boulder, Colo.: Westview Press, 2001).

15. Utsey and Ponterotto, "Racial Discrimination, Coping, Life Satisfaction, and Self-Esteem among African Americans."

16. Deborah Turner, "Letters to My Sister," in *Testimony: Young African Americans on Self-Discovery and Black Identity*, ed. Natasha Tarpley (Boston: Beacon Press, 1995), p. 71.

17. See Isabel B. Ferguson, "African-American Parent-Child Communication About Racial Derogation," in *Communication, Race, and Family*, eds. Thomas J. Socha and Rhunette C. Diggs (Mahwah, N.J.: Lawrence Erlbaum Associates, Inc., 1999), pp. 45–67 for a review of literature discussing the importance of racially socializing black children.

18. Ferguson, "African American Parent-Child Communication About Racial Derogation," p. 51.

19. Ibid., p. 61.

20. See Ferguson for a broader discussion of these strategies.

21. See ibid., p. 53 and passim.

22. Susan Toliver, *Black Families in Corporate America* (Thousand Oaks, Calif.: Sage, 1998).

23. John Hope Franklin, C. Eric Lincoln, Alvin F. Poussaint, Gaynelle Griffin Jones, and Anita L. Allen, "Black Scholars Recall Racism from Their Undergraduate Years," *Journal of Blacks in Higher Education* 14 (1996): 101–103. Italics added.

24. Joe R. Feagin, Hernan Vera, and Nikitah Imani, *The Agony of Education: Black Students at White Colleges and Universities* (New York: Routledge, 1996).

25. See Joe R. Feagin and Melvin P. Sikes, "How Black Students Cope with Racism on White Campuses," *Journal of Blacks in Higher Education* 8 (1995): 91–97.

26. James Baldwin, *The First Next Time* (New York: Dell, 1962–1963), p. 134.

7 Racism and the U.S. Health Care System

1. Ellis Cose, *The Rage of a Privileged Class* (New York: HarperCollins, 1993), p. 1.

2. S. S. Fluss, "International Public Health Law: An Overview," *The Scope of Public Health*, volume 1 of *Oxford Textbook of Public Health*, eds. R. Detels et al. (New York: Oxford University Press, 1997), pp. 371–390.

3. See *Jones et ux. v. Alfred H. Mayer Co.* 392 U.S. 409, 445 (1968).

4. See, for example, William J. Wilson, *The Declining Significance of Race* (Chicago, Ill.: University of Chicago Press, 1978).

5. Emile Durkheim, *The Division of Labor in Society*, trans. G. Simpson (New York: Free Press, 1933 [1893]).

6. Sheryl Gay Stolberg, "Race Gap Seen in Health Care of Equally Insured Patients," *New York Times*, March 21, 2002, p. A1.

7. Ibid.; and Steve Sternberg, "Study: Racial Disparities Persist in Medicine," *USA Today*, March 21, 2002, p. 6D.

8. See Sandra L. Gilman, *Difference and Pathology: Stereotypes of Sexuality, Race, and Madness* (Ithaca, N.Y.: Cornell University Press, 1985), pp. 131–149.

9. Thomas S. Szasz, "The Sane Slave: An Historical Note on the Use of Medical Diagnosis as Justificatory Rhetoric," in *The Production of Reality: Essays and Readings in Social Psychology*, eds. Peter Kollock and Jodi O'Brien, (Thousand Oaks, Calif.: Pine Forge Press, 1994), pp. 426–435; Donald H. Williams, "The Epidemiology of Mental Illness in Afro-Americans," *Hospital and Community Psychiatry* 37 (1986): 42–49; Charles B. Wilkinson and Jeanne Spurlock, "Mental Health of Black Americans: Psychiatric Diagnosis and Treatment," in *Ethnic Psychiatry*, ed. Charles B. Wilkinson (New York: Plenum Medical Book Company, 1986), pp. 13–50; Ezra E. H. Griffith and F. M. Baker, "Psychiatric Care of African Americans," in *Culture, Ethnicity, and Mental Illness*, ed. Albert C. Gaw (Washington, D.C.: American Psychiatric Press, 1993), pp. 147–173.

10. See, for example, W. M. Bevis, "Psychological Traits of the Southern Negro with Observations as to Some of His Psychoses," *American Journal of Psychiatry* 1 (1921): 69–78.

11. Ibid.

12. Arthur J. Prange, Jr., "Cultural Aspects of the Relatively Low Incidence of Depression in Southern Negroes," *International Journal of Social Psychiatry* 8 (1962): 104–112.

13. Mary Frances Poe, "The Negro as an Anesthetic Risk," *Anesthesiology* 14 (January 1953): 85. Italics added.

14. Ibid. Italics added.

15. Ibid., p. 87.

16. James H. Jones, *Bad Blood* (New York: Free Press, 1981), pp. 1–23.

17. We are indebted to Sheila Jeffers for this important point.

18. See Tom Junod, "Deadly Medicine," *Gentleman's Quarterly*, June 1993, pp. 164–169.

19. Richard A. Zmuda, "Ending Racism in Medicine," www.thehealthchannel.com, editorial team, 2001.

20. Linda A. Clayton and W. Michael Byrd, "The African American Cancer Crisis, Part I: The Problem," *Journal of Health Care for the Poor and Underserved*, 4 (1993): 98.

21. See Frank Michel, "Racism Can be Cancer on the Health System," *Houston Chronicle*, September 21, 1998, p. 18; Linda Chatters, "Physical

Health," in *Life in Black America*, ed. James S. Jackson (Newbury Park, Calif.: Sage, 1991), pp. 199–220; Wornie L. Reed, William Darity, Sr., Stanford Roman, Claudia Baquet, and Noma L. Roberson, "Cross-Cutting Issues in the Health of African-Americans," in *The Health and Medical Care of African-Americans*, ed. Wornie L. Reed (Boston: William Monroe Trotter Institute, University of Massachusetts at Boston, 1992), pp. 155–158.

22. Zmuda, "Ending Racism in Medicine."

23. John A. Rich, "The Health of African American Men," *Annals of the American Academy of Political and Social Science* 569 (2000): 149–160.

24. Zmuda, "Ending Racism in Medicine."

25. Reed, Darity, Roman, Baquet, and Roberson, "Cross-Cutting Issues," pp. 155–158.

26. Rich, "The Health of African American Men," pp. 149–160; see Chatters, "Physical Health," pp. 199–220.

27. [No author], "The Impact of Managed Care on Doctors who Serve Poor and Minority Patients," *Harvard Law Review* 108 (May 1995): 1625–1642.

28. See also D. R. Harris, R. Andrews, and A. Elixhauser, "Racial and Gender Differences in Use of Procedures for Black and White Hospitalized Adults," *Ethnicity and Disease* 7 (1997): 91–105; and the summary of studies in David R. Williams and Toni D. Rucker, "Understanding and Addressing Racial Disparities in Health Care," *Health Care Financing Review* 21 (Summer 2000): 75.

29. "Racial Disparities in Medical Care," *The New England Journal of Medicine* 344 (19) (May 10, 2001): 1471–1473.

30. M. Van Ryn and J. Burke, "The Effect of Race and Socio-Economic Status on Physicians' Perceptions of Patients," *Journal of Social Science and Medicine* 50 (March 2000): 813–828. We draw here on the summary of the study in National Medical Association, "Racism in Medicine and Health Parity for African Americans: 'The Slave Health Deficit,'" Second Annual National Colloquium on African American Health, March 12, 2001, p. 5.

31. The studies are cited in Robert Mayberry, Fatima Mili, and Elizabeth Ofili, "Racial and Ethnic Differences in Access to Medical Care," *Medical Care Research and Review* 57 (2000): 122.

32. Kevin A. Schulman et al., "The Effect of Race and Sex on Physicians' Recommendations for Cardiac Catherization," *New England Journal of Medicine* (February 25, 1999): 618–626; Peter B. Bach et al., "Racial Differences in the Treatment of Early-Stage Lung Cancer," *New England Journal of Medicine* (October 14, 1999): 1198–1205.

33. Mayberry, Mili, and Ofilii, "Racial and Ethnic Differences," p. 122.

34. G. Caleb Alexander and Ashwini R. Sehgal, "Barriers to Cadaveric Renal Transplantation among Blacks, Women, and the Poor," *JAMA* 280 (October 7, 1998): 1148–1152.

35. John Z. Ayanian et al., "The Effect of Patients' Preferences on Racial Differences in Access to Transplantation," *New England Journal of Medicine* 341 (November 25, 1999): 1661–1669.

36. Keith K. Key and Daniel J. DeNoon, "African Americans Receive Less Intensive Care—Fare Better than Caucasians," *Disease Weekly Plus*, August 12, 1996, pp. 19–21.

37. Ibid.

38. The studies are cited in Mayberry, Mili, and Ofilii, "Racial and Ethnic Differences," pp. 124–127.

39. "The New England Journal of Medicine Produces Flat-Out Proof of Racism in Medicare-Funded Medicine," *Journal of Blacks in Higher Education* 13 (Autumn 1996): 39.

40. Ibid.

41. See Jewelle Taylor Gibbs and Diana Fuery, "Mental Health and Well-Being of Black Women: Toward Strategies of Empowerment," *American Journal of Community Psychology* 22 (1994): 559–582.

42. See Nancy F. Russo and Esteban L. Olmedo, "Women's Utilization of Outpatient Psychiatric Services: Some Emerging Priorities for Rehabilitation Psychologists," *Rehabilitation Psychology* 28 (1983): 141–155; Griffith and Baker, "Psychiatric Care," pp. 147–173; Gibbs and Fuery, "Mental Health and Well-Being," pp. 559–582; Wilkinson and Spurlock, "Mental Health of Black Americans," pp. 13–50.

43. Doris Wilkinson, "Minority Women: Social-Cultural Issues," in *Women and Psychotherapy*, eds. Annette M. Brodsky and Rachel T. Hare-Mustin (New York: Guilford, 1980), pp. 295–297.

44. See Donald R. Atkinson, "A Meta-Review of Research on Cross-Cultural Counseling and Psychotherapy," *Journal of Multicultural Counseling and Development* 13 (1985): 138–153; Elaine J. Copeland, "Oppressed Conditions and the Mental-Health Needs of Low-Income Black Women: Barriers to Services, Strategies for Change," *Women and Therapy* 1 (1982): 13–26; Wilkinson and Spurlock, "Mental Health of Black Americans," pp. 13–50; Griffith and Baker, "Psychiatric Care," pp. 147–173; Gibbs and Fuery, "Mental Health and Well-Being," pp. 559–582.

45. Griffith and Baker, "Psychiatric Care," pp. 147–173; Charles R. Ridley, "Clinical Treatment of the Nondisclosing Black Client," *American Psychologist* 39 (1984): 1234–1244; Gibbs and Fuery, "Mental Health and Well-Being," pp. 559–582.

46. See Stanley Sue, "Psychotherapeutic Services for Ethnic Minorities: Two Decades of Research Findings," *American Psychologist* 43 (1988): 301–308; Ridley, "Clinical Treatment," pp. 1234–1244.

47. See, e.g., Raymond M. Costello, "Construction and Cross-Validation of an MMPI Black-White Scale," *Journal of Personality Assessment* 41 (1977): 514–519; Danielle Watts-Jones, "Toward a Stress Scale for African American Women," *Psychology of Women Quarterly* 14 (1990): 271–275; Gibbs and Fuery, "Mental Health and Well-Being," pp. 559–582.

48. Robert B. Hill, with Andrew Billingsley, Eleanor Engram, Michelene R. Malson, Roger H. Rubin, Carol B. Stack, James B. Stewart, and James E. Teele, *Research on the African American Family* (Westport, Conn.: Auburn House, 1993), p. 134; see also George Devereux, *Basic Problems of Ethnopsychiatry* (Chicago: University of Chicago Press, 1980); Victor R. Adebimpe, "Overview: White Norms and Psychiatric Diagnosis of Black Patients," *American Journal of Psychiatry* 138 (1981): 279–285; Harold W. Neighbors, James S. Jackson, Linn Campbell, and Donald Williams, "The Influence of Racial Factors on Psychiatric Diagnosis: A Review and Suggestions for Research," *Community Mental Health Journal* 25 (1989): 301–311; Griffith and Baker, "Psychiatric Care," pp. 147–173.

49. See Manuel Ramirez, III, *Psychotherapy and Counseling with Minorities: A Cognitive Approach to Individual and Cultural Differences* (New York: Pergamon Press, 1991); see also Wilkinson and Spurlock, "Mental Health of Black Americans," pp. 163–178, Robert L. Bragg, "Discussion: Cultural Aspects of Mental Health Care for Black Americans," pp. 179–185, and Richard I. Shader, "Discussion: Cultural Aspects of Mental Health Care for Black Americans: Cultural Aspects of Psychiatric Training," pp. 187–197, all in *Cross-Cultural Psychology*, ed. Albert Gaw (Littleton, Mass.: J. Wright, PSG, 1982); see also Enrico E. Jones, "Psychotherapy and Counseling with Black Clients," pp. 173–180 and Gerald G. Jackson, "Cross-Cultural Counseling with Afro-Americans," both in *Handbook of Cross-Cultural Counseling and Therapy*, ed. Paul Pedersen (New York: Praeger, 1985), pp. 231–237; see also Gerald G. Jackson, "Conceptualizing Afrocentric and Eurocentric Mental Health Training," pp. 131–149 and Evalina W. Bestman, "Intervention Techniques in the Black Community," pp. 213–224, both in *Cross-Cultural Training for Mental Health Professionals*, eds. Harriet P. Lefley and Paul B. Pedersen (Springfield, Il.: C. Thomas, 1986); Lawrence E. Gary, "Attitudes of Black Adults Toward Community Mental Health Centers," *Hospital and Community Psychiatry* 38 (1987): 1100–1105; Jewelle Taylor Gibbs, "Can We Continue to be Color-Blind and Class-Bound?" *Counseling Psychologist* 13 (1985): 426–435; James S. Jackson, "The Mental Health Service and Training Needs of African Americans,"

in *Ethnic Minority Perspectives on Clinical Training and Services in Psychology*, eds. Hector F. Myers, Paul Wohlford, L. Philip Guzman, and Ruben J. Echemendia (Washington D.C.: American Psychological Association, 1991), pp. 33–42; Atkinson, "A Meta-Review," pp. 138–153; Gibbs and Fuery, "Mental Health and Well-Being," pp. 559–582.

50. Griffith and Baker, "Psychiatric Care," p. 159; on contradictory evidence, see also Shae Graham Kosch, Mary Ann Burg, and Shifa Podikuju, "Patient Ethnicity and Diagnosis of Emotional Disorders in Women," *Family Medicine* 30 (1998): 215–219; George W. Comstock and Knud J. Helsing, "Symptoms of Depression in Two Communities," *Psychological Medicine* 6 (1976): 551–563; Ronald C. Kessler and Harold W. Neighbors, "A New Perspective on the Relationships among Race, Social Class, and Psychological Distress," *Journal of Health and Social Behavior* 27 (1986): 107–115; David R. Williams and Toni Rucker, "Socioeconomic Status and the Health of Racial Minority Populations," in *Handbook of Diversity Issues in Health Psychology*, eds. Pamela M. Kato and Traci Mann (New York: Plenum Press, 1996), pp. 407–423.

51. Kosch, Burg, and Podikuju, "Patient Ethnicity," p. 216.

52. See Mindy T. Fullilove, "Comment: Abandoning 'Race' as a Variable in Public Health Research—An Idea Whose Time has Come," *American Journal of Public Health* 88 (1998): 1298; Gibbs and Fuery, "Mental Health and Well-Being," pp. 559–582; David R. Williams, David T. Takeuchi, and Russell K. Adair, "Marital Status and Psychiatric Disorder among Blacks and Whites," *Journal of Health and Social Behavior* 33 (1992): 140–157; Raj Bhopal and Liam Donaldson, "White, European, Western, Caucasian, or What? Inappropriate Labeling in Research on Race, Ethnicity, and Health," *American Journal of Public Health* 88 (1998): 1303–1307.

53. "Eliminating Racial and Ethnic Disparities in Health: Overview," www.raceandhealth.hhs.gov/sidebars/sbinitOver.htm (retrieved on May 23, 2001).

54. "Racial Disparities in Medical Care," p. 1472.

55. Ibid., p. 1473.

56. Sternberg, "Study," p. 6D.

57. National Medical Association, "Racism in Medicine," p. 18.

58. See Joe R. Feagin and Clairece B. Feagin, *Racial and Ethnic Relations*, 7th ed. (Upper Saddle River, N.J.: Prentice-Hall, 2003), chapters 1. We are indebted to Sheila Jeffers for suggesting a number of points in this paragraph about the need for change in the medical school curriculum.

59. Joe Feagin had an experience with one major U.S. medical school in which he was invited to lecture by one faculty member (a sociologist) on problems of racism, only to have his talk canceled when some other faculty

members (medical doctors) learned that it would deal with the openly racist comments made by many white respondents in recent research. Over nearly forty years of lecturing, this is the only talk of many that Feagin has had cancelled by academic censors.

60. Harold E. Cheatham, "Empowering Black Families," in *Black Families: Interdisciplinary Perspectives*, eds. Harold E. Cheatham and James B. Steward (New Brunswick, N.J.: Transaction Publishers, 1990), pp. 373–393.

61. Harold W. Neighbors, Cleopatra Howard Caldwell, Estina Thompson, and James S. Jackson, "Help-Seeking Behavior and Unmet Need," in *Anxiety Disorders in African Americans*, ed. Steven Friedman (New York: Springer Publishing Company, 1994), pp. 26–39; Harold W. Neighbors and James S. Jackson, "The Use of Informal and Formal Help: Four Patterns of Illness Behavior in the Black Community," *American Journal of Community Psychology* 12 (1984): 629–644; Ruth L. Greene, "Mental Health and Help-Seeking Behavior," in *Aging in Black America*, eds. James S. Jackson, Linda M. Chatters, and Robert Joseph Taylor (Newbury Park, Calif.: Sage, 1993), pp. 185–200; Gibbs and Fuery, "Mental Health and Well-Being," pp. 559–582; Wilkinson and Spurlock, "Mental Health of Black Americans," pp. 13–50.

62. Griffith and Baker, "Psychiatric Care," pp. 147–173.

63. See Robert Joseph Taylor et al., "Changes over Time in Support Network Involvement among Black Americans," in *Family Life in Black America*, eds. Robert Joseph Taylor, James S. Jackson, and Linda M. Chatters (Thousand Oaks, Calif.: Sage, 1997), pp. 293–316; William W. Dressler, "Extended Family Relationships, Social Support, and Mental Health in a Southern Black Community," *Journal of Health and Social Behavior* 26 (1985): 39–48; Griffith and Baker, "Psychiatric Care," pp. 147–173; Harold W. Neighbors, James S. Jackson, Phillip J. Bowman, and Gerald Gurin, "Stress, Coping, and Black Mental Health: Preliminary Findings from a National Study," *Prevention in Human Services* 2 (1983): 5–29; Gibbs and Fuery, "Mental Health and Well-Being," pp. 559–582.

64. Ezra E. Griffith, John L. Young, and Dorothy L. Smith, "An Analysis of the Therapeutic Elements in a Black Church Service," *Hospital and Community Psychiatry* 35(5) (1984); see also Nancy Boyd-Franklin, "Group Therapy for Black Women: A Therapeutic Support Model," *American Journal of Orthopsychiatry* 57 (1987): 394–401; Vickie M. Mays, "Black Women and Stress: Utilization of Self-Help Groups for Stress Reduction," *Women and Therapy* 4 (1985–86): 67–79.

65. William W. Dressler, "Extended Family Relationships, Social Support, and Mental Health in a Southern Black Community," *Journal of Health and Social Behavior* 26 (1) (1985): 39–48.

66. National Medical Association, "Racism in Medicine," p. 22.

67. Ibid., pp. 21–23.

68. W. Michael Byrd and Linda A. Clayton, *An American Health Dilemma*, vol. 2 (New York: Routledge, 2002), p. 580.

69. Ibid., p. 586.

70. See "Doctors' Different Perceptions on Racism in Health Care," *The Race Relations Reporter*, June 15, 2002, p. 1.

71. "Washington Post/Kaiser/Harvard Racial Attitudes Survey," *Washington Post*, July 11, 2001, p. A01.

72. Lawrence D. Bobo, Michael C. Dawson, and Devon Johnson, "Enduring Two-Ness," *Public Perspective* (Roper Center), May/June 2001, pp. 12–16.

73. Lawrence Bobo, "Inequalities that Endure?: Racial Ideology, American Politics, and the Peculiar Role of the Social Sciences," paper presented at conference "The Changing Terrain of Race and Ethnicity," University of Illinois, Chicago, Illinois, October 26, 2001.

74. Richard Morin and David S. Broder, "The Big Issues; A Health Care Muddle; Voters Agree Only That It's Top Issue," *Washington Post*, July 28, 2000, p. A01.

75. See Wilson, *The Declining Significance of Race*; and Thomas B. Edsall, with Mary D. Edsall, *Chain Reaction* (New York: Norton, 1991–1992).

76. See Sharon M. Collins, *Black Corporate Executives: The Making and Breaking of a Black Middle Class* (Philadelphia, Pa.: Temple University Press, 1997); and Sharon Collins, "Blacks on the Bubble: The Vulnerability of Black Executives in White Corporations," *Sociological Quarterly* 34 (August 1993): 429–447.

77. See also Anthony J. Marsellas, "Work and Well-Being in an Ethnoculturally Pluralistic Society: Conceptual and Methodological Issues," in *Job Stress in a Changing Workplace*, eds. Gwendolyn P. Keita and Joseph J. Hurrell (Washington, D.C.: American Psychological Association, 1994), pp. 147–160.

78. See Roy Brooks, *Integration or Separation? A Strategy for Racial Equality* (Cambridge: Harvard University Press, 1996).

79. See Richard Delgado, "Affirmative Action as a Marjoritarian Device: Or, Do You Really Want to Be a Role Model?" *Michigan Law Review* 89 (1991): 1226.

80. See Keith James, "Social Identity, Work Stress, and Minority Workers' Health," in *Job Stress in a Changing Workforce*, eds. Gwendolyn P. Keita and Joseph Hurrell (Washington, D.C.: American Psychological Association, 1994), pp. 127–145.

81. We are indebted to Sheila Jeffers for these points about women workers. We refer here to her unpublished dissertation research.

82. Amnesty International Report, *United States of America: Rights for All* (New York: Amnesty International, 1998), pp. 109–111.

83. See Steven Keeva, "A Bumpy Road to Equality: Panelists Say Courts are Backpedaling on Minority Issues," *ABA Journal* 82 (1996): 32.

84. *Etter v. Veriflo Corporation*, 67 Cal.App.4th 457, 79 Cal.Rptr.2d 33 (1st Dist. Ct. App. 1998).

85. *Plessy v. Ferguson* 163 U.S. 537, 552 (1896). We are indebted to Roy Brooks for calling our attention to this point.

86. See *Meritor Savings Bank v. Vinson*, 477 U.S. 57, 66–67 (1986). This follows *Henson v. City of Dundee*, 682 F.2d 897, 902 (11th Cir. 1982).

87. *Harris v. Forklift Systems, Inc.*, 510 U.S. 17 (1993).

88. *Faragher v. City of Boca Raton*, 111 F.3d. 1530 (11th Cir. 1997), cert. granted, 118 S. Ct. 2275 (1998).

89. *Lopez v. S.B. Thomas, Inc.* 831 F.2d 1184, 1189 (2d Cir. 1987). This case is cited with approval in *Faragher*.

90. See Roy L. Brooks, *The Structure of Judicial Decision-Making From Legal Formalism to Critical Theory* (Durham, N.C.: Carolina Academic Press, 2002).

91. *Aman v. Cort Furniture Rental Corporation*, 85 F.3d. 1074 (3d Cir. 1996).

92. Barbara Flagg, "Fashioning a Title VII Remedy for Transparently White Subjective Decisionmaking," *Yale Law Journal* 104 (1995): 2009–2051.

93. Flagg, "Fashioning a Title VII Remedy for Transparently White Subjective Decisionmaking," pp. 2009–2051.

94. Charles R. Lawrence III, "The Id, the Ego, and Equal Protection: Reckoning with Unconscious Racism," *Stanford Law Review* 39 (1987): 317.

95. Joe R. Feagin, Hernán Vera, and Pinar Batur, *White Racism: The Basics*, 2d ed. (New York: Routledge, 2001), pp. 8–9.

96. Billy J. Tidwell, "More than a Moral Issue: The Cost of American Racism in the 1990s," *The Urban League Review* 11 (1991): 9.

97. "[Interview with] Laurence Thomas," in *African-American Philosophers: Seventeen Conversations*, ed. George Yancey (New York: Routledge, 1998), p. 297.

98. James Baldwin, *Notes of a Native Son* (Boston: Beacon Press, 1955), p. 175.

99. Ibid., p. 25.

Index

African Americans:
    Americanism of, 62–64
    challenges of, generally, 6–7
    collective memory of, 52–54, 119,
        129–30, 155
    communities of (*see* communities)
    empathy of, 51–54, 82–84, 126, 168
    families of (*see* families)
    health of (*see* health)
    life expectancy of, 30, 65–66, 188
    marginalization of, 34, 62–64, 90–91
    qualifications of, 51–52, 52–59, 81–82
    segregation of (*see* segregation)
    self-esteem of, 132–36, 145, 162–63,
        173–76
    slavery of (*see* slavery)
    socioeconomic classes of, 8–10, 35–38,
        52, 178–79, 197–98
    spirituality of (*see* spirituality)
    stereotypes about (*see* stereotypes)
    strengths of, generally, 97–100, 183–84,
        209
    work ethic of, 37, 77–78, 98, 107 (*see also*
        John Henryism)
aging, 142–43, 143–44
American Cancer Society, 188
American Civil Liberties Union (ACLU), 26
Americanism, 62–64
Anderson, Norman, 31

anger:
    age and, 142–43, 143–44
    blood pressure and, 77
    colonialism and, 41
    control of, 139–41
    cumulative, 52–54
    depression and, 54–59
    empathetic, 51–54, 82–84, 168
    families and, 111
    frequency of, 43–46
    internalization of, 120, 127–32
    personal, 46–51
    utilitarianism and, 164–67
    from workplace discrimination, 46–47,
        50–52.
    See also stress
attitudes, framing, 136–39, 145

Baldwin, James, 43, 104–5, 177–78, 210
Bellah, Robert, 52
Billingsley, Andrew, 98
Black Boy, 104
Black Enterprise, 141–42
blame, 12–13, 14, 40, 141, 204
Blauner, Robert, 99, 110–11
blood pressure, 76–82, 128
Blumenbach, Johann, 195–96
Brooks, Roy, 16, 206
Brown, Diane R., 61

Brown, Henry, 204
Byrd, James, Jr., 49
Byrd, W. Michael, 66, 187–88, 197–98

Centers for Disease Control and Prevention
(CDC), 65
Cheatham, Harold, 196
children:
    economic conditions and, 103–4
    racism and, 107–9, 109–10, 113–14
    self-esteem of, 134, 135–36
    socialization of, 173–76.
    See also families; youth
civil rights laws, 2, 15–17, 157–60, 203–208
civil rights movements, 118, 143
Clark, Rodney, 31
Clark, Vanessa, 31
Clayton, Linda A., 66, 187–88, 197–98
Clinton, Bill, 194
Cobbs, Price, 44, 54
collective memory, 52–54, 119, 129–30, 155
Collins, Patricia Hill, 19
colonialism, 20–23, 39–40, 41. *See also* slavery
communities:
    coping strategies and, 97, 99–100
    countering strategies and, 116–18,
        176–77, 178–79
    economic conditions and, 103–4
    health and, 29–31, 183–84
    racism and, 94–95, 114–18
    self-esteem and, 135–36.
    See also families
confrontation. *See* countering strategies
conservative conspiracy, 13–15
Constitution, 180–81
control, 139–41, 145, 175
coping strategies:
    addictive substances, 91–92, 133
    communities as, 97, 99–100
    control and, 139–41, 145
    desensitization, 125–27
    energy and, 62
    families and, 97–100, 170–76
    framing attitudes, 136–39, 145
    humor, 162–64
    internalization, 120, 127–32, 146

John Henryism, 77–78, 107, 111–12,
    128, 133
learning about, 119–20
mental illness and, 144–45
observation, 120
preparation, 124–25, 145
self-esteem, 132–36, 145, 162–63, 173–76
for sexism, 143, 144
spirituality (*see* spirituality)
tailoring, 120–21, 143–44
types of, 120–21, 122–23, 123–24,
    145–46
withdrawal, 167–69.
See also countering strategies
corporations, 4–5
Cose, Ellis, 30, 181–82
countering strategies:
    communities and, 116–18, 176–77,
        178–79
    energy and, 160, 169
    families and, 170–76
    humor, 160–62
    instruction, 151–53
    love, 87–88
    physical confrontation, 22–23, 50–51
    protests, 153–60
    for sexism, 156–57, 167
    shopping and, 148, 149–50, 151–52,
        153–55, 160–61, 168
    socialization about, 173–76
    support for, 169–77
    systemic racism and, 171
    tailoring, 147, 164, 169, 178
    taking the offense, 148–51
    types of, 34–35, 147, 153, 177–79
    utilitarianism and, 164–67
    verbal confrontation, generally, 73–74,
        88–89, 122, 123, 147–49
    workplace, 156–60.
    See also coping strategies
courts. *See* judicial system
Covey, 22–23

Davis, Angela, 22
democracy, 180–81, 201–203, 210
denial, 10–17, 126–27, 131, 181, 198–99

depression, 54–59. *See also* psychological costs
Derricotte, Toi, 105–7
desensitization, 125–27
discrimination:
    coping with (*see* coping strategies)
    copycat, 3
    countering (*see* countering strategies)
    covert, 3–4
    ending, 194–208
    examples of, 1–2, 26–28, 46–54
    gender (*see* sexism)
    harassment, 1–2, 15–17, 46–54,
        203–208
    health and, 29–34
    history of, 1–3, 20–25, 39–40, 180–81
    proving, 4, 15–17, 61, 203–208
    segregation (*see* segregation)
    stress and (*see* stress)
    tolerance of, 2, 3, 169–70
    woodwork (*see* woodwork
        discrimination)
    workplace (*see* workplace
        discrimination).
    See also racism
divorce, 112–14
documentation, 61, 127, 156–57
Donne, John, 118
Douglas, William O., 29, 93, 182
Douglass, Frederick, 21–22, 22–23, 119–20
Dow, Whitney, 49
drugs, 91–92, 133
D'Souza, Dinesh, 14, 131
DuBois, W. E. B., 23, 40, 63
Durkheim, Emile, 184

eating, 92
economic conditions:
    communities and, 103–4
    families and, 100–4
    health and, 67–68
    racism and, 8–10, 28–29, 52
    segregation and, 23–25, 28–29
    slavery and, 21
    stress and, 43
    white views of, 11, 36–37, 96–97, 131,
        198–99

education, 11, 99, 168–69, 173–76, 176–77,
    195–96
empathy, 51–54, 82–84, 126, 168
energy:
    communities and, 114–18
    countering strategies and, 160, 169
    families and, 107–9, 113
    health and, 33–34
    utilitarianism and, 164–67
    workplace discrimination and, 59–62
epithets, 15–17, 46–48, 84, 129, 138, 204
Equal Employment Opportunity
    Commission (EEOC), 1–2, 84
Essed, Philomena, 19
Etter, Robert, Jr., 15–16, 204

families:
    coping strategies and, 97–100
    countering strategies and, 170–76
    economic conditions and, 100–104
    energy and, 107–9, 113
    health and, 29–31, 183–84, 196–97
    ideological assault on, 95–97
    racism and, 94–95, 104–14, 133
    segregation and, 97
    self-esteem and, 135–36
    slavery and, 97
    spirituality and, 99
    stress and, 96, 97, 104–5, 111–12
    workplace discrimination and,
        107–14
Fanon, Frantz, 39–40
Faragher, Beth Ann, 205
Feagin, Joe:
    on cumulative discrimination, 33
    on desensitization, 127
    on frequency, 126
    on gendered racism, 19
    on sexism, 75
    on social costs, 208
    studies by, 6, 48
    on systemic racism, 100–101
Federal Housing Administration (FHA),
    102–3. *See also* housing
Flagg, Barbara, 207
focus groups, 35

Franklin, John Hope, 176–77
Frazier, E. Franklin, 96

gender discrimination. *See* sexism
genetics, 68–69
Gibbs, Jewelle Taylor, 71
glass ceilings, 4. *See also* promotions
God, 142. *See also* spirituality
Good Samaritan, 87–88
Grier, William, 44, 54

Hamer, Fannie Lou, 119–20
Hamilton, Charles, 18
harassment, 1–2, 15–17, 46–54, 203–208. *See also* discrimination
headaches, 71–76
health:
    of Americans generally, 65–67
    anger and, 54–59, 77, 120, 127–32, 164–67
    communities and, 183–84
    definition of, 7, 93, 182
    depression, 54–59
    discrimination and, 29–34
    drugs and, 91–92
    eating and, 92
    economic conditions and, 67–68
    empathy and, 82–85
    energy and, 33–34
    families and, 29–31, 183–84, 196–97
    genetics and, 68–69
    headaches, 71–76
    heart problems, 76–82, 128
    humor and, 162
    internalization and, 128
    life expectancy, 30, 65–66, 188
    mental (*see* psychological costs)
    racism and, 7–10, 65–67, 93, 109, 181–83
    segregation and, 29–34, 69, 182–83
    sexism and, 75, 92
    slavery and, 21–22, 41
    sleep, 69–71
    spirituality and, 80, 82
    stomach problems, 85–91.
    See also health care

health care:
    access to, 184–85, 187–89, 202–203
    history of, 185–87
    for mental illness, 192–93, 196–97
    provision of, 189–92
    reform of, 118, 194–200
    slavery and, 185
    spirituality and, 197
    white views of, 10–11, 13–15, 198–200.
    See also health
Health Policy and Research Institute, 197
heart problems, 76–82, 128
Hill, Robert, 98
Hirschfeld, Magnus, 17–18
hooks, bell, 41, 116–17
hostile work environment, 16, 203–208.
    See also workplace discrimination
housing, 9, 27–28, 102–3, 105–7
humor, 162–64
hypertension, 76–82, 128

icons, 1, 2, 3
ignorance, 137–39, 145
institutional racism. *See* systemic racism
internalization, 120, 127–32, 146
interviews, 36

Jackson, James S., 61
James, Sherman, 77
James, William, 34
John Henryism, 77–78, 107, 111–12, 128, 133
Jones, Camara, 68
Jones, James, 19
judicial system, 15–17, 61–62, 203–208

Kaiser Family Foundation, 198
Keith, Verna M., 61
King, Martin Luther, Jr., 88, 120, 143
Kovel, Joel, 90, 91
Krieger, Nancy, 76, 77
Ku Klux Klan, 1, 2, 3, 49

Lawrence, Charles, 208
life expectancy, 30, 65–66, 188
Lincoln, Abraham, 23

Lipsitz, George, 9
litigation, 15–17, 203–208.
  See also judicial system
love, 87–88
lynching, 2–3, 49

Malcolm X, 120
marginalization, 34, 62–64, 90–91
matriarchies, 98–99
McKinney, Karyn, 46
mental health. *See* psychological costs
Mirowsky, John, 54
Morrison, Toni, 102
Moynihan, Daniel Patrick, 96
Myers, Barbee, 128
Myrdal, Gunnar, 34

National Academy of Science (NAS),
  184–85, 189, 191, 194–95
National Medical Association (NMA), 7–8,
  187, 195, 197
National Study of Black Americans, 54
The Negro Family in the United States, 96
*The Negro Family: The Case for National
  Action*, 96
networking, 57–59, 90–91
Nixon, Richard, 102

O'Connor, Sandra Day, 205
Ollman, Bertell, 95
opportunities, 11–13, 24–25, 101

patriarchies, 98–99
Piper, Adrian, 120
Plessy, Homer, 204
Poe, Mary F., 186–87
police misconduct, 26
promotions, 4, 79–82, 83–84.
  See also workplace discrimination
protests, formal, 153–60
psychological costs:
  of colonialism, 39–40
  coping strategies and, 144–45
  depression, 54–59
  of discrimination, 30–34
  energy and, 33–34, 59–62
  health care and, 192–94, 196–97

marginalization and, 62–64
of racism, 6–7
of slavery, 21–23.
  See also anger; stress
public accommodations:
  discrimination in, 26–27
  payment in, 148, 149–50
  service in, 151–52, 153–55, 160–61, 168
Public Health Service, 187

qualifications, 51–52, 52–59, 81–82

racism:
  aversive, 90–91
  children and, 103–4, 107–9, 109–10,
    113–14
  communities and, 94–95, 114–18
  coping with (*see* coping strategies)
  countering (*see* countering strategies)
  denial of, 10–17, 126–27, 131, 181,
    198–99
  economic conditions and, 8–10, 28–29,
    52
  environmental, 9
  families and, 94–95, 104–14, 133
  health and, generally, 7–10, 65–67, 93,
    109, 181–83
  history of, 2–3, 20–25, 39–40
  systemic (*see* systemic racism).
  See also discrimination
rage. *See* anger
The Rage of a Privileged Class, 181–82
rape, 22
religion. *See* spirituality
research, social science, 35–38
respect, 73–74
restaurants. *See* public accommodations
Ross, Catherine E., 54
runaround, 164–65

Satel, Sally, 13–15
segregation:
  civil rights movements and, 118
  economic conditions and, 23–25, 28–29
  families and, 97
  health and, 29–34, 69, 182–83

history of, 23–25
housing and, 27–28
modern, 209–210
social costs of, 29–31
workplace, 200–202
Segura, Denise, 19
self-determinism, 12–13
self-esteem, 132–36, 145, 162–63, 173–76
sexism:
    coping strategies for, 143, 144
    countering strategies for, 156–57, 167
    gendered racism described, 19
    health and, 75, 92
    litigation concerning, 204–205,
        206–207
sexuality, 152
shopping. *See* public accommodations
Sidney, Stephen, 76
Sikes, Melvin, 6, 33, 127
slavery:
    badges of, 29, 182
    families and, 97
    health and, 21–22, 41
    health care and, 185
    history of, 21–23, 39
sleep, 69–71
Smith, Harrison, 101
smoking, 91–92
social costs, 29–31, 38, 208.
    See also communities; families
socialization, 173–76.
    See also communities; families
Social Security, 102
socioeconomic class, 8–10, 35–38, 52,
    178–79, 197–98
spirituality:
    coping strategies and, 141–44,
        145–46
    families and, 99
    health and, 80, 82
    health care and, 197
    workplace discrimination and,
        56–57
spouses, 110–11, 112–14, 171–72
Staples, Brent, 153
Steele, Claude, 132

stereotypes:
    aggressiveness, 70–71, 148
    blame, 12–13, 14, 40, 141, 204
    as ignorant, 137–39
    internalization of, 131–32
    medical, 185–87, 189–90, 192–93,
        195–96
    socioeconomic, 36, 37
St. Jean, Yanick, 19, 75
stomach problems, 85–91
stress:
    discrimination and, 2
    drugs and, 91–92
    economic conditions and, 43
    empathy and, 82–85
    families and, 96, 97, 104–5, 111–12
    headaches and, 71–76
    health and, generally, 31–34,
        42–43, 93
    heart problems and, 76–82
    humor and, 162
    sleep and, 69–71
    stomach problems and, 85–91
    systemic racism and, 33–34, 43
    workplace, 4–5, 13–14, 32, 42–43,
        44–45, 93
    See also anger; psychological costs
surveillance, 72, 85
systemic racism:
    countering strategies and, 171
    definitions of, 17–20, 100–101
    health and, 8–10, 93
    stress and, 33–34, 43

Texaco, 4, 84
Thomas, Laurence, 42, 153, 210
Thompson, Tommy, 65
Tidwell, Billy, 209
Toliver, Susan, 37, 107, 108
transparency phenomenon, 207
trust, 41
Tubman, Harriet, 119–20
Ture, Kwame, 18

United Nations, 28, 30
utilitarianism, 164–67

violence, 2–3, 22–23, 49–51

West, Cornell, 116–17
white Americans:
    epithets of, 15–17, 46–48, 84, 129,
      138, 204
    framing attitudes about, 136–39
    health care reform and, 198–200
    mistrust of, 41
    privileges of, 24–25, 51
    solidarity of, 159
    support from, 136–37, 150–51,
      169
    views of, 10–17, 36–37, 40, 95–97,
      131, 198–200
white supremacist organizations, 1, 2,
    3, 49
Wilkinson, Doris, 192
Willhelm, Sidney, 102
Williams, David, 31
Williams, Marco, 49
Williams, Trina, 24
withdrawal, 167–69
woodwork discrimination:
    definitions of, 4–5, 28
    desensitization and, 126
    health and, 9
    as systemic racism, 20
    workplace, 36–37, 207

work ethic, 37, 77–78, 98, 107
workplace discrimination:
    anger from, 46–47, 50–52
    countering strategies for, 155–60
    depression from, 54–59
    empathy and, 51–54, 82–85
    ending, 200–203
    energy and, 59–62
    epithets, 15–17, 46–48
    examples of, 1–2, 26, 46–47
    families and, 107–14
    headaches and, 71–76
    heart problems and, 76–82
    litigation concerning, 15–17,
      203–208
    networking and, 57–59
    promotions, 4, 79–82, 83–84
    segregation, 200–202
    sleep and, 69–71
    spirituality and, 56–57
    stomach problems and, 85–91
    stress and, 4–5, 13–14, 32, 42–43,
      44–45, 93
    withdrawal from, 167–68
    woodwork, 36–37, 207
World Health Organization (WHO), 7,
    93, 182
Wright, Richard, 104

youth, 168–69. *See also* children

About the Authors

JOE R. FEAGIN lives in Gainesville, where he is graduate research professor in sociology at the University of Florida. He is the author of forty-five books, two of which won the Gustavus Myers Human Rights Award—*Living with Racism* (1994) and *White Racism* (1995). He is coauthor of *The First R: How Children Learn Race and Racism* (2000). He is former president of the American Sociological Association, and his section on racial and ethic minorities recently gave him a special award for his book, *Racist America* (2000).

KARYN D. MCKINNEY is assistant professor of sociology at Penn State Altoona. Her research focuses on race, ethnicity, and gender. She is currently working on a book on young whites' understandings of race and racism (forthcoming, 2003), and on a book coauthored with Amir Marvasti on Middle Eastern Americans (forthcoming, 2003). She recently published a chapter in an edited book, *Race in the College Classroom* (2002).